DOUBTING

PHILOSOPHICAL STUDIES SERIES

VOLUME 48

DOUBTING

Contemporary Perspectives on Skepticism

Edited by

MICHAEL D. ROTH

Franklin & Marshall College, Lancaster, U.S.A.

and

GLENN ROSS

Franklin & Marshall College, Lancaster, U.S.A.

KLUWER ACADEMIC PUBLISHERS

DORDRECHT / BOSTON / LONDON

BD
201
.D68
1989

Library of Congress Cataloging in Publication Data

```
Doubting : contemporary perspectives on skepticism / edited by Michael
  D. Roth and Glenn Ross.
      p.   cm. -- (Philosophical studies series ; v. 48)
   Includes bibliographical references.
   ISBN 0-7923-0576-0
   1. Skepticism.   I. Roth, Michael David, 1936-   . II. Ross,
Glenn, 1953-   . III. Series.
BD201.D68  1989
121'.5--dc20
```
                                                          89-29547

ISBN 0–7923–0576–0

Published by Kluwer Academic Publishers,
P.O. Box 17, 3300 AA Dordrecht, The Netherlands.

Kluwer Academic Publishers incorporates
the publishing programmes of
D. Reidel, Martinus Nijhoff, Dr W. Junk and MTP Press.

Sold and distributed in the U.S.A. and Canada
by Kluwer Academic Publishers,
101 Philip Drive, Norwell, MA 02061, U.S.A.

In all other countries, sold and distributed
by Kluwer Academic Publishers Group,
P.O. Box 322, 3300 AH Dordrecht, The Netherlands.

Printed on acid-free paper

Printed in the Netherlands

TABLE OF CONTENTS

PREFACE

During the summer of 1986 one of the co–editors was a fellow at the Summer Institute in Epistemology held at the University of Colorado in Boulder. It was there that the idea for this volume was born. It was clear from the discussions taking place at the Institute that works such as Robert Nozick's *Philosophical Explanations*[1] and Barry Stroud's *The Significance of Philosophical Scepticism*[2] were beginning to have an impact and it was also clear that the debate over the issues surrounding skepticism had not gone away nor were they about to go away. Thinking that a new crop might be ready for harvest, the co–editors sent out a letter of inquiry to a long list of potential contributors. The letter elicited an overwhelmingly positive response to our inquiry from philosophers who were either writing something on skepticism at the time or who were willing to write something specifically for our volume. Still others told us that they had recently written something and if we were to consider previously published manuscripts they would permit us to consider their already published work. Out of all this material, the co–editors have put together the present collection. We believe that this anthology is not only suitable for graduate seminars but for advanced *undergraduate* classes as well.

Teaching philosophy to undergraduates in this, the golden age of pre–professionalism, is an enterprise open to considerable risks — psychic as well as financial. The cardinal tenet of the pre–professional, that knowledge is definitely *not* to be sought for its own sake, revitalizes the never–ending complaint that the study of academic philosophy is idle and pointless — devoid of significance for the real problems that real people encounter in the real world. If one happens to be a teacher of philosophy at a liberal arts college the enterprise can become downright perilous, for it is a distinctive and perhaps definitive property of such institutions that the primary criterion by which members of their faculties are deemed worthy is success in the classroom. Since both of the co–editors of this volume teach philosophy at a liberal arts college it would be fair to say that we are concerned.

It is our belief that not every response to the perilous situation outlined briefly above has been laudable. One of the most ubiquitous responses has been the proliferation of courses, almost all at the undergraduate level, designed to engage the interests of various student constituencies which would otherwise have little or no enthusiasm for studying the the traditional canon of philosophical issues. While we do not universally condemn such courses, we hold the view that at their worst such courses tend to be superficial and can blatantly pander to the most current and trendy concerns of college students, while at best they create a false impression in the minds of students as to what sort of enterprise philosophy professors and their graduate students are engaged in when they come together to do philosophy. More often than not these courses quickly become the most popular courses in the department's curriculum and those who teach them the most popular instructors. Consequently, what one of our contributors, Ernest Sosa, has labelled "serious philosophy"[3] is, apart from a cursory and necessarily condensed treatment in historical survey courses, fast becoming the exclusive preserve of graduate school courses where the students can be expected to have the requisite mixture of motivation and sophistication.

We find this situation not only unfortunate but deplorable. The logical rigor, clarity and overall acumen of Anglo–American philosophy in this century have combined to produce an extraordinary intellectual achievement which needs no apology. Since the exploration of the metaphysical and epistemological themes which have led to this achievement was and continues to be the dominant activity of English–speaking academic philosophers, we see no reason for excluding undergraduates from participating in the enterprise, at least to the point of allowing them to gain a clear sense of what the main business of academic philosophy in their own culture is all about. In our view, attaining such a level of understanding with respect to at least some of the important issues which are currently under discussion at the major research universities in the English speaking world should be an essential component of every ambitious under–graduate philosophy program.

In one sense then it is fair to say that this anthology is an attempt on our part to put our money where our mouths are. It is true that any success this anthology enjoys will come, most likely, from its adoption as a reader in graduate seminars. This is as it should be since the articles in the volume represent, we believe, the best of the current thinking on the famous philosophical problem which serves as the focus of this collection. But each of these articles is eminently teachable to undergraduates as well. The individual papers are, without exception, clearly written and while the various writing styles are diverse, they are uniformly lively and non–technical. Moreover, the substantive issues which are raised and analyzed in the papers collected here aptly provide the materials from which to construct a clear and compelling motivation for why philosophers have continued to be fascinated as well as frustrated by what may very well be the least tractable of all philosophical problems.

Finally, we have the pleasant task of acknowledging our debts: to Mr. Aristides Fokas and Mr. Eric Rubenstein, who helped with the preparation of this manuscript, and to Professor Keith Lehrer, teacher and friend to both of the co–editors, without whose encouragement and support this project could not have even begun.

NOTES

[1]Robert Nozick, *Philosophical Explanations*, Cambridge, Harvard University Press, 1981.
[2]Barry Stroud, *The Significance of Philosophical Scepticism*, Oxford, Oxford University Press, 1984.
[3]Ernest Sosa, "Serious Philosophy and Freedom of Spirit," *The Journal of Philosophy*, **84**, 1987, p. 707.

MICHAEL D. ROTH AND GLENN ROSS

INTRODUCTION

I

If there is a single issue about which undergraduates are skeptical it is skepticism. As soon as it occurs to them that they are being asked to take seriously a doctrine from which it immediately follows that they do not know their own names, or the name of the college they attend, or whether or not they are at present sitting in class listening to a philosophy lecture, their response is immediate and universal. Phrases like, "silly," "stupid," "this is all semantics," and "you're playing tricks with our heads," are fairly typical of the comments elicited by an introductory lecture on skepticism. Here is philosophy exposed as a useless and trivial enterprise, richly deserving of the ridicule heaped on it at the coffee shop and fraternity party.

How should a teacher of philosophy react to a classroom full of students for whom skepticism produces this sort of response? One could respond positively by accepting their reaction as a pedagogical challenge. A good way to begin is to acknowledge that at the level of common sense, the claims of the skeptic do appear ridiculous. But such an acknowledgement can be easily turned into a counter–challenge in the following way: if the skeptical thesis is so absurd, so laughable as to be dismissed out of hand, then it should turn out that if we consider what particular reasons people like Plato, Descartes and Hume had for taking skepticism seriously, we should discover, without too much difficulty, where they have made their mistake. At the very least, we should find out which intuitions seemed acceptable to them which are clearly not acceptable to us.

Once students accept this assessment of their situation as a fair one, it is a relatively easy matter to get them to see that if some particular claim to knowledge has any chance of being true it must be accompanied by some form of justification. One effective way to illustrate this is to point out that ordinarily when someone claims to know something it seems always legitimate to raise the question of how she knows it. The intuition that the claimer is then obliged either to come up with some sort of answer or forfeit her claim to know is one whose pull is deeply felt and is usually convincing. But once this is conceded the teacher has not only taken the offensive but has completed one half of a sort of pedagogical pincer movement and is now ready to close the trap. The crucial move involves introducing what is perhaps the most formidable and certainly among the most intuitively plausible of all the principles in the skeptic's arsenal. The principle, which has come to be known as the "Closure Principle" is one which is widely discussed in the papers which follow and it underlies the argument of the book which has stimulated much of the recent literature on skepticism, Barry Stroud's *The Significance of Philosophical Scepticism*.[1] The intuition which the Closure Principle captures can be brought out in the following example. If you know that Wilson is now in Cleveland and you realize that if Wilson is now in Cleveland it follows that she cannot now be in Pittsburgh, then it would appear to follow as well that you know that Wilson is not now in Pittsburgh. Thus, your knowledge remains "closed" under known

1

M. D. Roth and G. Ross (eds.), Doubting, 1–10.
© 1990 *Kluwer Academic Publishers. Printed in the Netherlands.*

logical implication. The persuasiveness of such examples makes it easy for students to accept that the following principle holds generally: For any propositions p and q, if one knows that p and knows that p entails that q, then one knows that q.

But now our students have no escape from the skeptic's clutches. It would be quite an effective move to remind them at this point that so far all the skeptic has asked them to accept is that knowledge requires justification and that the Closure Principle is true — neither of which is open to the charge of being silly or stupid. Armed with the reasonableness of these two modest proposals, a further reminder is in order — namely that the consequence of skepticism which elicited the most derisory response was the claim that we don't even know we are sitting here in philosophy class. Whatever we might or might not know, surely we know *that* — and whoever says we do not is obviously engaged in some form of intellectual legerdemain. But if we do know that we are really in philosophy class, then the Closure Principle requires us to accept that we must know that we are not merely dreaming we are in philosophy class. Clearly, the proposition that we are not merely dreaming we're in the class follows logically from the proposition that we really are there. And if we know we are not dreaming then, of course, it will be a simple matter to satisfy the justification requirement and tell the skeptic *how* we know that we are not dreaming. After seeing how many of their classmates admit to having had nightmares and having realized, upon awakening, that they thought the dream was really happening, students can be easily persuaded that satisfying the justification condition for knowledge in this case is not only extremely difficult, but may very well be impossible.

Of course, this is not the only scenario which generates a skeptical hypothesis. Perhaps the most famous of all such scenarios is the one proposed by Rene Descartes (1596–1650) in his *Meditations*. In that work Descartes asks us to consider the pos-sibility that we are being manipulated by a powerful and hostile "demon" whose intent is to deceive us by producing in us a set of beliefs which do not accurately reflect the real world, i.e., the way things actually are. Our beliefs would then represent a kind of global hallucination and it would not be up to us to decide whether to be so hallucinated. What we believe would be solely at the discretion of the demon. Once again, the twin props of the Closure Principle and the justification requirement support the conclusion that in order to claim knowledge of the world we must show somehow that we are not being deceived by an evil demon. In more recent times, a popular variation on this theme is the suggestion that we are nothing more than brains which are kept functioning in vats full of life–sustaining materials. These envatted brains are stimulated in various ways by, say, a sophisticated computer to produce in the brains the feeling of being in a philosophy class with other human beings discussing skepticism. What makes such a scenario thinkable is the widely held assumption that even if we really do have complete bodies situated in a real physical world, our consciousness of being in philosophy class etc. is nothing more than our brains being stimulated in certain ways. Thus our awareness of being in philosophy class would be exactly the same if we were envatted brains being stimulated in the appropriate ways. The scenario, like the previous one, demands a satisfactory explanation of how we come to know that we are not brains in vats. The usual response to these scenarios is one which is pedagogically gratifying. More often than not a student will raise her hand and ask, with a mixture of frustration and curiosity, "Well, how do we get out of this?"

In the recent literature, the answer which appears to have gained the most support relies on a principle which, like the Closure Principle, has a prominent role in the
subsequent papers. The principle, which we shall dub the "Relevant Alternatives
Principle" can be put as follows: In acquiring justification adequate for correctly
claiming knowledge it is not required that every possible contingency which would fal-
sify the knowledge claim be ruled out but only those which are relevant to the claim, as
determined by the context in which the claim is made.   While the formulation of this
principle is less elegant than that of the Closure Principle, the intuitions it captures are
equally compelling as is shown in the following illustration.   Given the way we ordinarily use the word "know" in English, it would be perfectly appropriate for you to
claim that you know that certain students were present in your class.   Among the ways
that you could turn out to be wrong would be if one or more of these students had an
identical twin who, unbeknownst to you, was standing in for the legitimately enrolled
twin.   Yet it seems obvious that in order for you to claim to know justifiably that, say,
Smith was in class this morning it is not required that you call the hospital where Smith
was born to see whether or not she has an identical twin.   In this case, the prospect of
Smith's being a twin is not one of the relevant alternative ways things might turn out,
relative to the quite ordinary context in which you claim to know that Smith was in
class.   You know Smith was there because you saw her and heard her speak.   But now
suppose that yesterday you had seen Smith with someone who looked exactly like her
and who obviously was her identical twin.   Suppose further that one of your friends had
told you that he had seen Smith's sister sitting in for Smith in her class.   Now the
prospect of Smith's twin rather than Smith being in your class this morning *is* a relevant
alternative relative to this somewhat unusual context in which you now wish to claim
knowledge.
    The point here is that while justification adequate for knowledge rules out some
of the ways you could turn out to be wrong it need not and does not rule out all of the
ways you could be wrong.   Which ways need to get ruled out by your evidence, the
so-called "relevant alternatives," are determined by the particular situation you happen to
be in.   However, in *normal* situations you don't need to check on whether or not you
are dreaming or whether your class has been kidnapped and replaced with clones, etc.
In an ordinary context such alternatives are not relevant to your acquiring justification
adequate for claiming knowledge.

II

The foregoing has consisted mainly of our attempt to provide a foundation for understanding the intuitions which motivate both the view of the skeptic and of her opponent.
If we have been successful, our readers should have little or no difficulty in seeing why
philosophers constantly refer to the *problem* of skepticism.   The question of whether one
should accept the intuitions behind the skeptical view or those behind her opponent's
view is one which can now be seen to be genuinely problematic.
    The papers in the present collection presuppose familiarity with the account set
out in the previous section in that they all approach skepticism from this point of view.
Each of them attempts to shed new light on the issues by uncovering a previously undetected flaw or improving an already existing argument or, in some cases, providing an

entirely new way of looking at one or more aspects of the issue. It should be obvious that we have left the relatively simple and easily explainable moves of the previous section behind us and are now entering into a somewhat more rarified atmosphere where we will encounter arguments which will embody much more subtlety and ingenuity than those we have previously considered. In what follows we make an effort to give a readable summary of the main points of each of the papers in our collection and to show how each paper fits into the overview presented in the previous section.

While the Relevant Alternatives Principle currently enjoys the widest support among the anti–skeptics, it is not a necessary component in the mounting of every anti-skeptical counterattack. One bold assault on the skeptic which does not rely on the principle is Thomas Tymoczko's "Brains Don't Lie: They Don't Even Make Many Mistakes." Tymoczko employs an argument of Hilary Putnam's to show that we cannot be brains in vats. Essential to the argument is the assumption that what we are thinking about is not wholly determined by what is in our heads — that such reference is partially a matter of the way the world is. Tymoczko purports to show that we could not be thinking of ourselves when we think of brains in vats. Thus we could not be mistaken in believing that we are *not* brains in vats. But couldn't brains in vats give exactly the same argument? Not only can they, but according to Tymoczko, their argument would be no less sound! For were brains in vats to think thoughts like ours of brains in vats, they would also not be thinking of themselves, for they would not be thinking about what we think about when we think of brains in vats. (Instead they would be thinking about computer subprograms, which are surely not brains.) Nor would their thoughts which are similar to ours of trees, tables, and tornadoes actually be about our world's trees, tables and tornadoes. Thus, their thoughts could be true of their vat–environment just as our thoughts can be true of ours. So, the skeptic is wrong to think that a brain in a vat believes what we believe but is always mistaken.

According to the skeptic, what makes knowledge so maddeningly unattainable is the requirement that our internal beliefs must be connected in the right sort of way to external reality, and there is no guarantee that our beliefs are hooked up to the world in the right way. Tymoczko's argument narrows the gap between belief and knowledge, by showing that the content of our belief is partly an external matter. Fred I. Dretske's "The Epistemology of Belief" gives added support to this thesis by showing that the characterization of someone as having representational powers (in particular, having beliefs) logically involves the capacity for reliably picking up and processing certain sorts of information. Facts about the sort of information available when we learn a concept determine just what concept we acquire. Were we to live in an environment in which it is impossible to distinguish between A and B, it will likewise be impossible for us to represent something as an A but not a B, and thus will be impossible to mistake a B for an A. Thus, if we are unable to know that something is X, we are also unable to believe that it is X.[2]

Perhaps the most direct reliance on the Principle of Relevant Alternatives to dismiss the possibility of global hallucination or deception is to be found in Paul Moser's "Two Roads to Skepticism." Moser argues that a skeptic who insists that knowledge requires all skeptical contingencies be excluded is guilty of a fallacy: confusing the fact that we do not know in an extraordinary sense with the claim that we do not know in our ordinary sense. Skeptics who commit this fallacy have taken what

Moser calls "the low road." Moser attempts to show that we can know *in the ordinary sense* that we are not dreaming or hallucinating, because the hypothesis of a real physical world causing our experiences is the best explanation of our experiences. He argues that alternatives such as the Dream Hypothesis are inferior, since they posit gratuitous entities — there is nothing in the subjective content of our ordinary experience to indicate that we are dreaming. Dorit Bar–On in "Justifying Beliefs: The Dream Hypothesis and Gratuitous Entities" joins Moser in criticizing low–road skepticism, but questions whether Moser has really answered those "high–road" skeptics who do not commit the above fallacy. She argues that if we characterize our experiences neutrally, without presupposing the cause of those experiences, then physical objects will be no less gratuitous than the items posited in skeptical scenarios.

The Principle of Relevant Alternatives is a subspecies of a more general anti-skeptical thesis known as *fallibilism*. Fallibilists hold that our justifications can be adequate for knowledge and still expose us to the risk of error. In order for us to aspire to empirical knowledge, we must make certain assumptions about the world and, as Richard Foley puts it, "We need the world to cooperate."[3] When it does, our aspirations to knowledge are fulfilled. The fallibilist believes that this happens a sufficiently large percentage of the time to allow us to ignore justifiably the very small possibility that the world, on some particular occasion, will not cooperate. This goes against the skeptical grain. Knowledge is not a matter of luck — not even if it's only a little bit of luck.

Despite whatever luck which may be ours in not being the victims of wholesale deception or hallucination, such possibilities are unlikely to motivate any genuine doubt in those fallibilists who have grown accustomed to dismissing such alternatives as irrelevant. Yet, even if we dispose of all of the above skeptical scenarios, the Closure Principle can still generate a skeptical challenge. As Robert Nozick has pointed out,[4] the skeptic need not present a *general* skeptical possibility entailing the falsity of almost all of our beliefs. It is enough if for almost all of the propositions that we take ourselves to know, there be various distinct skeptical possibilities undermining each. Thus, if we know whether the White House is in Washington, D.C., then we must know that a meteor has not just destroyed the White House.[5] But, according to the skeptic, we know no such thing.

A fallibilist might counter the skeptic by maintaining that our belief that the White House was not just hit by a meteor can be based on the fact that it is extremely unlikely that any particular location on the earth was hit in the last few minutes. It would seem unreasonable to doubt any belief on the basis of such a minuscule chance of error. But as several of our contributors argue,[6] our evidence in cases such as this seems no more impressive than our evidence that one's own ticket in a fair lottery will lose. Despite the high probability that one's ticket will not win, it seems plainly wrong to say that one *knows* that it will lose. Any reason that one has for denying that one's ticket will win will apply with equal force to the case of every other ticket. Thus, if we cannot be said to know that our own lottery ticket will lose, we cannot be said to know that a meteor did not just destroy the White House. And it would appear that the skeptic could generate similar doubts with respect to most of our beliefs about the world.

Peter Klein, in "Epistemic Compatibilism and Canonical Beliefs," concedes to the skeptic that each of our ordinary commonsense beliefs about the world (comprising what

Klein calls "the canon") is doubtful in the same way as is our belief in the present location of the White House. Klein further concedes that knowledge requires certainty and thus must be wholly immune from doubt. So, Klein agrees with the skeptic that we are mistaken in thinking that we know most of the ordinary things we take ourselves to know. Nonetheless, Klein argues that the meta–proposition that *the preponderance of beliefs in the canon is true* is absolutely immune from doubt, and hence can be known with certainty.[7] Klein's argument for this extraordinary result turns on his claim that even though for any belief in the canon there are propositions which we are not justified in rejecting that would lower the level of warrant for the belief, such doubts can only be accommodated into our belief system by raising the warrant of other beliefs we already possess. Richard Feldman, in "Klein on Certainty and Canonical Beliefs," argues that the above meta–proposition *is* doubtful, and thus is not certain in Klein's sense. Feldman contends that propositions such as "There are canons for people of which it is not the case that the preponderance is true and which are in every relevant way similar to my canon" cast doubt upon Klein's meta–proposition. Even if we are justified in accepting that the preponderance of beliefs in our own canon is true, the belief that others who are relevantly similar to us have less than a preponderance of true beliefs in their canons casts doubt on our own meta–proposition. Still, the fact that a proposition is not certain does not entail it is not known, unless knowledge requires certainty. Feldman sides with fallibilists in contending it does not.

Sooner or later, the skeptic must come face to face with the challenges posed by the Principle of Relevant Alternatives. The skeptic's replies to these challenges vary depending on which aspect of her position she takes the relevant alternativist to be attacking. Some anti–skeptics (e.g., Fred Dretske[8]) employ the Principle of Relevant Alternatives to attack the Closure Principle. Under this interpretation of the Principle, the relevant alternativist concedes that we do not know that the zebra we observe in a zoo is not a cleverly disguised mule, but that fact does not undermine our knowledge (in ordinary contexts) that we see a zebra despite our recognizing the clear implication from something's being a zebra to its not being a disguised mule. Thus the Closure Principle does not hold for every recognized logical implication of a proposition, but only for those whose denials are relevant alternatives to that proposition. If this view is correct then the Closure Principle should be reformulated as follows: for any relevant alternative q to a proposition p, if one knows that p and knows that p entails that $not–q$, then one knows that $not–q$.

Jonathan Vogel, in "Are There Counterexamples to the Closure Principle?," argues that the original Closure Principle can be defended against the attacks of Dretske and others.[9] If we follow Vogel and accept the Closure Principle, but still wish to avoid skepticism, then we must accept that we know all of the known consequences of our knowledge, including the claim that we are not now dreaming. Barry Stroud[10] contends that if knowledge that we are not merely dreaming is required for knowledge of the world, we cannot hope to fulfill that requirement. John Heil in "Doubts About Skepticism" argues that Stroud has not been careful to distinguish the satisfaction of conditions on knowledge from the determination that such conditions have been satisfied. The absence of a proof that we satisfy the conditions on knowledge can at best only show that we cannot *know that we know* we are not dreaming. Thus, skepticism is not demonstrated to be true, but only irrefutable.

Other philosophers[11] place the emphasis of the relevant alternatives doctrine on denying the justification requirement for knowledge. On this account, if having a justification for *p* is equated with being able to make a reasoned case for *p*, then clearly some things are known without justification. We are perfectly correct in disregarding the prospect that we might be dreaming, not because we have evidence that we are not dreaming, but simply because it is, given the context, an irrelevant alternative. Likewise for the prospect of identical twins in your class. It would be entirely proper to say we know such contingencies will not obtain (thus preserving the Principle of Closure) even though we have no *particular* evidence to support either claim. As long as one has no reason to think such skeptical possibilities obtain, one is entirely justified to ignore them. But why, the skeptic might ask, should we think an alternative to be irrelevant? One popular answer appeals to our ordinary standards for use of the verb "to know." If the skeptic requires that *every* possible alternative be ruled out with hard evidence in order to claim knowledge, then, of course, knowledge is unattainable. But the simple and undeniable fact is that those are not the standards we impose on ourselves when we seek to justify our claims to know. Fluent speakers of English can use the locution "I know" with perfect correctness while wholly ignoring the criteria proposed by such a skeptic. The skeptic then appears to be *recommending* a new standard for the correct usage of "I know," a recommendation which on the face of it seems absurd since if we were to accept the recommendation we could no longer use "I know" correctly, at least not with regard to statements about the world around us.

Stewart Cohen, in "Skepticism and Everyday Knowledge Attributions," argues that anti–skeptical appeals to ordinary language sometimes fail to distinguish between the conditions that make a claim *appropriate* to utter and those that make it *true*. For, if it is possible for a claim to be appropriate but nonetheless false, then the anti–skeptic cannot simply rest her case on the appropriateness of our ordinary knowledge claims. Nonetheless, Cohen thinks our ordinary attributions of knowledge deserve respect, since we feel their intuitive pull even in the face of skeptical arguments that we also find compelling. Cohen sets about the task of explaining why our intuitions are tugged in both directions. One of his explanations employs the Principle of Relevant Alternatives in a manner that is entirely consistent with the Closure Principle. In everyday contexts, we are content with standards that permit us to say, correctly, that we know much of what we ordinarily claim to know. But when certain skeptical possibilities are explicitly raised, our standards may shift and become stricter. Thus, the truth of knowledge claims is relative to the context of utterance. We can concede to the skeptic both the Closure Principle and the claim that knowledge requires justification. We can even charitably concede that, in *some* contexts, the skeptic is correct in claiming not to know what we ordinarily think we know, so long as we persist in maintaining that in other contexts the skeptic is wrong to deny our ordinary knowledge claims.

The skeptic will be singularly unimpressed with the relevant alternatives response to skepticism, unless some way to characterize what makes an alternative *relevant* can be spelled out that does not merely beg the question against the skeptic. Ernest Sosa, in "Knowledge in Context, Skepticism in Doubt," doubts that the relevant alternative theorist can escape this charge of making a merely *ad hoc* response to the skeptic. So, Sosa proposes an alternative fallibilist account of justification and knowledge that he believes has intrinsic merit. Sosa explicates the ability to achieve justification as an in–

tellectual virtue — a competence to distinguish truth from falsehood with a good (though not perfect) success ratio within a subject field. Thus, the skeptic needs to do more than appeal to the possibility of failure, or she will merely be begging the question against fallibilists such as Sosa.

Fallibilism is sometimes thought to entail the view that while we may in fact know many things about the world we really do not ever know that we know them. This view, which has been labeled "metaepistemological skepticism" by Richard Feldman in a previously published paper,[12] flies in the face of one of the most widely discussed proposals in recent epistemology — the so-called "K–K Thesis" which says that if you know something then you know that you know it. While most epistemologists would now reject a strictly literal reading of the K–K Thesis, there are those who would accept a somewhat weaker version which says that if you know then you can, by reflective introspection, come to know that you know. How plausible one finds this suggestion depends, on some accounts, on whether one has an "internalist" or an "externalist" conception of justification. To an internalist, one can consider internally one's own justification for claiming knowledge of something and on the basis of that consideration decide correctly whether that justification is a good one or not. For the externalist, one who believed, say, that one's beliefs are justified if they are produced via a reliable method for producing true beliefs, there would have to be a reliable method for discovering that the mechanisms which produced her true beliefs were reliably connected to the world, a discovery she presumably could not make by looking "inside" her head.

Yet, internalism may itself be vulnerable to a radical first–order skepticism, according to Richard Fumerton in "Metaepistemology and Skepticism." Fumerton argues that internalism entails that in order to be justified on the basis of evidence, one must be justified in believing that the evidence *is evidence*. But a requirement that the justification for this latter belief be based on evidence leads to an infinite regress. Thus, either we are able to identify *a priori* evidence to be evidence, or we are not justified on the basis of evidence. Fumerton doubts that our recognition of contingent, non–deductive evidentiary connections can be *a priori*. Thus, he worries that internalism may lead to skepticism concerning everything that depends upon such evidence — our beliefs about the external world, other minds, the past, and the future.

Several fallibilists contributing to this volume are willing to make significant concessions to the skeptic. Bredo Johnsen, in "Relevant Alternatives and Demon Scepticism" allows that we have no reason to believe vastly many of the beliefs we take for granted. But Johnsen contends that this fact does not offer a positive reason for changing our normal practices. Similarly, Steven Luper–Foy, in "Arbitrary Reasons" argues that our systems of justifying belief and action are ridden with arbitrary elements. Still, he denies the skeptic the further inference that this arbitrariness robs us of knowledge or of rationality in our actions or beliefs. Finally, Richard Foley, in "Skepticism and Rationality," grants that there is no non–question begging way to defend our intellectual practices and no guarantees that we will avoid massive error by believing what, by our lights, we deem rational. Nonetheless, Foley thinks we should not be troubled by this predicament. For, again, these facts do not provide us with any reason to abandon practices and beliefs that, by our lights, are reasonable.

Yet the existence of this attractive middle ground between skepticism and infallibilism is denied in Jonathan Adler's "Epistemic Universalizability: From Skepticism to
Infallibilism." The contention of fallibilists that the possibility of being mistaken, even
in easily imaginable and verifiable ways, need not defeat our knowledge claims has a
disturbing consequence: that two knowledge seekers can both possess exactly the same
degree and the same quality of evidence and one can turn out to know because the world
cooperated and the other not know because the world failed to cooperate. But a
knowledge–producing situation ought to be "universalizable" so that everyone in a situation epistemically indistinguishable from that of someone who knows should also
know. Adler concludes that we must either concede to the skeptic or adopt an infalli-
bilist account of knowledge.

Such are the issues which are raised and debated in the articles which follow.
We hope that our account will convince students that there is nothing ridiculous about
the skeptic's position. Still, their universal rejection of skepticism has been partially
vindicated by the fact that none of our contributors would wholly accept the label of
"skeptic." Clearly, though, there are marked differences in what is conceded to the
skeptic. (These differences neatly divide our papers into two types: those that include
significant concessions to skepticism and those that are primarily denials of key skeptical
assumptions.) We leave it then to our readers, serious students and professional
philosophers alike, to continue the discussion.

Franklin and Marshall College

NOTES

[1] Barry Stroud, *The Significance of Philosophical Scepticism*, Oxford, Oxford University Press, 1984.
[2] Some skeptics might be tempted to push skepticism to a new level by asking "How do we know what we
believe?" But it is not clear that this doubt is even coherent. (Tymoczko argues that it is not.)
[3] Richard Foley, "Skepticism and Rationality," this volume, p. 71.
[4] Robert Nozick, *Philosophical Explanations* , Cambridge, Harvard University Press, 1981, p. 244.
[5] Jonathan Vogel discusses similar examples in "Are There Counterexamples to the Closure Principle?"
(this volume).
[6] Jonathan Vogel, "Are There Counterexamples to the Closure Principle?," this volume, p. 16, Jonathan
Adler, "Epistemic Universalizability: From Scepticism to Infallibilism," this volume, pp. 89–90, and
Peter Klein, "Epistemic Compatibilism and Canonical Beliefs," this volume, p. 102.
[7] More precisely, it is immune from what Klein calls "internal doubt." It cannot be shown to be immune
from "external doubt" but it cannot be shown *not* to be either.
[8] Fred Dretske, "Epistemic Operators," *The Journal of Philosophy* 69, 1970, pp. 1015–1016.
[9] However, Vogel claims that the Closure Principle is inessential to the skeptic's case anyway. He suggests that propositions such as "A meteor did not just destroy the White House" appear to be analogous to
lottery propositions. If one accepts a principle of non–arbitrariness — that one cannot know any member
of a set of equiprobable propositions which one has good reason to believe contains at least one falsehood
— then that principle will be sufficient to establish a skeptical result without the assistance of the Closure
Principle.
[10] *The Significance of Philosophical Scepticism*, p. 23.
[11] For example, J. L. Austin in "Other Minds" *Philosophical Papers*, Oxford, Oxford University Press,
1961, and Gail Stine, "Skepticism, Relevant Alternatives, and Deductive Closure," *Philosophical Studies*
29, 1976, pp. 249–61.

12 Richard Feldman, "Fallibilism and Knowing that One Knows," *Philosophical Review* 90, 1981, p. 274.

PART 1

CONCESSIONS

JONATHAN VOGEL

ARE THERE COUNTEREXAMPLES TO THE CLOSURE PRINCIPLE?

Very often, a person can't know a proposition without knowing various logical consequences of that proposition. So, for instance, if you know that your friend is wearing a yellow tie, you can't fail to know that your friend is wearing a tie, period. In this case, the relation of logical consequence is obvious. When the relation isn't obvious, a proposition you know may have a logical consequence you don't know — for example, a suitably obscure mathematical theorem. In light of these considerations, it seems plausible to hold that if a person knows a given proposition, that person must also know any logical consequence of that proposition which he or she recognizes as such. Putting it differently, we might say that knowledge is closed under known logical implication.[1]

The problem of skepticism about the external world gives this epistemic principle (hereafter, the "Closure Principle") a special interest. When the skeptic argues that we have no knowledge of the world because we don't know that we aren't massively deceived in some way, he or she appears to assume that knowledge has the closure property. But if it is possible to find clear examples demonstrating that closure sometimes fails, a crucial piece of support for skepticism will be removed. The purpose of this paper is to show that even the strongest apparent counterexamples to closure don't hold up under scrutiny. To that extent, the problem of skepticism is still with us.

I DRETSKE'S ZEBRA CASE

In a widely read paper, Fred Dretske offered an intriguing example which is meant to show that the Closure Principle is invalid. It is worthwhile to quote Dretske's discussion at length:

> You take your son to the zoo, see several zebras, and when questioned by your son, tell him they are zebras. Do you know they are zebras? Well, most of us would have little hesitation in saying that we did know this. We know what zebras look like, and, besides, this is the city zoo and the animals are in a pen clearly marked "Zebras." Yet, something's being a zebra implies that it is not a mule and, in particular, not a mule cleverly disguised by the zoo authorities to look like a zebra. Do you know that these animals are not mules cleverly disguised by the zoo authorities to look like zebras? If you are tempted to say "Yes" to this question, think a moment about what reasons you have, what evidence you can produce in favor of this claim. The evidence you *had* for thinking them zebras has been effectively neutralized, since it does not count toward their *not* being mules cleverly disguised to look like zebras. You have some general uniformities on which you rely, regularities to which you give expression by such remarks as "That isn't very likely" or "Why should the zoo authorities do that?" Granted, the hypothesis (if we may call it that) is not very plausible, given what we know about people and zoos. But the question here is not whether this alternative is plausible, not whether it is more or less plausible than that there are real zebras in the pen, but whether *you know* that this alternative hypothesis is false. I don't think you do[2].

M. D. Roth and G. Ross (eds.), Doubting, 13–27.
© 1990 *Kluwer Academic Publishers. Printed in the Netherlands.*

According to Dretske, the Zebra Case is a counterexample to closure because you know (a) the animals in the pen are zebras, but don't know a clear logical consequence of (a), namely,(b) the animals in the pen aren't cleverly disguised mules. I find this de-scription of the situation implausible. Given what Dretske has said in laying out the example, I think it is more reasonable to conclude that if you know (a) you know (b) as well, and closure is preserved after all.

The reason you know that an animal in the pen is not a disguised mule (if you do know it's a zebra) is that you have a true belief to that effect backed up by good evi-dence. That evidence includes background information about the nature and function of zoos. You know that zoos generally exhibit genuine specimens, and that it would be a great deal of trouble to disguise a mule and to substitute it for a zebra. Only under the most unlikely and bizarre circumstances, if at all, would such a substitution be made, and there is no reason whatsoever to think that any such circumstances obtain. If you did feel there was a chance that a switch had been made, you would have reason to doubt that the animal you see is a *zebra*. You would not, then, know that it is a zebra, con-trary to what was assumed.

Dretske's motivations for denying that you know you aren't seeing a disguised mule are not fully clear. He himself grants that the "hypothesis" that the animal is really a mule is "not very plausible", yet adds

> But the question here is not whether this alternative is plausible, not whether it is more or less plausible than that there are real zebras in the pen, but whether *you know* that this alternative is false.[3]

One might have thought that if a belief is much more plausible than its denial, a person would be justified in accepting that belief. And, then, barring Gettier–like complications, that person's belief, if true, would be knowledge.[4]

Perhaps Dretske's point is this: When you look at the pen where the animal is, you have evidence that there is a zebra there, namely that the animal looks like a zebra. Your visual evidence does not, though, give any support to your belief that the animal you are seeing *isn't* a disguised mule. For, if it were a disguised mule, your visual ex-perience would be just as it is. As Dretske says, "The evidence you *had* for thinking them zebras has been effectively neutralized, since it does not count toward their *not* be-ing mules cleverly disguised to look like zebras".[5] The upshot is that you do know there is a zebra, since you have a true belief to that effect supported by evidence. You do *not* know that the animal isn't a disguised mule, since your belief in this case is true but not supported by available evidence. So, you know the first proposition, but don't know its clear logical consequence.

I indicated above why I think this analysis is incorrect. Your background knowledge does give you justification for denying that the animal is a mule, so you know that it isn't one. Still, it may appear that the possibility of failure for the Closure Principle arises out of the situation as I described it. It seems that the usual adequate evidence for the claim "It's a zebra" (i.e. visual evidence) is different from the back-ground evidence which supports "It's not a cleverly disguised mule." If so, you could conceivably be in a position where you had the visual evidence and knew there was a zebra, but lacked the background knowledge, and hence didn't know there wasn't a disguised mule. In such circumstances, the Closure Principle would face a counterexample. To my mind, this appraisal is based on an overly atomistic conception of evidence and justification. Your belief that the animal at the zoo is a zebra is justified in part by your visual evidence, but it is *also* supported by the background information that counts against the animal's being a disguised mule. By itself, the visual evidence wouldn't be sufficient to give you knowledge that there is a zebra. To see this, consider a case where the proper background knowledge is lacking. Imagine that you are driving through ranchland out West and for some reason or other stop by the roadside. Across the way you see a black and white striped equine creature tranquilly grazing in its pen. In a situation of this sort, it seems to me, it is far from clear that you could know the animal before you to be a zebra, even though it looks just as much like a zebra as the animal in the zoo does. The difference here is that you have no applicable background information which makes it more likely that a zebra–like animal really is a zebra rather than an oddly colored mule. So, even back at the zoo, your justification that what you see is a zebra depends on background information — just as the justification for your denial that it's a disguised mule would so depend.[6] There is no discrepancy here which provides grounds for thinking that the Closure Principle is false.

One might object that the defense of closure just given makes unrealistically high demands so far as evidence is concerned. A young child at the zoo, seeing an animal that resembles an illustration in a picture book might point and happily say "Zebra!". Despite the fact that the child knows nothing about how zoos work, doesn't that child know the animal is a zebra? The issues here are complex, but there are various reasons not to take this objection as decisive. First, even if it is granted that the child knows in the full sense that the animal is a zebra, if he or she isn't capable of drawing the inference about disguised mules, the child's case doesn't bear on the validity of the Closure Principle. Moreover, it's unclear that, under the circumstances, the child really ought to be described as knowing that the animal is a *zebra*. Suppose that the child can't conceptually distinguish between 'looks like an zebra' and 'is a zebra'. Perhaps the child knows only that the animal it sees looks like a zebra, and wouldn't know that the animal is a zebra without acquiring further conceptual resources and information.[7]

II CAR THEFT CASES

I have maintained that Dretske's Zebra Case does not furnish a counterexample to the Closure Principle. But what I have said so far bears largely on the particular details of the case as Dretske sets it up. His remarks point towards the formulation of examples which cannot be treated so straightforwardly. I call these "Car Theft Cases", for reasons which will become clear in a moment. It may be, in fact, that the Zebra Case properly understood is one of these.

Suppose you own a car which you parked a few hours ago on a side street in a major metropolitan area. You remember clearly where you left it. Do you know where your car is? We are inclined to say that you do. Now it is true that every day hundreds of cars are stolen in the major cities of the United States. Do you know that your car has not been stolen? Many people have the intuition that you would not know that. If this intuition is combined with the previous one, then it seems that the closure principle is violated. That is: You know the proposition (p) 'My car is now parked on (say) Avenue A'. You also know that that proposition entails (q) 'My car has not been stolen and driven away from where it was parked'. Yet, it seems, you do not know q, despite the fact that it is for you a clear logical consequence of p, which you do know. Since, in this instance, you (apparently) fail to know a clear logical consequence of a proposition you do know, the Closure Principle is (apparently) violated.

This example turns on a rather unusual feature of the clear logical consequence q. Given your evidence, that proposition is much more probable than not, and it is at least as likely to be true as p is. To that extent, it seems as though you should be as justified in believing q as you are in believing p. Nevertheless, even though your belief that p, if true, may be knowledge, your belief that q, if true, is not. You do not know that your car hasn't been stolen by someone and driven away, despite the high probability that your belief to that effect is true.

In this respect, your belief that q resembles someone's belief that a ticket, which he holds, will not win a fair lottery. No matter how high the odds that the ticket will not win, it strikes us that the ticket–holder doesn't *know* that his ticket will not win. In fact, the analogy between a subject's belief about holding a losing lottery ticket and one's belief that one's car has not been stolen goes even further than this and is quite illuminating.

A number of features of a lottery situation are especially relevant here. First, although winning a lottery on a particular ticket is unlikely or improbable, it would not be *abnormal* in some intuitive sense, for it to turn out that the ticket one holds happens to be a winner. Second, even though the weight of the evidence is certainly against any particular ticket's winning, there is still some *statistical* evidence in favor of the proposition that a certain particular ticket will win, i. e. there is some (small) reason to think a particular ticket–holder will win.[8]

A third important consideration is that, with respect to its chances of winning the lottery, each ticket is indistinguishable from every other one. So, any reason you have for thinking that your particular ticket will lose would be an equally good reason for believing of any other ticket in the lottery that it, too, will lose. Under these circumstances, it would be arbitrary to believe of some tickets (including your own) but not others that they will not win. So, if you are consistent rather than arbitrary, and you do conclude on the basis of the evidence available that *your* ticket will not win, you will conclude the same of every other lottery ticket. Nevertheless, you hold the belief that some ticket or other will win. On pain of arbitrariness, then, it seems that you can't justifiably hold both that your ticket will lose *and* that some ticket will win. A *fortiori*, you can't know that your ticket will lose and that some ticket will win.[9]

Now, in certain important ways, one's epistemic situation with respect to the lottery is like one's epistemic situation in the Car Theft Case.[10] In effect, when you park your car in an area with an appreciable rate of auto theft, you enter a lottery in which cars are picked, essentially at random, to be stolen and driven away. Having your car stolen is the unfortunate counterpart to winning the lottery. And, just as one doesn't know that one will *not* have one's number come up in the lottery, it seems one doesn't know that one's number won't come up, so to speak, for car theft.

To be more particular, believing that your car won't be stolen is like believing you won't win the lottery, in the ways just canvassed. (1) If you park your car in an area with a high rate of car theft, an area where it is virtually certain that some car like yours will be stolen, it would not be abnormal for your car to be stolen. (2) In the Car Theft Case, your knowledge that there is a considerable amount of auto theft gives you some real statistical reason to think you car will be stolen.[11] (3) It would be arbitrary of you to believe that your car, but not all the others relevantly similar to it, won't be stolen. In general, if a person fails to know a proposition because of considerations like these, I will call the proposition not known a *lottery proposition*.

The point of this extended comparison of the lottery and the Car Theft Case has been to try to characterize a family of apparent counterexamples to the Closure Principle. The essential feature of these examples is that they are cases in which the clear logical consequence of a known proposition is itself a lottery proposition meeting the criteria just discussed. What makes the Zebra Case, in my opinion, a weaker potential counterexample to the Closure Principle than the Car Theft Case, is just the fact that the clear logical consequence of the Zebra Case is harder to see as a lottery proposition. First, it *would* be abnormal for a disguised mule to be in a zoo enclosure marked "Zebras". Second, as Dretske describes the example, it isn't apparent that you have any reason (statistical or otherwise) to think that there might be a disguised mule in the zebra pen. These two weaknesses are related to the third: it is difficult to see the presence of a disguised mule in the zebra pen as the outcome of any lottery–like process. That is, it is not as though you know that a disguised mule has been placed in some zebra pen in some zoo chosen at random. In *that* case, any reason you had for thinking that the animal you happen to see isn't the disguised mule would apply in every other situation. You would, then, have to conclude that no zoo had a disguised mule running around — in contradiction with what you know to be the case, viz. there is a disguised mule in some zoo somewhere. However, this kind of lottery element isn't present in the Zebra Case as Dretske described it. So, it is unclear why, as Dretske maintains, you do not know that the striped animal before you isn't a disguised mule.[12]

III CAR THEFT CASES AND SKEPTICISM

I would like to turn now to the implications of the Car Theft Case. That case is supposed to count as a counterexample to the Closure Principle. For, in the Car Theft Case, you seem to know a proposition about where your car is, but you apparently fail to know another proposition which is a clear logical consequence of the first one. I will maintain below that taking the Car Theft Case in this fashion, as a counterexample to closure, is not the only, or the best way, to understand it. But, suppose that the Car Theft Case does stand as a counterexample to closure; does that really help us with the problem of skepticism?

The thought was that the Car Theft Case would show that closure isn't valid in general. Then the skeptic's reliance on that principle in the course of the argument from deception would be illegitimate, and the argument wouldn't go through. However, what the Car Theft Case really shows about the Closure Principle, if it shows anything at all, is that that principle is invalid when the clear logical consequence involved is a lottery proposition *with the features mentioned above*. The Car Theft Case gives us no reason to think that closure fails to hold for clear logical consequences which don't satisfy those criteria.

The question at this point is whether the clear logical consequence in the skeptic's argument is a lottery proposition in the specified sense. The clear logical consequence the skeptic invokes is something like 'I am not a brain in a vat thoroughly deceived by sinister neurophysiologists'. And this is clearly *not* a lottery proposition satisfying the three criteria having to do with abnormality, reliance on statistical evidence, and non–arbitrariness. Let me take these out of order. (1) If the skeptic's logical consequence were a lottery proposition, I would have to be an indistinguishable member of a class of subjects of which it is known that at least one member is a brain in a vat (making it arbitrary for me to believe that I'm not such a brain). This is hardly the case, since I don't know that there are any brains in vats anywhere. The lottery–like element which was crucial to the structure of the Car Theft Case is therefore lacking here. (2) Moreover, since there is no reason to think that some brains are put into vats as a matter of course, it might well be abnormal, in an intuitive sense, for someone to turn out to be a brain in a vat. (3) Finally, given (1), there is no basis for assigning a real, positive statistical probability to the proposition that someone is a brain in a vat.

The force of these observations is that the situation in which the skeptic invokes closure cannot easily be assimilated to situations like the Car Theft Case, in which there is some reason to think closure fails. Hence, the Car Theft Case as such gives little support to the claim that the Closure Principle fails when the skeptic appeals to it. This means that the Car Theft Case provides no convincing basis for rejecting the Deceiver Argument.

It may be that, if Cartesian skepticism is the issue, no more needs to be said about the Zebra Case or the Car Theft Case. I will, however, pursue the question of whether the Car Theft Case is a genuine counterexample to the Closure Principle. Aside from whatever intrinsic interest that question may have, it is worth seeing that the results strengthen, rather than weaken, the conclusion that these examples do not undercut skepticism.

IV THE INTERPRETATION OF INTUITIONS ABOUT THE PROBLEM CASES

The Car Theft Case and its analogues provide counterexamples to the Closure Principle if we take our intuitions about such cases at face–value. For, then, it seems that in the circumstances described, a person may know some proposition (e.g. 'My car is on Avenue A, where I parked it') yet not know a clear logical consequence of that proposition (e.g. 'My car hasn't been stolen and driven away from where it was parked'). It's worth noting, though, that some additional reactions people have suggest that closure is preserved in these situations after all. Often, when faced with the possibility that their cars might have been stolen, people withdraw, at least temporarily, their initial claims to know where their cars are. Such a response is just what the Closure Principle would require.

Now, I think it must be admitted that the intuitions we have here are weak. It would be difficult to find decisive support for closure in the tendency people have to change their minds in the way just mentioned. Still, the fact that the Closure Principle seems to be respected to the extent that it is provides a motivation for analyzing that case in a way that doesn't presuppose the failure of closure.

The problem facing any such analysis is to accommodate or discredit the intuitions that produce the impression of closure failure in the first place. Those are the intuitions which lead us to say, first, that a person, under certain circumstances, would know some proposition, and, second, that the person doesn't know a clear logical consequence of that proposition. One way of trying to reconcile these intuitions with closure is to argue that some kind of shift takes place between these responses. The claim would then be that, for no *fixed* set of circumstances, do we regard a subject as knowing a proposition while failing to know one of its clear logical consequences.

Certain psychological studies provide independent reasons to believe that a shift of this kind takes place. These studies concern people's attitudes towards improbable events. They are relevant to the Car Theft Case because of the essential role played in that case by the unlikely possibility that your car has been stolen. If closure does fail here, it is because the possibility of theft, though highly improbable, undercuts the claim that you *know* that your car hasn't been stolen, even while that possibility somehow leaves intact your knowing that your car is at a certain spot. In the studies mentioned, it has been found that people may treat improbable events either as likelier than they really are or as having essentially no chance of occurring. Moreover, these assessments are unstable, and subjects can easily be influenced to grant a possibility more weight than otherwise, if that possibility is made salient to them.[13]

Such psychological considerations provide an explanation for our intuitions about the Car Theft Case. Initially and generally, in evaluating the knowledge claims in that case, we treat the chance of your car's being stolen as essentially zero. You can, then, be as sure as you need to be that your car is where you left it; you are fully justified in that belief. Thus, we are likely to say without hesitation that in the situation described you know where your car is. Later, however, when we dwell on the rate of car theft, the chance of your car's having been stolen is lent more weight. Given a (now) significant possibility that you may be wrong in believing that your car hasn't been stolen, we are no longer prepared to say that you *know* it hasn't been stolen. And, viewing the situation in this light, giving weight to the chance that the car isn't where you left it, we may be inclined to go on to say that you don't know where the car is after all. That is, there seems to be a motivation to deny your initial knowledge claim in a set of circumstances where you cannot claim to know a clear logical consequence of what you thought you knew. In that way, the Closure Principle is respected.

In short, the fact that at one time we would say that you know the location of your car, and that *shortly thereafter* we might say that you don't know your car hasn't been stolen, does not establish the invalidity of the Closure Principle. For, it may be that at no *one* time do we affirm that you know something yet fail to know one of its clear logical consequences. It is doubtful, then, that the Car Theft Case, when properly understood, provides a counterexample to the Closure Principle.

I have suggested that the anomalous character of our intuitions about the Car Theft Case may be due to some kind of epistemically important shift rather than to closure failure. My conjecture has been that the shift is a change in a probability assignment, but other mechanisms may be at work instead. An alternative explanation of our intuitions is that we are somehow induced to shift our sense of the degree of assurance knowledge requires. Thus, our estimation of the chance the subject could be wrong because of car theft would remain constant, but we would change our minds as to whether knowledge is consistent with that level of epistemic risk. There are still other forms the shift could take. It might even be that the movement in the Car Theft–type situations is between wholly distinct notions of knowledge embodying different sets of necessary and sufficient conditions.

For my purposes, the details of what actually occurs are relatively unimportant. The main point I wish to make is that there are explanations other than closure failure for our intuitions about the Car Theft Cases.[14] Or, to put it differently, a straightforward appeal to those intuitions is insufficient to establish that the Closure Principle does not hold without restriction.

V THE PROBLEM OF SEMI-SKEPTICISM

I have just argued that a simple inspection of our intuitions about the Car Theft Case does not conclusively refute the Closure Principle. The advocate of closure can claim that the Closure Principle only *appears* to fail, as the result of an epistemically important switch that takes place in the course of our thinking about the example. However, a claim of this sort leaves open what a subject, in fact, does and doesn't know in Car Theft–type situations. The Closure Principle faces a strong objection to the effect that it is incompatible with any acceptable account of what is known in Car Theft Cases.

If closure holds, and some uniform standard of knowledge applies across the board, either you don't know where your car is, or you do know that it hasn't been stolen. The latter claim seems hard to sustain. This impression is strengthened by the similarity between the Car Theft Case and a real lottery situation. Knowing that your car hasn't been stolen would be, in the ways I've mentioned, like knowing someone will lose a fair lottery. And *that* seems like the sort of thing one doesn't know. So, given the untenability of saying that you know your car hasn't been stolen, the Closure Principle will require that, contrary to what we might have thought, you don't know where your car is.

This result seems unwelcome, and things worsen quickly. It turns out that, of the propositions about the external world which we take ourselves to know, a great many entail lottery propositions as in the Car Theft Case. (The propositions with these consequences are, specifically, propositions about the current state of the world beyond our immediate environments). To see the range of Car Theft–type cases consider some other examples:

Bush Case:

        Q. Do you know who the current President of the United States is?
        A. Yes, it's George Bush.
        Q. Do you know that Bush hasn't had a fatal heart attack in the last five minutes?
        A. No.

Luncheonette Case:

        Q. Do you know where I can get a good hamburger?

A. Yes, there's a luncheonette several blocks from here.
Q. Do you know that a fire hasn't just broken out there?
A. No.

Meteorite Case:

Q. Do you know what stands at the mouth of San Francisco Bay?
A. Yes, the Bay is spanned by the Golden Gate Bridge.
Q. Do you know that the Bridge wasn't just demolished by a falling meteorite?
A. No.

It's apparent that variations on these cases can be constructed for any number of propositions about people, things, or activities. That is to say, all the propositions about such matters, which we take ourselves to know, entail lottery propositions which, it seems, we do not know. If closure holds, along with the intuition that we do not in fact know the clear logical consequences in question, the result is that we have a great deal less knowledge of the world than we had supposed. In other words, the Closure Principle leads, even without the argument from deception, to a fairly strong and unpalatable semi–skepticism. The case against closure appears that much the stronger.

But does the threat of semi–skepticism really count against the Closure Principle? The key idea here is that there is supposed to be some feature which the lottery propositions in Car Theft Cases share with propositions about genuine lotteries, in virtue of which we can't be correctly described as knowing those propositions. What is that feature? One answer is that, because of the statistical probability that your ticket may win in a genuine lottery, there is a "real" possibility of error in believing that you will lose. In other words, the crucial belief in these circumstances lacks a kind of certainty, and hence can't count as knowledge.[15] Similarly, the lottery propositions which figure in Car Theft Cases are such that a "real" possibility exists that they are false. Since, therefore, the subject can't be certain of the truth of these lottery propositions, the subject can't know them. By the Closure Principle, it would follow that the subject can't have knowledge of the propositions which he knows to entail those lottery propositions. This would result, as we have seen, in a pervasive semi–skepticism.

The important thing to realize about this way of viewing matters is that it doesn't really justify concluding that the Closure Principle is invalid. For, according to the objection, the lesson of the genuine lottery examples is that a belief can't be knowledge if there is a "real", and not merely logical, possibility that the subject is wrong about it. If this is correct, then semi–skepticism follows *without* the Closure Principle. After all, there is a "real" possibility that, e. g. you may be wrong in believing that your car is at a certain spot; it is possible that your car has been stolen. The same point applies, *mutatis mutandis*, to any other Car Theft Case. So, perhaps, there is a legitimate epistemological problem in the threat of a semi–skepticism derived from a certainty requirement for knowledge. However, since rejecting closure won't avoid that problem, that problem doesn't provide a reason for denying the Closure Principle's validity.

On another way of analyzing the lottery examples, the unknowability in these contexts of propositions like 'My ticket will lose' is due to the arbitrariness of accepting any proposition of that form. By analogy, in the Car Theft Case, you wouldn't know the proposition 'My car has not been stolen'; there is reason to think that some car or cars similar to yours will be stolen, and you have no non–arbitrary ground for believing that your car in particular won't be the one (or one of the ones) stolen. Once more, it looks as though *all* knowledge claims about lottery propositions in other Car Theft cases would be undercut by similar considerations. Then, semi–skepticism will be inevitable if closure holds.

Here again, though, I am inclined to think that there is no argument to be found against the Closure Principle as such. The analysis of the lottery effect now being entertained makes the following assumption: all other things being equal, it is unjustified to accept any member of a set of propositions L, such that the members of L are equiprobable and the subject knows (or has good reason to believe) that at least one member of L is false.[16]

It turns out that this principle is sufficient to establish semi–skepticism regardless of the validity of the Closure Principle. To see why this might be so, let's take the Car Theft Case as the basic model. The present attempt to attach the burden of semi–skepticism to the Closure Principle amounts to the claim that the non–arbitrariness requirement just stated defeats your claim to know the lottery proposition that your car hasn't been stolen — while it leaves intact your claim to know a proposition (i.e. 'My car is on Avenue A, where I parked it') clearly entailing that lottery proposition. But the entailing proposition is itself a member of a set of equiprobable propositions which, you have good reason to believe, contains at least one falsehood. That set contains, along with 'My car is on Avenue A, where I parked it', propositions like 'My neighbor's car is where he parked it', 'The postman's car is where he parked it', and so on. You may not be able to state all the members of the set explicitly, but you still have very good reason to think that there is such a set L. By the non–arbitrariness requirement, it would follow that you don't know the original proposition 'My car is on Avenue A, where I parked it'.[17]

The same line of thought would seem to apply to any case of the Car Theft–type where knowledge of a lottery proposition is blocked by the non–arbitrariness constraint. So, if the non–arbitrariness condition is strong enough to establish ignorance across the board for lottery propositions, it is also strong enough to establish ignorance of the propositions which, in Car Theft cases, entail the lottery propositions. That is to say, if the non–arbitrariness condition *plus* closure generates semi–skepticism, so too does the non–arbitrariness condition alone. Therefore, the opponent of closure cannot use that condition as the basis for an argument that the Closure Principle is invalid because *it* would lead to semi–skepticism.

The preceding discussion makes clearer what would be required in order to make the case against closure work. The critic of the Closure Principle has to identify some way in which beliefs in lottery propositions are epistemically defective, and this defect must not be shared by the mundane beliefs whose contents, in Car Theft cases, are known to entail those lottery propositions. It isn't easy to see what such a defect would be, if not the ones just considered.[18]

In this section, I have tried to show that our anomalous intuitions about Car Theft Cases and the related threat of semi–skepticism really have little to do with closure. No attempt has been made here to give a fully acceptable positive account of what really known in these cases, and I suspect that such an account may not be available at all. For it may be that the Car Theft Cases together with the problem of semi–skepticism reflect deep–seated, unresolved conflicts in the way we think about knowledge.[19]

VI CAR THEFT CASES AND RELEVANT ALTERNATIVES

It is tempting to think that the omission of a positive account of what we know could be made good by adopting a version of the relevant alternatives approach to knowledge.[20] This approach promises all the advantages, without the defects, of the treatment just given. In my view, a turn to the relevant alternatives approach is not advisable, but the proposal is interesting and deserves consideration.

According to the relevant alternatives theorist, the demands for knowledge are restricted and contextual. On one version of the theory, S knows that p just in case S possesses evidence which counts against all relevant alternatives to p; on another formulation, S knows that p just in case S would be right about p over some class of relevant alternative situations. A major problem for the relevant alternatives approach is to explicate the crucial notion of relevance it invokes. Relevance of alternatives will vary according to the subject's situation; it may also (depending on the details of the theory) be determined by the content of the subject's belief and the context of attribution for the knowledge claim. If the standard of relevance obeys certain constraints, the relevant alternatives theory may be used to explain intuitions about the Car Theft Cases in a way that doesn't deny the validity of the Closure Principle.

How would this go? Suppose the facts are as described in the Car Theft Case. Initially, we operate with a standard of relevance according to which the possibility of Car Theft is too remote to be considered. At this point, the fact that you would be wrong about the location of your car, had it been stolen,[21] doesn't impair the claim that you know where your car is. Moreover, since the possibility of car theft is remote, that possibility doesn't undercut the claim that you know your car hasn't been stolen. Closure is maintained. What produces the impression to the contrary? When the possibility of car theft is explicitly raised, somehow a new, more generous standard of relevance is instated, according to which the possibility of car theft is relevant. By this standard, you know neither where your car is nor that it hasn't been stolen. Closure is still preserved, as before.[22]

There are several drawbacks to analyzing the Car Theft Cases in this fashion. First, the supposed virtue of the analysis is that it provides an account of what you would and wouldn't know in the circumstances given. But in giving such an account, the relevant alternatives theorist must say that, in some sense or from some standpoint, you would know that your car hasn't been stolen. This seems plainly wrong, and the intuition that it is wrong is just what makes it so hard to give an adequate treatment of the Car Theft Case and its analogues. The relevant alternatives approach really doesn't accommodate the body of our intuitions in an unforced, convincing way, contrary to what one might have hoped.

Let me turn to a further point. The relevant alternatives theorist hypothesizes that, in the problem cases, there is a shift in the standard of epistemic relevance. In the Car Theft Case specifically, the possibility of car theft is supposed to be, alternatively, too remote and not too remote to be relevant. It is natural to presume that "remoteness" here is to be understood in probabilistic terms. Thus, at one time, the chance of car theft is treated as small enough to be ignored; later, in a more scrupulous frame of mind, we find even that little probability of error sufficient to undercut knowledge. Relevance, then, is a function of an alternative's probability.

This probabilistic criterion of relevance seems attractive, but it leads to trouble, especially if knowledge requires having evidence that excludes relevant alternatives. Suppose you know a proposition k. Let l be an alternative probable enough to be relevant to k, and let m be any other alternative to k which should count as irrelevant. Consider, in addition, the disjunction $(l \lor m)$, which is logically incompatible with k. This disjunction is at least as probable as its disjunct l, so it is probable enough to be relevant to your knowing k. Now, since $(l \lor m)$ is relevant to your knowing k, you have to have good evidence against it. That is to say, you have to have good evidence for the negation of $(l \lor m)$, namely the conjunction $(not-l \text{ \& } not-m)$.

Why is this a problem? If you have good evidence for $(not-l \text{ \& } not-m)$, you presumably have good evidence for $not-m$ alone.[23] Thus, your being in this favorable position with respect to $not-m$ is a condition for your knowing k. So, m isn't irrelevant to your knowing k, contrary to what we originally supposed, and there is a threat of contradiction.[24] In the face of this objection, the relevant alternatives theorist may eschew a probabilistic criterion of relevance as such. Yet, it's hard to see what alternative, and otherwise satisfactory, standard of relevance would yield the desired conclusions about the Car Theft Cases, and the value of the relevant alternatives approach in dealing with such cases seems questionable.

An important motivation for pursuing that approach is the hope that this would contribute, down the line, to a solution of the problems raised by Cartesian skepticism. Typically, a relevant alternatives theorist takes the position that we can have knowledge of the external world even though we may be victims of massive sensory deception. On this view, the possibility of such deception leaves our knowledge of the world intact because, with respect to such knowledge, the possibility of deception is an irrelevant alternative. Of course, it won't help just to declare skeptical alternatives irrelevant — that evaluation has to be made in a principled way. Now, suppose that the relevant alternatives approach really did provide an acceptable account of the Car Theft Cases. Such success would mean that relatively pedestrian possibilities like car theft are, in some contexts at least, epistemically irrelevant. All the more reason, then, to hold that the outlandish possibilities raised by skeptics are irrelevant as well.

The envisioned anti–skeptical strategy is to try to assimilate the problem of skepticism to the problem of knowledge in the Car Theft Cases. Such an attempt seems misguided, in light of considerations raised above. The issues arising in the Car Theft Cases have to do with knowledge on the basis of statistical evidence and, perhaps, the requirement of non–arbitrariness in forming justified beliefs. As I have argued, these are not the issues raised by Cartesian skepticism, and there is no reason to expect that a solution to one set of problems will have any bearing on the other set. To be more specific, let's imagine that a preponderance of statistical evidence can create situations in which some alternatives are irrelevant. This is not the situation in which we confront the skeptic (i.e., it's not as though we know, antecedently, that just a handful of the sentient creatures in the universe are massively deceived). So, it isn't easy to see here any basis for the claim that the possibility raised by the skeptic is, for us now, an irrelevant alternative.

VII CONCLUSIONS

I have argued for a number of points concerning the Closure Principle. First, Dretske's Zebra Case does not, on my view, provide a genuine counterexample to the Closure Principle. It seems more plausible that there is a violation of closure in examples like the Car Theft Case. However, even if the Closure Principle does fail in cases of that sort, there is, I maintain, no reason to believe that such a failure carries over to the contexts where the skeptic may appeal to closure. Finally, in my view, serious questions may be raised as to whether the Car Theft Cases really do demonstrate any failure of the Closure Principle at all.[25]

Amherst College

NOTES

[1] This formulation stands in need of further refinements. For, suppose someone knows both *p* and (*p* entails *q*); if that person doesn't put these things together, he or she might fail to infer, and hence not know, *q*. This kind of complication doesn't affect what I want to say below, so I will disregard it. Where a logical consequence is properly recognized as such, I will call it a "clear" logical consequence.

[2] Fred Dretske, [3], p. 1015–1016. Dretske also employs the example in his more recent [5], p. 130.

[3] Dretske, [3], p. 1016.

[4] The problem can't be that you aren't certain that what you see isn't a mule. For, any chance or possibility that the animal is a mule is a chance that it's not a zebra. If this chance makes you uncertain of 'It's not a mule' it should make you equally uncertain of 'It's a zebra'.

[5] Dretske, [3], p. 1016.

[6] Someone might maintain that you don't need this sort of background in formation at the zoo; such information is required out West only because *there* you have information which conflicts with the claim that the animal is a zebra (viz. zebras aren't generally found on Western ranchland). My first response would be that the zoo and ranchland situations are still analogous. If you happen to be at, say, the Bronx Zoo, you have evidence that conflicts with the claim that the animal in the pen is a zebra, namely, the information that zebras aren't native to New York City. In any case, the example could be further modified. Suppose you are in a situation where you mean to identify an animal by sight, but you have no information at all about whether such animals are found in your location, nor about the presence or absence of similar looking but different creatures in the area. Under those circumstances, I think, you couldn't know that the animal is of the sort you would take it to be. I am indebted here to Robert Audi.

[7] For a discussion of these issues, see Robert Stalnaker, [10], especially pp. 63–68.

[8] When I say that there is a statistical reason or statistical evidence in favor of the proposition, I mean roughly the following. Let us say that a statistical probability of an *A*'s being a *B* is one that is assigned on the basis of relative frequencies, counting cases, and so forth. On the basis of such statistical probabilities, a statistical probability may be assigned by direct inference to the proposition 'This *A* is a *B*'. If this statistical probability, in turn, is not zero, we have, other things being equal, some reason—perhaps very small—to think that the *A* in question is a *B*. I am calling such a reason a statistical reason. (My usage here follows John Pollock, [10], p. 231–252).

9 This analysis will seem misguided to those who doubt that justified acceptance is closed under conjunction. However, it might still be that the existence of the relevantly similar tickets, one of which is known to win, somehow undercuts justification (and knowledge) regardless of how things stand with conjunction. For such a view, see Laurence Bonjour, [1]. The role of the non–arbitrariness constraint in situations like this is also clouded by the fact that someone may fail to know that his or her ticket will lose in lotteries in which the winning chances of the tickets are uneven. I hope to pursue these issues in a further paper; for now, it would be sufficient for my purposes if nothing beyond statistical probability and abnormality enters into the proper characterization of these examples. My conclusions below should remain unaffected by dropping any assumptions about the significance of non–arbitrariness in these contexts.

10 The connection between lottery–like situations and situations where closure (apparently) fails has also been noticed by Jeffrey Olen in [8], p.521–526. I am indebted to David Shatz for this reference.

11 Compare this set of circumstances with those of a crime–free small town. In a locale where cars are never stolen, you would have no reason at all to think that your car in particular has been stolen, and you can know that it's where you left it. Notice, too, that in such circumstances your car's being taken would be abnormal.

12 Interestingly enough, the Zebra Case can be made more convincing by filling it out so that a lottery element is introduced. The example could be developed in this way:

Q. Do you know what the animal in the pen is?
A. Sure, it's a zebra.
Q. Do you know for a fact that members of some college fraternity didn't steal the zebra last night as a prank, leaving behind a disguised mule?

The reason one might hesitate to claim to know that such a prank wasn't carried out may be that there is some reason to think that successful, temporarily undetected college pranks are brought off from time to time. Then, in turn, you may not be entitled to say that you know that there isn't a cleverly disguised mule before you. So, it may be that, properly understood or properly filled out, Dretske's Zebra Case should be taken as a member of the family of cases for which the Car Theft Case was the paradigm.

13 These findings are summarized and discussed by Daniel Kahneman and Amos Tversky, [6].

14 Which is not to say, of course, that alternative explanations, involving closure failure, can't also be devised. I am indebted here to Richard Feldman.

15 By a "real" possibility, I mean just one for which there is a positive, even if small, statistical probability; this is a richer notion than plain logical possibility. The associated notion of certainty is the absence of any real possibility of error. This notion of certainty is weaker than the conception of certainty according to which one must have evidence that entails the truth of a belief for that belief to be certain. It is questionable whether the stronger standard of certainty represents a condition for knowledge, since it *ipso facto* rules out the possibility of knowledge by induction. I should make it clear here, though, that I don't intend these glosses to serve as a substantive account of real possibility or of certainty.

16 The statement of this principle is rough, since it doesn't rule out that the members of L could be entirely unrelated in content. Some stipulation is needed to ensure that L be suitably natural or appropriate; this problem is, of course, closely related to that of choosing an appropriate reference class for direct inference about probabilities.

17 A similar point is made by Bonjour, [1], p.73n.

18 Jeffrey Olen suggests that you know the mundane proposition because there is a "nomic connection" between the state of affairs picked out by the propositions which are your evidence and the state of affairs you believe to obtain; in the case of your belief in the clear logical consequence, however, the connection is merely probabilistic and not nomic, and you don't know. Notice, though, that in the Car Theft Case, it is nomologically possible for you to have the evidence you have and yet be wrong in your belief about both the initial proposition and the clear logical consequence. So, it is at least obscure exactly how Olen means to draw the crucial distinction. See Olen, [8]. Another explanation of closure failure that would fit the Car Theft Cases is that you "track", in the sense discussed by Nozick, the truth of initial proposition but not that

of the clear logical consequence. Nozick's account is presented in his *Philosophical Explanations* (Cambridge: Harvard University Press, 1981); however a discussion of Nozick's work lies outside the scope of this essay.

[19] For more discussion of this possibility, see my doctoral dissertation "Cartesian Skepticism and Epistemic Principles" (Yale University, 1986), Chapter II.

[20] Important early statements of the relevant alternatives theory are found in Fred Dretske, [3] and [4], and in Alvin Goldman [5].

[21] Or, alternatively: the fact that your evidence doesn't exclude the possibility of car theft.

[22] A sophisticated version of this line of thought has been developed by Stewart Cohen in [2].

[23] The relevant–alternatives theorist can't balk at this point, since we're assuming that he or she endorses the Closure Principle.

[24] A related argument may be given to show that the probabilistic criterion of relevance is unacceptable when the relevant alternatives theory is couched in terms of reliability over a range of counterfactual situations.

[25] I'm grateful to many people for help in thinking about the issues raised here: Robert Audi, Phillip Bricker, Anthony Brueckner, Fred Dretske, Richard Feldman, John Martin Fischer, Harry Frankfurt, and David Shatz. Recently, I have benefited greatly from conversations with Stewart Cohen.

BIBLIOGRAPHY

[1] Bonjour, Laurence. "The Externalist Conception of Knowledge" in P. French, T. Uehling, and H. Wettstein, eds. *Midwest Studies in Philosophy, Vol. V: Studies in Epistemology* (Minneapolis: University of Minnesota Press, 1980).

[2] Cohen, Stewart. "How To Be A Fallibilist", in J. Tomberlin, ed. *Philosophical Perspectives, Vol. II: Epistemology* (Atascadero: Ridgeview Publishing Company, 1988).

[3] Dretske, Fred. "Epistemic Operators", *The Journal of Philosophy* 69 (1970), p. 1015–1016.

[4] Dretske, Fred. "The Pragmatic Dimension of Knowledge", *Philosophical Studies* 40 (1981), p. 363–368.

[5] Dretske, Fred. *Knowledge and the Flow of Information* (Cambridge: Bradford Books, 1981).

[6] Goldman, Alvin. "Discrimination and Perceptual Knowledge", *The Journal of Philosophy* 73 (1976), p. 771–791..

[7] Kahneman, Daniel and Tversky, Amos. "Choices, Values, and Frames", *American Psychologist* 39 (1984), p. 341–350.

[8] Nozick, Robert. *Philosophical Explanations* (Cambridge: Harvard University Press), 1981.

[9] Olen, Jeffrey. "Knowledge, Probability, and Nomic Connections", *The Southern Journal of Philosophy* 15 (1977), p. 521–526.

[10] Pollock, John. "Epistemology and Probability", *Synthese* 55 (1983), p. 231–252.

[11] Stalnaker, Robert. *Inquiry* (Cambridge: MIT Press, 1984)

BREDO C. JOHNSEN

RELEVANT ALTERNATIVES AND DEMON SCEPTICISM[†]

The degree of rigor we expect of ourselves and others in making claims to knowledge varies with context, and perhaps also with the speaker's intentions. This has seemed to many to provide, at long last, the basis for a definitive response to the sceptic. Roughly, the idea is that the sceptic attempts to impose extremely high standards of rigor, and that this yields two possibilities: either those standards are contextually inappropriate, in which case we may simply reject his claims that we don't know; or they are appropriate, in which case that very fact shows the context to be extremely unusual, even bizarre, and therefore of little concern — most of our claims are not made in such contexts, and are therefore not threatened. This perspective on central epistemological questions has become known as the relevant alternatives view. According to this view, again roughly, to know the truth of some proposition is to be justified in rejecting those alternatives that are relevant by contextually appropriate standards.

It is common to find philosophers tracing the intellectual ancestry of this view back to Wittgenstein and Austin, but something very much like it is certainly to be found as early as Peirce, with his full–scale attack on the concept of radical, i.e., context–independent, doubt, and his insistence that questions are answered definitively when no one in fact challenges the consensus. But while there is no doubt some truth to such genealogical claims, one thing that distinguishes the self–styled relevant alternativists is their contention that their view provides a basis for a straightforward and definitive refutation of radical scepticism. That is, they see radical scepticism as a coherent, but demonstrably mistaken, view. I shall argue that the relevant alternativists are on to something important, but that, paradoxically, they themselves have failed to see what it is. My guess is that the bogey of scepticism has pushed these philosophers into a serious distortion of their own central insight, but whether or not this hypothesis is correct, there can be no doubt that something extraordinary has happened, since given that insight, it is finally possible to see with real clarity that the sceptic is right! Or so I shall argue.

A closely and importantly related approach to the problem is associated primarily with Robert Nozick, though it has precedents in the work of Fred Dretske and others. The focus here is on showing that knowledge is not closed under known logical implication. That is, it is not true in general that if S knows both that p, and that p implies q, then S knows that q. (In Nozick's view, all sceptical arguments rely on this principle, so that its refutation would suffice to refute all those arguments.)

But though these positions are intimately related, their relations to scepticism and its possible refutation are quite distinct. This is a result of their incorporating radically different conceptions of knowledge, which in turn are the objects of quite distinct sceptical challenges. In a word, Nozick's view is an instance of so–called "externalist" theories of knowledge, a category it shares with reliability and causal theories, among others. I shall consider Nozick's view first, and then devote the bulk of the paper to the relevant alternativist position.

[†] Reprinted by permission of the author and the editors from the Journal of Philosophy 84 (1987), pp. 643–653. The author has made some modifications to the original version.

29

M. D. Roth and G. Ross (eds.), Doubting, 29–37.
Kluwer Academic Publishers. Printed in the Netherlands.

Nozick[1] holds the following:

    S knows p iff i) p,
                     ii) S believes p,
                    iii) $\sim p \rightarrow \sim(S$ believes $p)$ and
                    iv) $p \rightarrow S$ believes p.

iii) and iv) are subjunctive conditionals, which may be glossed as follows, using the term "*not–p* world" to refer to a possible world in which p does not hold: iii) is true just in case S does not believe p in those *not–p* worlds which are closest to the actual world, and similarly, *mutatis mutandis*, for iv). Nozick argues that given this conception of knowledge, one can show that the principle of closure is false. I know that I am now typing because: I am, I believe that I am, in the nearest possible worlds in which I am not, I do not believe that I am, and in the nearest possible worlds in which I am, I believe that I am. However, I do not know, what I know to be implied by my typing, that *I am not being deceived by an Evil Demon into falsely believing that I am typing*, because even though that proposition is true, and I believe it, in the nearest possible worlds in which it is false, I still believe it, which violates condition iii).

This argument simply begs the question against the sceptic.[2] Nozick, though he takes himself to be giving serious consideration to the sceptic's views by conceding that the Evil Demon hypothesis is possible, in fact *assumes* that it is possible *but not actual*! To say, in the relevant sense, that that hypothesis is possible, is to say not only that it is logically consistent, but also that *it may in fact be true*. But if one concedes that, then one is in no position to determine what one's beliefs are like in those possible worlds closest to the actual one. Since the actual world may be Evil–Demon–governed (and may be any one of an infinite number of other possibilities), one simply has no idea of the truth or falsity of the subjunctive conditionals iii) and iv), whose truth is required for knowledge.

Relative to a Nozickean account of knowledge, the sceptic's position is that *we have no idea* whether we know our typical contingent beliefs to be true or not; that is, *we have no reason whatever* for thinking we have any such knowledge. Unless confused, he does not claim that we do not have such knowledge. How could he possibly be in a position to determine that? He has no idea what this world and its nearby neighbors are like, hence no idea whether the relevant subjunctives are true, hence no idea whether any of our beliefs constitute knowledge. This is, or should be, characteristic of the sceptic's position with respect to externalist views of knowledge, but not internalist ones. In spite of admirable sensitivity on the part of many philosophers to the distinction between scepticism with regard to the existence of (contingent) knowledge and scepticism with regard to our knowledge that we have such knowledge, it is an insufficiently noted consequence of the sceptic's scepticism that he cannot consistently take himself to know whether "external conditions" of knowledge obtain. *Relative* to an externalist *conception* of knowledge, he has no business denying that we possess knowledge, or even that we possess a great deal of it; he can only point out, or argue, that we have no reason whatever to think we do.

The relevant alternativist's conception of knowledge differs sharply from Nozick's on this score. Relative to that conception, knowledge of p requires that *I be able to justify* the rejection of all relevant alternatives to p. And here the sceptic's position will be that I can be *shown* to be in no position to do so; hence, I can be *shown* to lack knowledge. It is time now to turn our attention to this view.

I shall begin by considering an essay of Gail Stine's, which raises all of the right questions, while at the same time revealing crucial difficulties with the view.[3] (The difficulties emerge more clearly in her work than elsewhere principally because she worked out the position more completely than have others; these problems are inherent in the approach, as it has been understood thus far.) Stine develops her position in partial contrast to that of her fellow relevant–alternativist, Fred Dretske. Dretske, like Nozick after him, had argued against the closure of knowledge under known logical implication, but on classic relevant alternativist lines: we do not have any evidence on the basis of which to reject any number of hypotheses of varying degrees of wildness, but that is of no concern, since those hypotheses are not relevant alternatives to our actual beliefs.[4] Thus I know that the animals I see in the cage at the zoo are zebras, even though I have no grounds for rejecting the alternative hypothesis that they are mules painted to look like zebras, and I know that I am typing, even though I have no grounds for rejecting the alternative hypothesis that I am being deceived by an Evil Demon into falsely believing that I am.

Stine thinks that sceptical possibilities cannot be so flatly and definitively dis-missed. According to her, the Evil Demon hypothesis *is* sometimes a relevant alternative in the context of a knowledge claim. The sceptic, as she puts it, has "an opening wedge" — "tighter criteria are appropriate in different contexts. It is one thing in a street encounter, another in a classroom, another in a law court — and who is to say it cannot be another in a philosophical discussion? ...by some extreme standard, there is some reason to think there is an evil genius, after all" (254). The reason the sceptic fails to carry the day is that most knowledge claims are not made in philosophical discussions, hence the Evil Demon hypothesis is not *usually* a relevant alternative, and need not be ruled out: "a sceptical philosopher is wrong if he holds that *others* are wrong in any way ... when they say they know a great deal" (254). Those others are right provided only that they have adequately ruled out the alternatives that are relevant in the contexts of their claims.

We must consider briefly the question of how the relevance of an alternative is determined, which is recognized on all hands to be a difficult problem. After faulting Dretske's proposal on the subject, Stine settles on the idea that an alternative is relevant if and only if there is some reason to think it is true. Thus in discussing the question whether Henry knows that what he sees is a barn (in an "ordinary" situation she has described for illustrative purposes), Stine says that the possibility that it is a papier–mâché fake is clearly relevant if there are such fakes in the immediate vicinity. It is less clearly relevant if there used to be such, but no longer are; or if there are none here, though there are some elsewhere; or if there are none now, though there used to be (here, or elsewhere). Stine is well aware that the matter of when there is some reason to think an alternative true is quite vague, but she thinks that for her purposes this is not problematic. The crucial point, as she sees it, is that there is *no reason whatever* to suppose that there is an Evil Demon; or so, at least, she holds when expounding this matter: "...it seems safe to say [Descartes] was wrong if he thought there was some reason to think there *was* an evil genius. ...the whole thrust of the relevant alternatives position, as I conceive it, is that such an hypothesis is not relevant" (253).

But we have already seen Stine say that "by some extreme standard, there is some reason to think there is an evil genius... ." What are we to make of this conflict? There is an air of self–referential paradox about any attempt to sort these matters out. A philosophical essay on scepticism is presumably a paradigm case of a philosophical context, and Stine herself has rhetorically asked the question, "Who shall say" what the appropriate standard is for such a context? Indeed, she has conceded that by some (extreme) standard the Evil Demon hypothesis is a relevant alternative, and it's clear that on the sceptic's view, at least, it is precisely such a standard that is appropriate for such a discussion. Hence in discussing with the sceptic whether Henry knows the object to be a barn, we must apparently take the Evil Demon hypothesis into account as a relevant alternative; we must, at any rate, if we are to be justified in claiming to take the sceptic seriously (as Stine does). Further, we must *conclude* that Henry does *not* know it is a barn unless we can show that this alternative can be justifiably eliminated. It is pre–sumably this situation Stine has in mind when she says, "In truth, *in some sense*, scep–ticism is unanswerable" (254). The harsh truth seems to be that if Stine is right in conceding the sceptic "an opening wedge," then we must ultimately conclude that the sceptic cannot be refuted *at all*, and not only "in some sense."

But though she sometimes makes this apparently fatal concession, it appears to be her more settled view that *nothing at all* need be conceded, and here we find a second significant disagreement with Dretske. Though she goes to great lengths to defend the relevant alternatives position, with its aim of somehow isolating the sceptic, she *also* holds that the sceptic is *wrong* in claiming that his extreme standards cannot be met: she argues that *we know his radical alternatives to be false*. She takes Dretske to be right in thinking that we have no *evidence* that they are so, but wrong to abandon deductive closure on those grounds: we know they are false, because "one does know what one takes for granted in normal circumstances .. The evidence picture of knowledge has been carried too far." If this last is right, then we simply have no reason not to adopt the sceptic's standards: we can cheerfully admit his challenges as legitimate, since they are adequately met by the fact that we take the falsity of his outrageous alternatives for granted, and hence know them to be false.

To my knowledge, others have not openly followed Stine in this last, somewhat desperate proposal. One reason is perhaps obvious enough: in the history of the race, any number of false views have been taken for granted by any number of people. But if we do not follow her here, we are left with the tensions which, I surmise, originally motivated the proposal, to wit, the inconsistency of her other views: i) there is no reason whatever to suppose that there is an Evil Demon; ii) by some standard (or in some con–texts) the existence of a Demon is a relevant alternative; and iii) an alternative is relevant if and only if there is some reason to think it true.

Before turning to work these matters out, I want briefly to consider a recent effort to provide some independent support for relevant alternativism. Stewart Cohen has ar–gued that whether an individual possesses knowledge is a function of the intellectual capacities of a relevant epistemic community: S knows p provided S truly believes p and S possesses no defeater of his justification for p, whose status as a defeater is intersub–

jectively obvious within that community. In his view, it is possible for a speaker to determine deliberately which community, with its accompanying standards of obviousness, is the relevant one, simply by intending to use its standards, though "routinely our own personal/social perspective determines which standards we intend."[5] This has the consequence that I can correctly claim to know p, while insisting that a member of a genius society possessed of exactly the evidence available to me may not know p, since by the standards of his society that evidence may include a defeater whose status as a defeater is intersubjectively obvious in the genius community. In the other direction, I could attribute knowledge to a member of a moron society by intending my claim to be evaluated by the standards appropriate to that society, while simultaneously denying that I, who possess exactly the same evidence, have knowledge, since by my standards there is a defeater whose status as a defeater is intersubjectively obvious to the members of my society. This conclusion is reached independently of any considerations of scepticism, and Cohen argues that this provides support for the relevant alternativists' parallel response to scepticism, to wit, the claim that S knows p if and only if S truly believes p and is in a position to rule out all the relevant alternatives to p.

My argument against all of this will consist primarily of my positive account, but in passing several things should be noted. First, Cohen's theory of knowledge, developed independently of sceptical considerations, carries a very high price — it makes knowledge a negative function of intellectual capacity — and this makes it quite unpromising as the basis for an independent defense of the relevant alternatives position. Second, Cohen shares in the widespread confusion concerning how an alternative's relevance is determined: he indicates first that the mere presence of papier–mâché barn replicas in the vicinity makes relevant the alternative that what S sees is a barn replica; subsequently, he suggests that more is needed, e.g., knowledge that a reliable source reports the existence of the replicas; and finally, he says that there are contexts in which the Evil Demon hypothesis can be made a relevant alternative, simply by our lowering the probabilistic standards in effect, clearly suggesting that relevance is relative to standards of probability which in turn are to some extent discretionary. These various proposals, for which Cohen claims no particular originality, along with a number of others, have been subjected to a variety of criticisms in the literature.[6] But the criticisms, even if sound, show only that the strongly intuitive notion of a relevant alternative is hard to spell out with precision. This detracts no more from the interest of this view than would similar difficulties in spelling out the precise parameters of "the inherited background against which I distinguish between true and false" detract from the interest of Wittgenstein's earlier view (see *On Certainty*, par. 94). These terms may be (irremediably) vague; they are not *ipso facto* devoid of meaning or interest. What *is* seriously problematic, I shall argue, is Cohen's idea (shared by others, including, at least at times, Stine) that in a given context or situation the Evil Demon hypothesis can be transformed from irrelevant to relevant by a change in probabilistic standards. I shall argue below that the Evil Demon hypothesis has no probability whatever relative to any available data; its sometime relevance has nothing to do with its having any finite probability relative to anything.

It is time to try to separate the relevant alternativists' insights from their confusions, and to see to what extent the insights can be preserved while drawing out the sceptical consequences I take to be implicit in their view. In "Scorekeeping in a Language Game,"[7] David Lewis has provided an elegant account of how the presuppositions operative in a conversation can shift with the course of that conversation: "If at time t something is said that requires presupposition P to be acceptable, and if P is not presupposed just before t, then — *ceteris paribus* and within certain limits — presupposition P comes into existence at t." One of his illustrations of this phenomenon is an imagined dispute with a sceptic over the appropriate standards for the use of such vague terms as "flat" and "certain." Here the idea is that the presupposed standards of precision for use of these terms vary with the context, and that in the course of a conversation with the sceptic the standards get raised extremely high — perhaps to the point that the terms have no application at all. Lewis' point is that such a turn of events has no relevance to the truth of claims made earlier in the conversation, or in other conversations, when the presupposed standards were lower.

Imagine now a discussion following a presentation of Lewis' paper, in the course of which an innocent who happens to be present asks Professor Lewis, "Well, are you saying that billiard tables (in good condition) are flat, or not?" or simply, "Are billiard tables (in good condition) flat?" This brings out vividly a central Lewisian point — the answer to such a question is determinate only in a conversation in which some relevant presupposition or other exists. The innocent's question *has no answer*, precisely because no such presuppositions are in place. But the flatness of billiard tables is not of much interest; we must now try to understand the implications of this view for questions concerning human knowledge.

I am much taken with Thomas Nagel's idea that often, in grappling with philosophical questions, we are trying to reconcile two views of the world, one subjective and one objective.[8] It seems to me that the relevant alternativists are doing just that. They see that in any concrete conversation, we are guided in what we say by certain relatively clear presuppositions, which may or may not govern other conversations, and seeing this, they hope to portray the sceptic as either i) failing to understand this point, and trying to impose a particularly rigid set of presuppositions on every conversation in which anyone's knowledge of anything comes in for mention, or ii) making claims which are true (since his presence and activity determine the relevant presuppositions), but which have no bearing on ordinary claims to knowledge which appear superficially to be in conflict with them.

But all of this is more or less on the subjective side of the ledger. It emphasizes the legitimacy of our attending to the practical aspects of our commerce with the world, and that is all to the good, perhaps. Its failure lies in giving inadequate recognition to our pull toward objectivity, as reflected in another question we might have put in the mouth of our innocent: "Do we know there's a physical world we inhabit, or not?" It is just this tension, I suggest, that leads Stine to say both that there is no reason to think there is an Evil Demon, and that by some extreme standard there is after all some reason to think there is an Evil Demon.

Let me say, then, how I think sense is to be made of all of this. So far as I know, no relevant alternativist has noticed that the Evil Demon hypothesis (that is, Descartes' classic one, according to which nothing exists or ever has existed but an Evil Demon and my disembodied mind with its myriad (subjective) states) can never be a relevant alternative except in one very special context, or at any rate one special sort of context, namely, one in which *I presuppose nothing except the existence of my own mental states.* The reason for this is that the existence of anything other than those states is *logically incompatible* with the Evil Demon hypothesis! Consequently, in *any* context in which *any* other existential presuppositions are in place, the sceptic cannot make the Demon hypothesis a relevant alternative by raising standards of *probability* so high that even that vastly "improbable" hypothesis cannot be ruled out. It is *completely* ruled out, on logical grounds alone, by the presence of such presuppositions.

But there are, I have just said, special contexts in which that hypothesis is a relevant alternative. What is its fate in such contexts? Even there, as Stine sometimes sees, *there is no reason whatever* to suppose that such a Demon exists. But what has seldom if ever been noticed is that *neither is there any reason to think there is a physical universe* which we inhabit. Relative only to the existence of my subjective states, there is an infinity of hypotheses about what else reality may comprise, and each of them has the same standing: there is no reason whatever to accept any of them. The relevance of the Demon hypothesis stems not from the application of some extreme standard of probability, but from its membership in an infinite set of hypotheses all of which are equally and completely devoid of support.

The situation is quite analogous to the one in which Pascal found himself: taking for granted the existence of a physical universe, he recognized that he was "infinitely ignorant" with respect to the question of God's existence. (Notoriously, he failed to see the full force of his own argument, but that is another matter.)

Elsewhere I have argued, somewhat unfashionably, that my (largely unspoken and unconscious) beliefs about how things seem to me to be and to have been hold a privileged place in my larger body of beliefs – they are, as I have put it, forced on me (in just the way that philosophers since the time of the Greek sceptics have tried to say they are).[9] It is a coherent possibility, no matter how absurd, that I am not now sitting at a typewriter, but *for me* it is not a coherent possibility that it does not *seem* to me that I am. Thus, I suggest that the fact that it seems to me that things are a certain way, and not others, is an *unavoidable* presupposition in each of my conversations. (But notice that it is *my* presupposition, and not *ours.*) The sceptic, therefore, has a strong basis for claiming that the context which interests him is of special importance — it is the one in which I make no presuppositions except those which are utterly unavoidable. And in that context, he claims, it is clear that *either* I have absolutely no knowledge of contingent matters of fact beyond those which I presuppose (in case the concept of knowledge is to be cashed out in terms of justification), *or* I have absolutely no reason to believe that I have any such knowledge (in case the concept of knowledge is to be cashed out in terms of reliable processes, subjunctive conditionals analyzable in terms of possible worlds, etc.).

But what, then, of other contexts? Is the sceptic prepared to agree with the rel-evant alternativists that there need be nothing wrong with knowledge claims made there? Yes; but that is less of a concession than might be supposed. Stine was wrong to claim that we know whatever we take for granted, but there is an important truth in the neighborhood: we *take ourselves* to know what we take for granted, and against that background we take ourselves to be seeking further knowledge. And now we are in a position to make good sense of the relevant alternativists' principal insight. The crucial point is that I take for granted that you, as I, exist, and that we both continuously take for granted a four–dimensional world which is our common home, and indeed that we both continuously take for granted a good deal more — that our individual and collective powers of observation and memory are more or less reliable, and so forth. Thus I take for granted both that we mutually take for granted that we continuously share this vast range of things taken for granted, and that we have devised a way of speaking which is consonant with this situation: we attribute knowledge to each other and to ourselves provided that we can see that those alternatives to our beliefs which are relevant, given what we mutually take for granted, can be ruled out. (Incidentally, this perspective on knowledge helps make clear that the Gettier problem and the problem of scepticism about "the external world" are entirely independent of one another, so that recent attempts to solve both in one grand sweep were always doomed to failure. The Gettier problem is a baffling problem about how to assess knowledge claims in contexts in which much is taken for granted; a solution to that problem would have no bearing whatever on the sceptic's claim that relative only to the unavoidable presupposition of our knowledge of our own conscious mental states, we know nothing at all about the existence of an external world.)

Philosophical reflection is a late arrival on the human scene — certainly arriving much later than the development of a more or less comprehensive language. The sceptic's contribution to our understanding of ourselves, when finally and properly understood, consists in pointing out that at best we have no reason to think we know the vast number of things we continuously take for granted. But once it is recognized on all hands that our knowledge claims are (almost) universally to be taken as relative to some body of presuppositions, and that we have no reason to think we know our deepest optional presuppositions to be true, since they are entirely unsupported by our unavoidable presuppositions, it would be both mistaken and churlish of the sceptic to object to our continuing to speak in the ways we always have. He should be satisfied to have us concede that the Evil Demon hypothesis is no more outrageous than our own favored hypothesis, and he should then be prepared to let us continue with our normal practice of taking for granted our familiar world.

University of Houston

NOTES

[1] *Philosophical Explanations* (Cambridge, MA: Harvard University Press,1983).

[2] I have argued this point somewhat more fully in "Nozick on Scepticism, "*Philosophia*, **XVI**, 1 (April, 1986): 65–69. In "Demon Scepticism," *American Philosophical Quarterly*, **XIII**, 3 (July 1986): 209–216, Doug Odegard repeats Nozick's mistake by taking it that the Evil Demon hypothesis is possible, but false, while purporting to provide an independent argument against it.

[3] Gail Stine, "Scepticism, Relevant Alternatives, and Deductive Closure," *Philosophical Studies*, **XXIX**, 4 (April, 1976): 249–261. Parenthetical page references are to this paper. Limitations of space prevent me from taking up here the earlier, closely related views of Wittgenstein, especially in On Certainty (Oxford: Basil Blackwell, 1969), and of J. L. Austin, especially in "Other Minds," in his *Philosophical Papers* (Oxford: Oxford University Press, 1961).

4 See "Epistemic Operators," *Journal of Philosophy*, LXVII, 24 (Dec., 1970): 1007–1023; "Contrastive Statements," *Philosophical Review*, LXXXI, 4 (Oct., 1972): 411–430; "Conclusive Reasons," *Australasian Journal of Philosophy*, XLIX, 1 (May, 1971): 1–22; and *Seeing and Knowing*, (Chicago, Ill.: Univ. of Chicago Press, 1969).

5 "Knowledge and Context," *Journal of Philosophy*, LXXXIII, 10 (October 1986): 574–583; p. 580.

6 See, for example, Ernest Sosa, "Knowledge in Context, Scepticism in Doubt," in *Philosophical Perspectives: Epistemology* (2) , (Atascadero, CA: Ridgeview Publishing Company), ed. James Tomberlin, and Palle Yourgrau, "Knowledge and Relevant Alternatives," *Synthese*, 55 (1983), pp. 55–70, and sources cited therein.

7 In David Lewis, *Philosophical Papers*, Vol. 1 (Oxford and New York: Oxford University Press, 1983).

8 *The View from Nowhere* (Oxford and New York: Oxford University Press, 1986).

9 "The Given," *Philosophy and Phenomenological Research*, XLVI, 4 (June, 1986): 597–613.

STEVEN LUPER–FOY

ARBITRARY REASONS

We should avoid any action or belief that is arbitrary, not based on a reason, which is a consideration suggesting that we ought to perform that action or adopt or maintain that belief. This claim seems central to our lives as rational creatures, yet I shall argue against it. Doing so will allow me to resist the threat of skepticism the claim initiates. On the one hand, it unleashes the threat of theoretical skepticism, which says that since ultimately we have no reason to believe anything about the way things are, our views should all be dropped. On the other it motivates practical skepticism, which says that because we ultimately have no reason to do one thing rather than another, we should do nothing. The so–called regress argument is perhaps the most prominent source of the threat of theoretical skepticism. Since we should eschew any arbitrary belief, the regress skeptic says, we should never in the first place have believed the most fundamental claims we use as support for other views. We had no reason to believe them. Justification must *begin* somewhere, yet all beginnings are arbitrary and hence unacceptable. The practical skeptic can reason analogously: since we ought never to do anything arbitrarily, we ought never to have adopted the most fundamental goals we use as the basis for our less fundamental desires and as the ultimate rationale for all of our acts.

Most of my essay will deal with theoretical skepticism, which is far more commonly encountered than the practical sort. Much of my discussion will be concerned with foundationalism and coherentism, the most popular responses to the theoretical skeptic's regress argument. Both are ways of trying to show that since our beliefs need not be arbitrary, the skeptic has no grounds for saying we should abandon them. Neither questions the skeptic's fundamental assumption that we ought to avoid all arbitrary beliefs and acts. Precisely this assumption is my target. Once it is rejected, we can say that *even if* our beliefs and acts ultimately are arbitrary, the skeptic cannot conclude that we should stop believing and acting. The skeptic's position no longer will be a threat to knowledge claims.

Nonetheless, I think skeptics should welcome the suggestion that we ought not avoid acts and beliefs simply because they are arbitrary. Perhaps the most common complaint against skepticism is that in a practical sense it is self–refuting; that is, anyone who wants to live cannot be either sort of skeptic, and anyone who proselytizes in its name cannot take it seriously. Skeptics are bad company for the same reason as are those who live a long life advocating suicide on the grounds that nothing is worth doing. If skeptics stopped suggesting that we ought never act or believe without a reason, however, they could avoid self–refutation. Skeptics do not refute themselves in making their central point that ultimately acts and beliefs are arbitrary.

In fact, that central point is correct. Foundationalism and coherentism notwith–standing, skeptics are correct when they emphasize that knowledge and rational belief are shot through with inescapably arbitrary elements. Unfortunately, I shall be able to offer

M. D. Roth and G. Ross (eds.), Doubting, 39–55.
© 1990 Kluwer Academic Publishers. Printed in the Netherlands.

only the hint of an argument for this claim; I hope to do a more thorough job arguing that at some junctures it would be rational to do and believe things without reason.

REGRESSING WITH SKEPTICS

The forms theoretical skepticism takes are of course many; however, I shall limit my attention to two, namely the sort that relies on the regress argument and an offshoot thereof. Some clarification of these arguments will position us to refute them.

According to the regress argument, a reason to believe something is a consideration suggesting that it is true. Moreover, all justification of my views, including views concerning what I ought to do, is *inferential* in the following sense: it takes the form of an argument with premises I believe, a conclusion, and a rule of deductive or inductive logic which says that the latter is probable given the truth of the former, or entailed by the former. If I am justified in some belief, I must have observed that it is 'probabilified' by my other beliefs, and this observation is at least part of my basis for believing what I do — or at least such an observation *would* be available to me if I were to seek it out. But the same holds for these other beliefs, and similarly for any belief on which I base *them*. Given that human beings cannot sustain infinitely regressing chains of beliefs, then my beliefs must ultimately rest on claims that are arbitrary. Yet arbitrary claims are unacceptable. I ought not believe them. But if I ought not believe my foundational views, then I ought not use them as a basis for other beliefs. Hence I ought to unravel my entire scheme of beliefs from the bottom up. Let us call this argument *regress skepticism.*

What I shall call *rule skepticism* also assumes that reasons to believe something are considerations suggesting that it is true, and that justification is always inferential. But instead of worrying about regresses of premises, the rule skeptic points out that the trustworthiness of rules of implication and probabilification must be justified or at least justifiable if the use of these rules is to result in justified beliefs. Yet the only way the rules *can* be justified is to take for granted the sorts of conclusion for which those rules are the guidelines. The idea is that if we assume we have a set of good conclusions, then we can use them to test the rules that endorse those conclusions. Unfortunately, justifying rules this way is circular; we can either justify conclusions using rules whose trustworthiness we take for granted, or justify the trustworthiness of rules by taking conclusions for granted; either way our starting point involves completely arbitrary assumptions, claims not based on reasons. Since arbitrary assumptions won't do, we ought to abandon our beliefs.

Two main theses are involved in rule and regress skepticism. The first is one defended by almost all if not all skeptics; it is the view that our ultimate beliefs are arbitrary. We may as well call it the *arbitrariness thesis.* The second tenet is of more recent vintage: we ought not assent to arbitrary claims, where an arbitrary claim is one that, even upon some reflection, we cannot link to a consideration that suggests it is true. Recently Gilbert Harman labeled this tenet the *principle of negative undermining.*[1] I shall follow his lead, except that I shall usually shorten Harman's label to 'the negative principle.'

Rule and regress skeptics, with their commitments to the arbitrariness thesis and the negative principle, will be the targets of my essay. I do not claim that any particular historical figures adopted either form of skepticism. Still, while the fits are not perfect, regress skepticism has much in common with Pyrrhonism while rule skepticism shares a good deal with Humean skepticism.

Sextus's Pyrrhonism is neatly summed up in the following passage:

> The Skeptic's end is quietude in respect of matters of opinion and moderate feeling in respect of things unavoidable. For the Skeptic, having set out to [decide which] sense impressions. . .are true and which false, so as to attain quietude thereby, found himself involved in contradictions of equal weight, and being unable to decide between them suspended judgment; . . .there followed, as it happened, the state of quietude in respect of matters of opinion.[2]

As this passage reveals, Pyrrhonians did recommend avoiding any beliefs concerning the way things are. But they did not do so on the grounds that arbitrary beliefs ought to be eschewed. Instead, they did so on the grounds that avoiding factual judgments is the way to achieve equanimity.[3] The Pyrrhonians's point was that if we are concerned to make factual judgments we cannot escape being tormented by the worry that our views are wrong, while if we drop the whole matter we can base our lives on the way things seem and thus achieve the happiness brought by not caring about what is really going on. To help us become carefree "in respect of matters of opinion," they prescribed a device that had worked for them: each time we are tempted to infer that things *are* some way on the grounds that they seem that way, we should take note of the fact that there are *other* ways things seem that appear to support a contrary judgment about the way things are. Such juxtapositions of the appearances caused the Pyrrhonians to suspend belief concerning reality, and they hoped the juxtapositions would work for us.

It seems clear that the upshot of such juxtapositions of the appearances is that they reveal the arbitrariness of each of our factual beliefs, and so it is tempting to explain any power they had to eliminate the beliefs of the Pyrrhonians by saying that the Pyrrhonians implicitly thought that we should never believe the arbitrary and that we typically act on this implicit thought. M. F. Burnyeat gives Pyrrhonism this sort of explanation in his influential essay "Can the Skeptic Live His Skepticism?", and he says that in the course of discussing Pyrrhonism Hume adopts it as well.[4] Burnyeat claims that he and Hume agree on the core of an interpretation of Sextus's Pyrrhonism: Sextus thought that (1) our claims are demonstrably unfounded, (2) we should abandon unfounded claims, and (3) we *will* abandon our claims, "in the normal case," once we realize they are unfounded.[5] Burnyeat goes on to claim that Hume's criticism of Pyrrhonism consisted in an undefended rejection of (3), that Hume ignores the argument Sextus gives for (3), and that he, Burnyeat, can make good on the rejection of (3): he can show that it is impossible to live without belief.

However, Burnyeat ought not attribute (2) to Sextus.[6] True, it is difficult to understand how Sextus's juxtaposed appearances could wash away the beliefs of anyone other than those who subscribe to (2), those who do not think they ought to believe what they cannot show more likely to be correct than not. But Sextus would have considered (2) a piece of "dogmatism". So he said that steering clear of factual claims seems to help people who yearn for quietude reach their goal, and that suitable juxtapositions seem to have the causal power to rid us of these distressing claims, but was careful not to explain how, nor to say that his was the only doxicide capable of relieving us of pesky beliefs.[7] Perhaps other devices would also work — such as a lobotomy.

Pyrrhonian skepticism is thus quite different from its modern counterpart, regress skepticism; the former, unlike the latter, offers a prescription for living a worthwhile life. If it worked as promised, the prescription would not make our lives worthwhile, as Hume and Burnyeat pointed out, since a life without any beliefs is too much like a vegetable's existence. It is worth noting, however, that one way to think of my attempt to refute the modern skeptics's negative principle while leaving their arbitrariness thesis intact is to think of it as an attempt to fashion a livable form of skepticism. (There is another respect in which Pyrrhonian skepticism is unlivable; a less ambitious form of skepticism would help here as well: Pyrrhonianism suggests that once we give up the effort to reach the truth, we can live by the appearances. Yet if each appearance is paired to another which suggests a contrary view about what is going on, then we cannot base our lives on the way things seem after all.)

How about Hume's own skepticism? He did think that the trustworthiness of induction could be defended only if we take for granted claims whose defense requires induction, so that either our *a posteriori* views or our belief that induction is trustworthy is arbitrary. So he was to that extent a rule skeptic, though he limited the arbitrariness thesis to *a posteriori* beliefs and the rules of probabilification associated with such beliefs. Our knowledge of necessary truths he thought immune to skeptical doubt.

What about the rule skeptic's negative principle? Would Hume have said that we should avoid arbitrary beliefs since it is always irrational to believe something whose truth has not or cannot be shown likely? This would explain why he seemed worried about the discovery that all of our inductive inferences are based on an assumption that cannot itself be justified, namely the proposition that the future will resemble the past. But he did not use the "rational–irrational" terminology, and he never on *any* grounds (a fortiori on grounds of irrationality) recommended that we *stop* believing that the future will resemble the past. Instead, he famously claimed that we *must* make use of inductive argument, and we must believe various views with its help.[8]

So much for the historical roots of rule and regress skepticism. Now I want to assess the merits of these arguments, starting with the negative principle on which they both rely. I shall give skeptics the arbitrariness thesis and whatever follows from it. The negative principle is my quarry. It should be rejected, I shall maintain, because honoring it is epistemically irrational. Epistemic rationality and irrationality, in turn, are defined in terms of what contributes to the goal of purely cognitive beings. So to defeat the negative principle, I must first discuss that goal.

THE NEGATIVE PRINCIPLE AND THE GOAL

Several philosophers, starting with Aristotle, have offered a rough characterization of rationality as efficient goal seeking. I accept this characterization. But our goals are many, and some of them have nothing to do with the aim of the purely cognitive beings who are the concern of epistemologists. These beings are a useful fiction, a simplifying device, invented for the purpose of clarifying ideal theoretical inquiry. We can characterize cognitive beings as ones whose efforts to fulfill their goal are efficient, and who are so narrow–minded and ruthless as to ignore all other aspirations (such as the various concerns of daily life); at least, we can do so once we have identified the aim of purely cognitive beings. The conduct of these fictional agents then defines a kind of rationality

— call it epistemic rationality. Epistemic rationality therefore includes a 'practical' element: it is designed to achieve the cognitive end.

Unfortunately, those who discuss this goal have not been especially careful. BonJour's description of the epistemic goal — truth — is definitely not very clear, and by no means complete.[9] Are we supposed to maximize the total number of accurate claims we accept? Won't that call for too much tolerance of false beliefs? An alternative description of the epistemic goal is one I, Richard Foley, and others before us have offered: to maximize one's true beliefs while minimizing one's false beliefs.[10] Unfortunately even this description is unacceptable because it is impossible to make sense of counting beliefs, and it is by no means obvious that the trade–off between truths and falsehoods should be numerical rather than a matter of the importance of the belief as a component of one's whole belief scheme. Compare the following candidates for belief:

(1) All physical objects attract each other inversely as the square of the distance sepa–
    rating them.
(2) Some sand is on my porch.

Is the inverse square law one belief, and hence no more nor no less important a com–ponent of a belief scheme than a belief about the dirt on my stoop? And if so, then should the epistemic goal lead us to stop searching for laws of nature like the inverse square law once we notice that it is far easier to crowd our brains with trivial but un–controversial beliefs like my observation about my sandy porch?

Talk in this context of 'numbers' of beliefs should be dropped altogether. If we do so we can provide a better characterization of the cognitive goal, I suggest: a com–plete and accurate understanding of what is the case. One could have a great number of correct beliefs (say ones about the sand on the beach), but they may amount to a terribly incomplete view of what is the case; they may amount to an accurate picture of trivial features of a small corner of the universe. Similarly, when put together, a collection of just a few of one's beliefs might be so encompassing and accurate that it amounts to a very complete and accurate view. And this may be so even if *none* of them is strictly true, given the fact that accuracy is a matter of degree while truth is not: even if every–thing Newton claimed about the laws of nature were strictly speaking false since it needed correction in light of Einstein's innovations, the Newtonian version is still quite accurate. Surely purely epistemic creatures should prefer a scheme of beliefs that in–cludes Newton's versions of the laws of nature over a scheme that focuses on trivial features of grains of sand even if all of the beliefs in the former are strictly speaking false while all of the beliefs in the latter are strictly speaking true. What the Newtonian claim lacks in accuracy it more than makes up in comprehensiveness.

Nothing I have said implies that our *attaining* the cognitive goal is necessary for us to be epistemically rational. I have characterized the goal of cognitive beings; I did not provide a set of necessary and sufficient conditions for rational belief. If we fail to meet the conditions in such a set we are considered irrational. By contrast, failing to meet the *goal* of rationality does not make us irrational. We are rational to the extent that our efforts to attain the cognitive goal are efficient given our resources.

In my formulation of the cognitive goal, I refer to what is the case, but I am as–suming that one of the things that *is* the case is that various things *ought* to be the case, where 'ought' is understood in its broadest sense.[11] Some philosophers would argue that only the 'fact' component of the above goal is the concern of purely cognitive beings. Yet a cognitive being is concerned with *any* kind of truth, so unless we want to deny that there is such a thing as an ethical truth we must understand cognitive beings to be interested in ethical truths. Those who draw a sharp fact–value distinction can still adopt my statement of the cognitive goal, of course. They have only to reject my assumption, which must remain undefended here, that no sharp distinction exists.

If, as I have assumed, rationality is efficient goal seeking, and if, as I have also assumed, the goal of a purely cognitive being is a complete and accurate understanding of what is the case, then purely cognitive beings ought to do their best to achieve that goal. When we show that to some extent an action or belief helps achieve that end, to that extent we have proven it epistemically rational. When we show that to some extent an action or belief prevents us from reaching the cognitive goal, to that extent we have shown it irrational. Methods that help us achieve the cognitive end would be codified by what we may call *principles of rational belief management* (what Harman would call a "rule of belief revision"[12]).

It turns out that if the skeptic's negative principle is correct at all then it must itself be one of these belief management principles. Certainly it cannot be a principle or rule of implication or probabilification. Examples of such rules are modus ponens (p, and *if p then q*, taken together, imply *q*) and perhaps the following inductive rule: *All of the many A's observed have been B's*, together with *Here is an A*, probabilifies *Here is a B*. Instead, the negative principle is supposed to spell out a policy that rational agents conform to in conducting their affairs. Certainly rational agents will be *interested in* rules of implication, since those rules help determine how to apply principles of belief management. But those rules do not tell us what we ought to do when confronted with the implications of our views. Suppose I believe *Whenever I whistle, Spot shows up* and *I whistled.* Suppose also that I look around and come to believe *Spot has not shown up.* Modus ponens tells me that the first two beliefs imply that Spot has shown up, but that rule of implication does not itself tell me whether to believe *Spot has shown up, Spot has not shown up, I did not whistle,* or Spot does *not always show up when I whistle.* For this choice I need principles of rational belief management.

Given that the negative principle is offered as a belief management principle, we would assess it the same way we would assess any putative belief management principle: by ascertaining its utility from the standpoint of the cognitive goal. When we do we will find that the negative principle should be rejected as irrational.

In rejecting the negative principle, we will be following the example of Harman, who notes that if we had to abandon all of those beliefs with which we do not associate a justification, we would have to abandon most of them, since as a matter of psychological fact people can rarely keep track of the justifications by which they arrive at their views. (Nor would it help to say that the negative principle does not force us to abandon beliefs we can justify *on the spot;* if we can rarely keep track of the justifications for our views, it is unlikely that we can provide very many of our thoughts with fresh justifications on the spur of the moment.) Harman rejects the negative principle on the grounds that this result is "absurd," and I agree that the result itself is so strikingly implausible that it constitutes grounds on which to reject the negative principle.[13] But he was not discussing skepticism, and since some (including Harman himself) would say that showing a view leads to skeptical results is itself a reductio ad absurdum, antiskeptics cannot rest much on avoiding absurdity.

We can rest a great deal, however, on considerations about our goal as cognitive beings, which is an approach Harman did not take. Given the negative principle, we must do something even more drastic than drop beliefs whose justifications we have forgotten. Assuming that the ultimate bases for belief are arbitrary, as we have granted the skeptic, the negative principle would require us to stop believing *anything*. Yet an injunction against believing anything (or even one against believing very much) would obviously make it impossible to achieve the goal of arriving at a complete and accurate understanding of what is the case. The negative principle has turned out to be quite unattractive.[14]

Indeed, given that our ultimate beliefs are arbitrary, it is rational to adopt man-agement principles that allow us to retain these fundamental yet arbitrary views, since the alternative is to simply give up on the attempt to achieve the epistemic goal. One policy for dealing with arbitrary beliefs that is far milder than the negative principle is given by the *principle of positive undermining* ('the positive principle'), according to which we should abandon a belief if we positively think that our reasons for believing it, if any, are misleading; that is, either the belief at hand is not justified and we are able to probabilify its negation, or we are convinced that our reasons for assenting to it involve indispens-able false claims.[15] Needless to say, if we have no reason to think something, then our reasons cannot be misleading, and the mere fact that we have not provided evidence *for* a view does not mean we have evidence against it. Indeed, it would be difficult to find convincing evidence against our most fundamental claims, simply because they are fun-damental. So the milder principle would not automatically enjoin abandoning arbitrary beliefs. On the other hand, if we really had positive evidence against a view, or we saw that it rests on false assumptions, our cognitive goal would almost certainly be served by abandoning that view.

Obviously, the positive principle could not stand as the sole belief management principle. The epistemic goal motivates cognitive beings to adopt other principles. One additional management principle would instruct them to increase the *coherence* of their belief scheme (since they want to *understand* reality, and do so accurately). I take it that this vague principle implies the positive principle, so no tension exists between the two. Another management principle would direct cognitive beings to increase the *scope* of their belief scheme (since they want a *complete* picture of reality). This principle *is* in tension with the others, since it is sometimes possible to increase scope by knowingly adopting far–reaching beliefs that conflict with other beliefs and hence lower the overall coherence of one's scheme. When management principles conflict, cognitive beings must work out the best compromise they can.

At any rate, providing a complete set of management principles is beyond the scope of this essay. For our present purposes focusing on the positive principle is good enough, since in almost all cases our desire for a complete and accurate understanding is served by avoiding any claim based on misleading grounds, and since the positive principle avoids the difficulty that so thoroughly undermines the negative. And note that principles instructing us to increase the scope and coherence of our belief scheme no more force us to abandon fundamental yet arbitrary beliefs than does the positive principle. Even though our fundamental beliefs are arbitrary it is epistemically rational to tolerate them through the application of something like the positive principle rather than to abandon them through the application of the negative.

SKEPTICISM AND THE POSITIVE PRINCIPLE

The loss of the negative principle bodes ill for the regress skeptic, who argues first that our ultimate beliefs are arbitrary and then uses the negative principle to show that we should abandon them and everything resting on them. Deprived of that principle, regress skeptics cannot complete their argument. Suppose they try to appeal to the *positive* principle instead. As we have already noted, the positive principle does not motivate us to revise our views just because their justification happens to be claims that are themselves arbitrary. So far as that principle is concerned, a justification that begins with an arbitrary view is a perfectly good justification. Hence the positive principle is useless to regress skeptics.

Rejecting the negative principle also stops the rule skeptic. For suppose we continue to blunt the impact of the arbitrariness thesis with the positive principle, saying that arbitrary beliefs are fine so long as there is no good reason to regard them as mistaken. To be sure, applying this principle involves the need to identify evidence so that we can tell when we have such overwhelming evidence against a belief that it must go. Since we identify evidence using rules of induction and deduction, we need these rules to apply the positive principle. Even if we grant rule skeptics that these rules are necessary, however, they still cannot complete their argument. They can claim that to defend rules of inductive or deductive logic we must take a set of conclusions for granted, while to defend conclusions we need to take the trustworthiness of rules of logic for granted, but this admission of the inevitability of an arbitrary starting point is no longer worrisome once we replace the negative principle with the positive.

It is instructive to connect together the elements of the case against rule skepticism in a slightly different way. Given our goal as cognitive beings, we want a complete and accurate understanding of reality. If the only ways to get started on that project are to arbitrarily adopt a set of claims or to arbitrarily accept the trustworthiness of a set of logical rules, then that is what we should do. From the standpoint of rationality, some picture (whether internally consistent or not) is necessarily better than none, for adopting no picture whatever guarantees that we will completely fail to meet our goal, and a picture adopted through initial moves that are themselves arbitrary is certainly more likely to be a closer approximation to a complete and accurate understanding of reality than no picture at all. Even a set of claims (such as 'There is a dollar on the table' and 'There is a pen one foot from my foot', etc.) each of which is false (since in fact the bill on the table is counterfeit, and the pen is thirteen inches from my foot, etc.), may contain a great deal of information about the world (as we said earlier). And inconsistent views may have individually accurate components that we can exploit without exploiting the contradictions themselves — that is, without going on to believe anything we like on the grounds that a contradiction 'entails' everything.

I have accepted the awkward claim that some beliefs we have no reason to think true are rational. This is awkward because people tend to define a 'justified' *and* a 'rational' belief as one we have reason to believe true. Most of the awkwardness can be avoided, however, if we drop the regress skeptic's assumption that we are justified in thinking things only when we have reasons to think those things true. Let us accept the usual convention that a rational belief is the same thing as a justified belief, but let us understand a reason to be a consideration suggesting that a claim is true or that an action is one we ought to undertake. Then we may say that we are justified in believing things that are not based on reasons.

It is time to sum up. Since the negative principle would force us to give up all of our views, it prevents us from meeting the definitive goal of cognitive beings, namely a complete and accurate understanding of what is the case. A far better belief management principle, from the point of view of epistemic rationality, is the positive principle, according to which we ought to avoid consenting to claims when we think that our reasons for accepting them are misleading. Through this principle we may rationally believe claims that are fundamental yet arbitrary.[16]

While defending the positive principle, and defusing skepticism, I have assumed that our ultimate beliefs are based on no reasons whatever. It is time to consider whether that strong assumption is plausible. I shall do so by asking whether foundationalists and coherentists, who hold the leading approaches to justification, manage to show that arbitrary beliefs are escapable. Needless to say, I cannot consider all of the many accounts of justification available, nor even all of the versions of foundationalism and coherentism. But I hope that my sketch of the main reasons foundationalists and coherentists cannot escape arbitrary beliefs can be extended to cover other approaches to justification, so that the arbitrariness thesis is at least rendered plausible.

THE ARBITRARINESS THESIS

The most familiar moves that have been offered to block the regress argument, at least in discussions of fact skepticism, are foundationalism and coherentism. Proponents of both approaches think it important to block the regress, and presumably that is because they think the skeptic is correct in saying that arbitrary beliefs should be avoided since such views are irrational. Contemporary philosophers who have endorsed the negative principle include Lawrence BonJour and Richard Foley.[17] BonJour uses it in the course of justifying coherentism; Foley uses it while justifying foundationalism. Thus BonJour says

> One's cognitive endeavors are epistemically justified only if and to the extent that they are aimed at [the truth], which means very roughly that one accepts all and only those beliefs which one has good reason to think are true. To accept a belief in the absence of such a reason. . .is to neglect the pursuit of truth; such acceptance is, one might say, *epistemically irresponsible*.[18]

Aside from their agreement on the negative principle, however, foundationalism and coherentism overlap very little. The former says that justification begins with *basic* beliefs, that is, ones that are self–supporting (though not incorrigible) in the sense that having them makes it likely that they are true. The claim that some beliefs are basic is likely to lead foundationalists to deny the skeptic's assertion that all justification is inferential, but whether or not they reject the inferential conception of justification, foundationalists deal with skepticism by saying that some beliefs support themselves. Coherentists are far more likely to agree that all justification is inferential. Whereas foundationalists say that basic beliefs support both themselves and everything else, co–herentists say that each belief is paired to others in the scheme that support it, though none is foundational.[19] On the coherence theorist's view, justification involves the whole of a big belief scheme: these schemes themselves are self–supporting, in that having them makes it likely that they are roughly correct.

The most obvious way to defend the arbitrariness thesis against foundationalists would be to reject their claim that all of our views rest on a foundation of basic beliefs. Instead, we could say, it makes no sense to say that our foundational views are self–supporting. Either they are simply arbitrary, or else they are not really basic and instead are justified on the basis of some picture of how we arrived at them. I shall not take this approach, however, even though I think it is correct. Instead, I shall adopt a simpler tactic. I want to give foundationalists their basic beliefs. Let us suppose that our beliefs really do rest on ones whose very presence ensures that they are probably true, so that they are self–justifying. With basic beliefs as a head start, can foundationalists hope to silence skeptics who say that arbitrary beliefs are unavoidable?

They cannot. They can bypass regress skepticism if we give them basic beliefs, but the baton is then passed, relay–style, to the rule skeptic. To be useful, basic beliefs must be our link to other claims about the world, for basic beliefs are highly restricted. I presume that an example of a basic belief would be a percept statement like 'I seem to see a flamingo now'. It takes a greater stretch of the imagination to call an observation statement like 'There *is* a flamingo now' self–justifying, but let us say it is. Our interest in percept statements is due to their utility toward getting us to other percept statements and to nonpercept statements, so that prediction, retrodiction and claims about the world become possible. And a good deal of our interest in observation statements is their utility toward getting us to theoretical statements, including 'Flamingos are tasty,' and 'The structure of all water molecules is the same.' If we think that there is such a thing as inductive *logic*, that is, a set of *formal* rules specifying when the premises of an argument probabilify its conclusion without entailing it, we might say that the link is made by these ampliative rules or principles of induction. If we doubt that there is such a logic, we must still grant that there is such a thing as inductive *reasoning*, which involves inferring a conclusion from premises that do not entail it. Accordingly, we might say that the link is the simple belief that given the nature of the world (and given, perhaps, the nature of our specific circumstances), the truth of one of the things we believe is a reliable indicator of the truth of another; for example, the truth of 'I seem to see a flamingo now' reliably indicates the truth of 'There is a flamingo now.'

Suppose we find ourselves skeptical about inductive logic, and admit only inductive reasoning. Nonetheless, as Hume would have pointed out, to take the truth of one claim as a reliable indicator of the truth of a second (not entailed by the first) is to take it for granted that ours is the sort of world in which the one sort of fact reliably indicates the other. Perhaps we can justify that claim about the world, but only if we take for granted other claims about the world. One way or another we take a great deal for granted.

Now suppose that we grant the existence of inductive logic. As Hume *did* point out, the only way we can justify one inductive logic over an alternative one is to take for granted some of the claims that may be justified only with the use of an inductive logic. Roughly, to justify an inductive logic involves arguing that it is truth–conducive. Given our end as cognitive beings, we want it to be likely that our inductive logic will get us from accurate claims about aspects of the world to other accurate claims about the world, where the former do not entail the latter. To the extent that we have argued persuasively that our inductive logic is truth–conducive, to that extent we have justified it. However, the claim that our inductive logic is truth–conducive is itself a substantial claim about the world. As such, it can be justified only by taking for granted a substantial set of as–sumptions about the world, assumptions support for which it is the very purpose of our inductive logic to provide.

So either we take our inductive logic for granted, and use it to defend claims about the world, or else we take for granted a picture of the world that is substantial enough to provide grounds for thinking that our logic is truth–conducive. Either way, extensive arbitrariness is central to our belief scheme.

A way to resist this rule–skeptical defense of the arbitrariness thesis is to suggest that we can avoid taking *either* an inductive logic or world picture for granted since we can justify *both* through reaching what John Rawls has called a reflective equilibrium. One of the earliest descriptions of this mechanism was provided by Nelson Goodman in *Fact, Fiction, and Forecast.*[20] Concerning deductive inference Goodman wrote:

> Rules and particular inferences alike are justified by being brought into agreement with each other. A rule is amended if it yields an inference we are unwilling to accept; an inference is rejected if it violates a rule we are unwilling to amend.[21]

He then extended his conclusion to inductive inference:

> An inductive inference, too, is justified by conformity to general rules, and a general rule by conformity to accepted inductive inferences.

What Goodman described is a process whereby a rather narrow equilibrium is reached between accepted inductive inferences like 'I have seen 99 thousand gophers living in holes and none who did not, so all gophers live in holes' and general rules like 'From: large numbers of observed F's are G's and no observed F's are *non–G*'s, infer: all F's are G's.' However, a 'wider' equilibrium could be reached if we throw in other convictions of which we are confident, including claims about the world, like 'When I seem to see a gopher, usually one is really there.' I take it that this notion of reaching a wide reflective equilibrium is at the heart of the coherence theory of justification; the idea is that the initial confidence we have in some claims transfers over to other claims and to our rules of deductive and inductive logic, and vice versa.

I do not doubt that our confidence in a whole scheme of beliefs can be bolstered if we make mutual adjustments leading to a state of reflective equilibrium. Unfortunately, reaching reflective equilibrium does not eliminate the arbitrariness we underlined when discussing foundationalism. We certainly can pick out claims about the world and par–ticular inductive inferences in which we feel confident and use them as a guideline for adjusting the rules of our inductive logic. We could even introduce a notion of arbitrariness–relative–to–such–and–such, and say that relative to our background assumptions about the world, our inductive rules are not arbitrary. But these moves still involve taking the background assumptions for granted. Similarly, if we swear by some inductive logic, we can use it to adjust our inductive inferences and claims about the world, but we are still taking its truth–conduciveness for granted. To say that the arbitrariness vanishes if we make *both* kinds of adjustment — from rules to inferences and back again — is absurd. What happened is that the coherentist takes one thing for granted at one time, then something else at another, depending on which element in our scheme of beliefs is under scrutiny. Indeed, this very point is admitted by coherentists; as soon as they have explained that our belief scheme is analogous to Otto Neurath's ship in that any part of it may be rebuilt but only while borne by other parts, they always acknowledge that circularity is involved, though they quickly add that the circularity 'is not vicious' — whatever that means.[22]

Connecting issues up differently reveals another way to show that coherentism does not eliminate the arbitrary elements in our scheme of beliefs. The coherentist presumes that the practice of reaching reflective equilibrium helps ensure that a belief scheme is a complete and accurate understanding of reality. But why presume that? Here coherentists are in the same sort of predicament as foundationalists. Coherentists can use a world picture to defend the truth–conduciveness of reaching equilibrium, or they can simply take that truth–conduciveness for granted. Either way, extensive arbitrariness is inescapable.[23]

SKEPTICISM ABOUT GOALS

My discussion of theoretical skepticism has been based on the assumptions that rationality is, roughly, efficient goal pursuit, and that our goal as cognitive beings is a complete and accurate understanding of reality. But what's to stop skeptics from raising doubts at a deeper level? Why not imagine a kind of skeptic who argues that our fundamental goals in general and the cognitive goal in particular are arbitrary in the sense that we have no reason to adopt or retain them, and so we ought not? Such goal skepticism, as I shall call it, would be a kind of practical skepticism. Goal skeptics say that when we have no reason to have some goal, no consideration suggesting that we ought to adopt or retain it, we should drop it. It is not unrelated to the theoretical skepticism we have already discussed, for on the assumption that we cannot drop all beliefs concerning what ought to be the case unless we also avoid seeking anything, radical theoretical skepticism would entail goal skepticism. Yet we have already refuted the theoretical skeptic's negative principle; won't the same strategy work against goal skepticism as well? Perhaps, but it is by no means clear.

Until now our response to skeptics has involved saying that to the extent that an action is useful toward our cognitive goal, to that extent it is epistemically rational; since even arbitrary beliefs are a crucial part of our effort to achieve our goal, yet the negative principle prevents us from retaining any of them, we ought not honor it. Applied to goal skepticism, this strategy would have us say that even if the cognitive end is arbitrary, having it plays a key role in our effort to achieve our goal as cognitive beings, so if a version of the negative principle forces us to abandon arbitrary goals, we ought instead to abandon that principle. The version of the negative principle used here by the goal skeptic, one that is more general than its predecessor (since believing things is only one kind of act), says that we ought to avoid doing anything arbitrarily, and that includes adopting or retaining goals. This strategy seems ineffective against goal skeptics. It amounts to saying that we must *have* the cognitive goal if we expect to *achieve* the cognitive goal, so any principle of goal revision that stops us must go. While that is (trivially) true, it is useless, since the status of the cognitive goal is precisely what the skeptic questions.

But wait. True, showing that we must have a goal if we expect to achieve it is no reason to have that goal in the first place. But our response to the skeptic was not *intended* to be a reason to adopt or retain the cognitive goal. We admitted that that goal is arbitrary. What we were trying to show was that it is epistemically rational to retain the cognitive goal in spite of its arbitrariness. For that purpose, it *is* effective to point out that retaining our goal helps us achieve it, since by definition it is epistemically rational to do what serves the cognitive end. We have a response to goal skeptics after all. Their argument against our cognitive goal was that it, like any other arbitrary goal, should be abandoned. Our response is that the skeptics's general negative principle — never act arbitrarily — interferes with our cognitive goal. From the standpoint of epistemic rationality, we would do well to prefer something more like a general *positive* principle: never do what you have reason not to do. This principle does not inveigh against having or adopting arbitrary goals. So the general negative principle and not our arbitrary cognitive goal is what we should abandon.

Let me put my objection to the skeptic's case against arbitrary goals differently. The goal skeptic thinks that the arbitrariness of a goal suggests that that goal is not to be valued. But why should the skeptic, of all people, assume that arbitrariness is of disvalue rather than of value or neither? After skeptics find that our ultimate reason to want or value what we do is arbitrary, why should they conclude their finding supports indifference or nihilism? Mustn't skeptics admit that our ultimate reason to *avoid* or *disvalue* what we do is arbitrary as well? So mustn't they admit that ultimately we have no reason *not* to continue to want and value the things we do, or even to create new desires, values and projects for ourselves without pretending to have any reasons for doing so?

Our response to goal skeptics gave them much of the ground they claimed. It involved admitting that the cognitive goal is arbitrary, so that rationality itself is in the service of an arbitrary end. Perhaps we ought not admit any such thing. Why not at least delay, by making fairly standard moves? I doubt that the cognitive goal is ultimate for everyone. Whether it is ultimate for us or not, however, we might still try to deny the arbitrariness of the cognitive goal by noting its instrumental value toward *other* ultimate goals we have, such as surviving, or enjoying ourselves.

It little avails us to respond this way, however. One problem is that to do so is to change the subject. We have been concerned with epistemic rationality, defined in terms of fictional agents who efficiently pursue the cognitive end and who ignore all others. To invoke other sorts of ends is to leave the context of the purely epistemic and to enter the context of a more general sort of rationality, namely rationality as concerned with all of our goals, not just the epistemic end. This broader sort would lead us to take roughly the attitude that all of our goals ought to be achieved efficiently, though when they conflict a compromise of some sort must be worked out either by eliminating a suspect goal, or by designing our lives as best we can to fulfill even the goals that conflict.

Changing the subject is, however, not much of a problem, given the extreme artificiality of *purely* epistemic rationality. No one (except perhaps Schopenhauer[24]) would want to be the cold mirror of reality that a purely cognitive being aims to be. Even those of us for whom the cognitive end is an ultimate aim have other interests that compete for our attention and energies. Some of these lead us to regard many aspects of a complete and accurate picture of reality (perhaps most — how can we tell?) as trivial. No one, for example, should care how many blades of grass were growing on the White House lawn on August 1, 1981. So let us extend the scope of our discussion, and ask whether the arbitrariness thesis can be refuted from the standpoint of rationality in general.

Included in the more generous supply of goals might well be some that constitute reasons to pursue the cognitive end. But defending it this way only serves to delay the inevitable. The skeptic will only ask why we pursue *those other* goals.[25] If (though we probably could not do this) we managed to show that our ultimate goals are mutually supporting, the skeptic will ask why we pursue our *package* of ultimate ends rather than some other. We might respond by suggesting that our cognitive goal or our package of ultimate ends are hard–wired in, so that we could not abandon them even if we wanted to. Yet the retort would be immediate: that does not make them any less arbitrary. Suppose we *did* have the ability to change our goals; suppose that through genetic engineering or with the potions of a clever chemist we could give ourselves any profile of ultimate desires we wanted to. The fact is that we have no reason to prefer one profile over another. Perhaps there are other gambits to delay the skeptic, but eventually we must agree that our ultimate goals are arbitrary.

A POSSIBLE PARADOX

I have assumed that in the theoretical sphere, a reason to believe something is a consid–eration suggesting that it is true. I argued that it is rational to believe some things even when we have no reason to think them true, and I did so by saying that something like the positive principle should feature prominently among the belief management principles. But if I defend the positive principle as I have, and say it is rational to hold a belief through the application of this principle, haven't I given a *reason* to hold that belief? In arguing that the positive principle is better from the standpoint of the cognitive end than the alternative, so that it is rational to believe arbitrary claims endorsed by that principle, haven't I given a consideration suggesting that we ought to believe those claims?

I *have* given a practical reason to adopt the positive principle, but I have given neither a practical nor a theoretical reason to believe particular arbitrary claims rather than others. The positive principle is indiscriminate among beliefs; it does not pick out par–ticular ones and say we ought to believe them. So far as that principle is concerned, any of an unlimited range of beliefs will do just as well. Moreover, nothing I have said singles out one set of arbitrary beliefs as more useful than an unlimited range of others as a means for achieving the epistemic goal. Hence my argument that it is rational to be–lieve fundamental arbitrary claims does not show that those claims are not arbitrary after all.

One final point. Even if we *could* show that one set of beliefs is more useful than any other as a means for achieving the epistemic goal, that would not show that our cognitive scheme is devoid of crucial arbitrary elements. For as we saw earlier, even the epistemic goal itself is arbitrary. However, since an arbitrary goal can still be a reason to act, we need not deplore our predicament in the way that existentialists did.[26]

Trinity University

NOTES

[1] He does so in Chapter 4 of his excellent book *Change in View: Principles of Reasoning* (Cambridge, MA: MIT Press, 1986). Harman's version of the negative principle is this (p. 39) : One should stop believing *P* whenever one does not associate one's belief in *P* with an adequate justification (either intrinsic or extrinsic). Incidentally, Charles Peirce adopts something resembling the positive principle and rejects something resembling the negative in "The Fixation of Belief," reprinted in J. Buchler, ed., *Philosophical Writings of Peirce* (New York: Dover Publications, 1955); see especially "erroneous conception" number 2, p. 11.

[2] Sextus Empiricus, *Outlines of Pyrrhonism*, Chapter 12.

[3] One way to read Richard Rorty's *Philosophy and The Mirror of Nature* (Princeton: Princeton University Press, 1979) has it offer the Pyrrhonian advice that we ought to stop worrying about facts, about correctly mirroring the world.

[4] M. F. Burnyeat, ed., *The Skeptical Tradition* (Berkeley: University of California Press, 1983), pp. 117–149.

[5] As Burnyeat says on p. 119 (ibid.),

Sextus defends exactly the proposition Hume challenged the Pyrrhonist to defend, the proposition that he should, can, and does give up his belief in response to the skeptical arguments. . . .

[6] Hume never ascribed to the Pyrrhonian skeptic the claim that we *should* abandon views when we realize they are unfounded. According to his interpretation, Pyrrhonians thought (or hoped) that we *would* drop unfounded views when we identify. Here is the passage in which Hume lodged his complaint against Pyrrhonism: A Pyrrhonian cannot expect that his philosophy will have any constant influence on the mind. . . . On the contrary, he must acknowledge. . .that all human life must perish, were his principles universally and steadily to prevail. . . . [People] must act and reason and believe; though they are not able, by their most diligent enquiry, to satisfy themselves concerning the foundation of these operations, or to remove the objections, which may be raised against them. (*Enquiry*, Sect. XII, 128; quoted by Burnyeat, ibid., p. 117). Nothing said here is inconsistent with the possibility that on Hume's reading (like mine) Sextus has (falsely) reported that juxtaposing the appearances is desirable since as a matter of fact it eliminates factual belief and thereby produces peace of mind.

[7] For a more extensive exposition, see J. Annas's and J. Barnes's excellent discussion in *The Modes of Scepticism* (Cambridge: University Press, 1985), especially p. 49ff.

[8] For a discussion that does a good job of turning aside some recent silly interpretations of Hume's position on skepticism, see Robert Fogelin's book *Hume's Skepticism in the Treatise of Human Nature* (London: RKP, 1985).

[9] See his book *The Structure of Empirical Knowledge* (Cambridge, MA: Harvard University Press, 1985). Cf. Alvin Goldman, *Epistemology and Cognition* (Cambridge, MA: Harvard University Press, 1986), p. 3: "The central epistemological concepts of appraisal, I argue, invoke *true belief* as their ultimate aim."

[10] Steven Luper–Foy, "The Causal Indicator Analysis of Knowledge," *Philosophy and Phenomenological Research* 47 (1987); Richard Foley, *The Theory of Epistemic Rationality* (Cambridge, MA: Harvard University Press, 1987). See also Bernard Williams's *Descartes* (New York: Pelican Books, 1978), Chapter 2, and Roderick Chisholm's *Theory of Knowledge*, Second Edition (Englewood Cliffs: Prentice–Hall,

1966), p. 15, where he suggests that each person must meet two "purely intellectual requirements": (1) he should try his best to bring it about that if that proposition is true then he believe it; and (2) he should try his best to bring it about that if that proposition is false then he not believe it." He also points out that in *The Will to Believe and Other Essays in Popular Philosophy* (New York: David McKay Co., Inc., 1911), p. 17, William James had said that our "duty in the matter of opinion" is that "we *must know the truth*: and we *must avoid error.* . . ."
Incidentally, the talk, in these passages, about epistemic "duties" is preposterous unless it is figurative. Flouting one's *duties* makes one immoral. Not doing one's best to get the truth and to avoid the false makes one ignorant.

11 As clarified by Bernard Williams, *Ethics and the Limits of Philosophy* (Cambridge, MA: Harvard University Press, 1985), Chapter 1.

12 Op. cit., Chapter 2.

13 Op. cit., p. 39.

14 The restrictions Harman places on "tentative" and "full acceptance" of hypotheses seem to force him to say that it is always irrational to tentatively or fully accept arbitrary claims: "one needs a special positive reason to keep on accepting something as a working hypothesis" (op. cit., p. 47), "[to be justified in fully accepting *P*,] it is not enough to look for positive evidence in favor of a hypothesis; one must also try to find evidence against the hypothesis." (p. 48) However (because of the positive principle discussed later), he would also say that once we *do* act irrationally and tentatively then fully accept an arbitrary claim it is rational to *continue* believing that arbitrary claim. Harman's restrictions are unacceptable given that fully accepting fundamental arbitrary claims is the means to achieving the cognitive goal.

15 A version of this principle, too, was named by Harman (op. cit.), Chapter 4. Harman's version is "One should stop believing *P* whenever one positively believes one's reasons for believing *P* are no good"

16 If successful, my argument against the negative principle obviously would also show that Barry Stroud and Michael Williams are mistaken in accepting a "conditional" form of skepticism. In his essay "Epistemological Realism and the Basis of Scepticism," *Mind 47* (1988), p. 417, Williams states this version of skepticism as follows: "if we hand the sceptic his foundationalist presuppositions, there is no refuting him. . . ." For Stroud's version, see his book *The Significance of Philosophical Scepticism* (New York: Oxford University Press, 1984). As the next section of my essay will make clear, I would also reject Williams's claim that skepticism presupposes foundationalism (ibid., p. 418).

17 Foley:

> For a proposition *p* to be genuinely uncontroversial for *S* . . .it is not enough for him to lack an argument for *not–p*. He must also have reasons in favor of *p*. For if *S* were to have no good reason to think that *p* is true (as well as no argument for not*p*), withholding judgment on *p* would be his best option. (op. cit., p. 49)

I might add that in "Evidentialism" (*Philosophical Studies* 48 [1985]), Richard Feldman and Earl Conee, while defending a view called 'evidentialism', write

> The paranoid person epistemically ought not believe that he is being spied upon when he has no evidence supporting this belief. We hold the general view that one epistemically ought to have the doxastic attitudes that fit one's evidence. We think that being epistemically obligatory is equivalent to being epistemically justified.

18 Op. cit., p. 8.e

19 Nor are coherentists and foundationalists the only epistemologists who adopt the skeptic's negative principle. Even reliabilists like Alvin Goldman do (as in his essay "What is Justified Belief?" *Justification and Knowledge* [Dordrecht: D. Reidel, 1979] 1–25), though in other ways they disagree quite fundamentally with coherentists and with those foundationalists who say that only beliefs may justify beliefs. Reliabilists suggest that being justified is not merely a matter of having beliefs that support themselves or one another; instead, it is at least partly a matter of how we are related to the world. But while our relationship to the world sometimes ensures that our views are justified, beliefs still must be justified to be rational, and if they are not rational they should be abandoned.

[20] (Indianapolis: Hackett Publishing Company, 1979), Chapter III.

[21] Ibid., p. 64.

[22] Neurath introduced his metaphor in "Protokollsatze," *Erkenntnis* 3 (1932) 206.

[23] BonJour would characterize the situation of the coherentist as follows: (a) if our knowledge of those metabeliefs of ours that (more or less) accurately detailed our first–level beliefs were unproblematic, so that we could detect how coherent they are, and if these first–level beliefs *were* coherent, then we could show that our first–level beliefs were not arbitrary. (b) However, we cannot know or justify ourselves in thinking that these metabeliefs are correct since the only possible style of justification for them is a coherence justification, and such a defense, extended to metabeliefs, is viciously circular. Our metabeliefs are arbitrary. We merely *presume* they are true; we make what BonJour calls the Doxastic Presumption. So (c) a very radical skepticism is in order (op. cit., p. 105). We cannot justifiably believe that we have a rough idea of what it is that we believe, and so we cannot justifiably believe anything at all. Given what BonJour says about epistemic irresponsibility—that is, given the negative principle—it follows that we ought to abandon all of our beliefs. However, BonJour never draws this consequence, and instead suggests that we investigate what we could justify if we *had* unproblematic access to our metabeliefs. Unfortunately, BonJour's point about skepticism is buried in his book; it comes in the space of a couple of paragraphs on p. 105, where BonJour's discussion could be clearer. Occasionally he has been misinterpreted (e.g., by Anthony Brueckner, *Philosophical Studies* 54 (1988) 153–160); he does not intend to imply that the Doxastic Presumption allows us to bypass skepticism when he says that once we make that presumption we can go on to show that our commonsense beliefs are probably true.

[24] "Knowledge. . .can. . .throw off its yoke, and, free from all the aims of the will, exist purely for itself, simply as a clear mirror of the world. . . . If this kind of knowledge reacts on the will, it can bring about. . .resignation. This is the ultimate goal, and indeed the innermost nature of all virtue and holiness, and is salvation from the world." *The World as Will and Representation*, Vol. 1, E. F. J. Payne, trans. (Indian Hills: The Falcon's Wing Press, 1958), Sect. 27, p. 152.

[25] In his useful essay "Reflective Equilibrium, Analytic Epistemology and the Problem of Cognitive Diversity," *Synthese* 74 (1988) 391, Stephen Stich argues that we ought to reject the analytic epistemologist's proposal "to arbitrate between competing [criteria for evaluating cognitive processes] by seeing which one accords best with the evaluative notions 'embraced by everyday thought and language'" (p. 409). Stich's thesis supports my own since it defeats one possible type of argument for the claim that the epistemic goal is not arbitrary. Moreover, I agree that the analytic epistemologist's methodology is misleading if taken to provide critique–proof criteria for evaluation. After all, commonsense evaluative notions are themselves subject to evaluation. Still, devising clear accounts of the commonsense evaluative notions is useful if we want to work out a sharp picture of the conception of rationality approximating the one we actually hold. Nothing stops us from then criticizing it, or simply embracing it while recognizing its arbitrariness. (Stich's thesis is anticipated by various authors including Wesley Salmon and Brian Skyrms; see his acknowledgements in his note 29.

[26] This essay of a colloquium at the University of Texas at Austin, December 2, 1988. I thank the members of the philosophy department there for their advice and criticism. I also thank Jonathan Vogel and Curtis Brown for helpful comments on an earlier version of this essay.

RICHARD FUMERTON

METAEPISTEMOLOGY AND SKEPTICISM

Although the terminology is relatively new, it has been possible for some time now to distinguish two quite different sorts of questions in epistemology — metaepistemological questions and normative epistemological questions. The terminology is borrowed from and the distinction parallels the metaethical/normative distinction in ethics. Just as in doing metaethics one is concerned with analyzing concepts fundamental to ethical thought, so in doing metaepistemology one is concerned with analyzing concepts fundamental to epistemological thought, such concepts as knowledge, evidence, and justification. Similarly, just as in doing normative ethics one is concerned with deciding to what if anything the ethical concepts apply, so in doing "normative" epistemology one is trying to determine what one knows, what one is justified in believing, what constitutes good evidence for believing what. Classical issues concerning skepticism seem to fall most naturally into "normative" epistemology. The arguments of the skeptic most often *presuppose* metaepistemological positions but there is often far too little explicit discussion of the nature of knowledge or justified belief. Those of us who think that metaethics always takes logical priority over normative ethics will no doubt feel that metaepistemology takes logical priority over normative issues in epistemology and we may understandably feel that the way to get to the bottom of traditional skeptical problems is to first arrive at the correct metaepistemological position.

The issue is complicated, however, by the fact that at least some philosophers insist that one evaluate metaepistemological views in part by their implications concerning skepticism. Thus philosophers like Roderick Chisholm have indicated unequivocally that they will reject a metaepistemological account if skepticism is the inevitable result.[1] A sufficient reason for rejecting a Cartesian account of knowledge, some would argue, is that within such an account we do not know much, if anything, of what we think we know. A sufficient reason for rejecting a Humean account of legitimate reasoning is that it makes the vast majority of the beliefs we take to be justified unjustified. Again the argument has its parallels in metaethics. At least some philosophers, for example, reject consequentialist conceptions of morally right action because given such accounts it follows that it would be right to do certain things (break promises, lie, punish innocent people etc.) that we pre–philosophically take to be obviously wrong.

We might call the view that rules out skepticism from the start and evaluates metaepistemological views in part by the way in which they will allow one to avoid skepticism, epistemological commonsensism. While my concern is not to evaluate the view in any sort of detail here, I do want to make at least one comment on one sort of argument for it. The most obvious question the skeptic will ask is *why* we should assume at the outset that the beliefs we take to be justified are justified. The answer that we must start somewhere will no doubt not please a skeptic who is not inclined to start a careful re–examination of all of our beliefs with the presupposition that most of those we take to be justified are justified. A somewhat more sophisticated answer involves

M. D. Roth and G. Ross (eds.), Doubting, 57–68.

appeal to science and evolution. We can assume, the argument goes, that most of our beliefs are justified because it is obviously evolutionarily advantageous to have justified beliefs and science tells us that that which is evolutionarily advantageous has a high probability of occurring other things being equal. Such an argument will not impress traditional skeptics, of course, because they will correctly point out that the pronouncements of science can be used to refute skepticism only if they are justified. Their justification, however, presupposes solutions to the various problems the skeptic presents. Whether or not science can refute traditional skepticism will, as we shall see, depend itself on the plausibility of certain metaepistemological views. But for now I also want to remind the reader that even if we give ourselves full access to the pronouncements of science, it is not clear that science does tell us that it is evolutionarily advantageous to have justified beliefs. Many of the empirical conclusions of science seem to suggest that much of what we expect or take for granted is "programmed" into us through evolution. If children had to reason deductively and nondeductively to the various conclusions they take for granted, their chances of survival would, no doubt, be rather slim. There is no reason to believe that we are not programmed to simply respond to certain stimuli with certain intentional states, just as lower life forms appear to be programmed to respond to certain stimuli with appropriate behavior. Now given certain metaepistemological views, the causal origin of these spontaneous unreflective beliefs might be sufficient to make them justified, but one might also conclude that nature has simply no need to satisfy the philosopher's desire for the having of fully justified belief. One might, in other words, argue that if what science tell us is true, one might well expect that nature has probably not constructed us to believe only that which we have good reason or evidence to believe. Commonsense science might well tell us that through evolution nature has decided that it would be better for us to have true beliefs than justified beliefs.

Now of course if we could *know* this we would again have reason to believe that most of our beliefs are true. My only concern is to point out that our scientific *beliefs* are perfectly compatible with the conclusion that those beliefs are quite unjustified, and may well even suggest it. It is probably just this thought that led Hume to observe with respect to the question of whether or not man should believe in a physical world that:

> Nature has not left this to his choice, and doubtless esteem'd it an affair of too great importance to be trusted to our uncertain reasonings and speculations.[2]

It what follows I will not presuppose from the outset that skepticism is false. But I do want to explore the implications of certain metaepistemological views for the possibility of refuting traditional skeptical challenges. Again I do so not to reject those views that make it difficult to refute skepticism but to understand clearly the way in which metaepistemological views will shape our approach to skepticism. While my main purpose is to see the interconnections between certain views, I am myself inclined to a certain version of internalism which makes skepticism very difficult to avoid and I want to make clear what I take the possibility of avoiding skepticism to depend on within the framework of that internalism.

I THE INTERNALISM/EXTERNALISM CONTROVERSY AND ITS IMPLICATIONS FOR
SKEPTICISM:

Perhaps the dominant metaepistemological controversy today is the Internalism/Externalism controversy. It is a controversy with potentially enormous implications for traditional skeptical problems. I think it is fair to say that almost all traditional skeptical challenges simply presupposed at least one version of internalism and that if externalist metaepistemological views are correct it changes the entire way in which one would address the skeptical challenge.

To make this point we should begin by defining the internalist/externalist controversy. Unfortunately, however, it is notoriously difficult to find a way of defining the issue that puts paradigm internalists and externalists in the appropriate categories. I have discussed the problem of defining the controversy in some detail elsewhere[3], so I will confine myself to only a few remarks that particularly concern the issue of skepticism. The internalist is sometimes characterized (particularly by the externalist) as someone who maintains that one can satisfy the necessary and sufficient conditions for knowledge and justified belief only if one has access to the fact that they are satisfied. "Access," of course, is itself an epistemic term, so on this way of understanding internalism, the internalist might be thought of as someone who is committed to the view that knowledge entails knowing (perhaps directly) that one knows; having a justified belief entails justifiably believing that one has a justified belief. Paradigm externalists like Goldman, Dretske, Armstrong, and Nozick would of course reject this view.[4] In one way or another all attempt to understand knowledge and justified belief in terms of nomological connections (connections defined in part by reference to causation, universal or statistical laws, contingent subjunctive conditionals). On a primitive causal theory of knowledge, for example, one knows that P when the fact that P is a cause of one's belief that P. Obviously on such a view the belief that P might constitute knowledge even though one's belief that one knows that P does not. One's belief that P might be caused by P even though one's belief that one's belief is caused by P is not caused by the fact that one's belief that P is caused by P. On Goldman's first reliability analysis of justified belief (in "What is Justified Belief?"), a sufficient condition for my belief that P being justified is that it is caused by a belief–independent process that generates (not accidentally) mostly true beliefs (complications that need not concern us here are added both to the account of reliable belief–independent processes and to the recursive analysis that defines justified beliefs resulting from belief–dependent processes). Again it is clearly possible for my belief that P to be reliably produced even though my belief that P is reliably produced is not reliably produced. Given the view, having a justified belief would have no implications for the possibility of having a justified belief that one has a justified belief. To consider one last example, Nozick wants to understand knowledge in terms of the truth of certain contingent subjunctive conditionals. He starts with the idea that one knows that P when one has a true belief that P employing some method M and one would believe that P via M if P were true and one wouldn't believe via M that P if P were false. Modifications that we can ignore are introduced to cope with the availability of alternative methods and the results that would occur from using them. Again if anything like Nozick's account were correct, one could clearly know that P without knowing that one knows that P.

If we do understand the internalist as someone who believes, the externalist as someone who denies, that knowing entails knowing that one knows and having a justified belief entails having a justified belief that one has a justified belief, it is small wonder that the internalist is often charged with inviting skepticism. On the face of it the skeptic need only point out the apparently vicious regress that arises on the internalist's view. To know or have a justified belief one must be capable of having infinitely complex intentional states. The regress is in some respects worse than the traditional regress foundationalism is designed to avoid which involves only the having of an infinite number of different justified beliefs. As long as one allows that one can have justified *dispositional* beliefs, after all, it is not clear that there is any difficulty in one's having an infinite number of justified beliefs (that 2 > 1, that 3 > 1, that 4 > 1 and so on). But even if finite minds can have an infinite number of different beliefs, it is doubtful that a finite mind can have even a dispositional belief in a proposition having infinite complexity, and that is what the extreme internalism defined above involves. (Notice that this problem affects even weaker forms of internalism that assert only that knowledge entails the *capacity* to know that we know). There may be ways of avoiding the conclusion that this internalism involves a vicious regress but I am not prepared to defend any. Rather, if internalism is defined this way, I will abandon internalism.

Let us call the above internalism global internalism, and distinguish it carefully from what I shall call inferential internalism. I do not think that classical skeptical arguments in general presuppose global internalism. Rather such arguments typically presuppose only a principle that I call the Principle of Inferential Justification:

To be justified in believing one proposition *P* on the basis of another *E* one must be 1) justified in believing *E* and 2) justified in believing that *E* makes probable *P*.

To accept such a principle is *not* to accept the claim that having a justified belief entails having a justified belief that one has a justified belief. It is to accept the claim that one cannot have evidence *E* justifying one in believing *P* unless one at least is justified in believing that evidence *E and* one is *aware of*, i.e. has a justified belief in, the evidential connection between *E* and *P*. It is this enormously plausible principle that underlies many traditional skeptical arguments but also seems at play in relatively commonplace discussions about the rationality of certain positions. When the astrologer offers the alignment of planets as evidence for the existence of an era of prosperity, one naturally enough raises questions concerning the astrologer's evidence for thinking that there is any connection between the positions of planets and prosperity here on earth, and to the extent that we reach the conclusion that the astrologer has no such evidence we reject the idea that his conclusions are justified or rational. Hume's arguments for skepticism with respect to the physical world directly parallel the above more mundane discussion. Having reached the conclusion that all of our beliefs about the external world are based ultimately on what we know about the character of our sensations, Hume wonders how we established, i.e. came to know or justifiably believe, that our sensations are reliable indicators of the presence of physical objects. He correctly concludes that one could never inductively establish sensations as evidence for the existence of physical objects for one could never *observe* the necessary correlations between sensations and objects necessary to get knowledge of the premises of an inductive argument. Since he was further convinced that the only *candidate* (and not a very good one at that) for the source of such knowledge is inductive reasoning, Hume argued that one could never establish sensation as evidence for the existence of physical objects and thus concluded (implicitly relying on the second clause of our principle of inferential justification) that one could never be justified in believing anything about the physical world based on sensation. The traditional skeptical problem about knowing the past just is the problem of satisfying the second condition of the principle of inferential justification for inferences we make to the past from present memory experiences. How, the skeptic wants to know, did you discover that memory experiences were reliable indicators of past events? An inductive argument will involve premises describing correlations between the having of memory experiences and their being veridical but we can then invoke the first clause of the principle of inferential justification to question the justification for accepting the premises of such an argument. When we refuse to allow memory as a source of knowledge of the truth of such premises, we seem to have nowhere to turn and the skeptic is in a powerful position indeed. Just as the principle of inferential justification together with gaps between sensation and the physical world, and memory and the past, generate the classical problems of skepticism with respect to the physical world and the past, so the principle together with the existence of evidential gaps between behavior of other bodies and their mental states, the past and the future, the characteristics of objects in the macroworld and the theoretical entities of the physicist's microworld generate their own skeptical problems.

Notice that on this reconstruction of classical skeptical arguments we can easily de-emphasize the importance of the familiar skeptical scenarios — dreams, hallucinations, brains in a vat, evil demons, and the like — for the force of the skeptical challenge. Indeed, it seems to be a serious error to suppose that the force of skeptical positions derives somehow from the intelligibility of hypothetical situations that are consistent with our evidence and in which our commonsense beliefs would be false. As I reconstruct the skeptical challenge, the skeptical scenarios serve two primary purposes. First they vividly demonstrate that the evidence from which we infer conclusions about the past, the external world, other minds, the future, and so on, never precludes the conceptual possibility of error. Put another way one will never be able to *deduce* the vast majority of our commonplace beliefs from the available evidence. Such an observation by itself will generate only a very weak and, I believe, uninteresting sort of skepticism. *If* we understand knowledge, or *absolute* knowledge, or knowledge with *certainty*, as belief with justification so strong that the justification is logically or formally inconsistent with the belief being false, then to be sure appeal to the intelligibility of skeptical scenarios demonstrates quite effectively that there is no such knowledge. As we all know, while such a conclusion might strike one as initially startling, even our students in "Intro" classes soon shrug their shoulders and adopt a "Well what did you expect anyway?" sort of attitude. The most interesting sort of skepticism with respect to a certain class of propositions, is skepticism with respect to the possibility of having a *justified* belief in propositions of that sort. The most interesting skeptic challenges even the possibility of acquiring justification that makes more probable than not the propositions we believe about the past, the external world, other minds, and the future. And pointing out the intelligibility of skeptical scenarios is only a preliminary step in an argument for that sort of skepticism. Once we have agreed that the occurrence of our sensations is perfectly compatible with there being no physical world, the skeptic can then invoke the principle of inferential justification in order to request some positive reason to suppose that there is a *probabilistic* connection between the occurrence of certain sensations and the existence of certain objects.

There is here no burden of proof. Many discussions of skeptical challenges begin with a frantic jockeying for position. The anti–skeptic wants the skeptic to give some positive reason for supposing that there is no physical world and in the absence of such argument, proposes that we continue with the beliefs we are in any event disposed to have. The skeptic, however, armed with the principle of inferential justification, can adopt the clearly correct attitude that the principle of inferential justification plays no favorites, recognizes no special burdens of proof. The astrologer and the astronomer, the Gypsy fortune teller and the economic forecaster, the druid priest examining entrails and the physicist looking at tracks in cloud chambers are all expected to have reason to believe that their respective evidence makes probable their conclusions if their conclusions are to be rational.

Now one attempt to satisfy the second condition of the principle of inferential justification often gives rise to a second purpose served by skeptical scenarios. While earlier in this century philosophers tended to emphasize the prominence of enumerative induction as the most obvious candidate for legitimate non–deductive reasoning, contemporary philosophers who realize the limitations of inductive reasoning as a means of regaining commonsense beliefs about the world, have often turned to so–called reasoning to the best explanation. The physical world, the past, other minds, lawful regularities, theoretical entities, are posited, the argument goes, as the best explanation for the order in which sensations come and go, the existence of memory experiences, the behavior of other bodies, observed regularity and phenomena in the macroworld. In response to this gambit the skeptic will often request criteria for "best explanations" and turn again to skeptical scenarios to argue that there are always explanations that compete with our "commonsense" hypotheses and that satisfy equally well criteria of good explanations. For example, if one posits physical objects as the best explanation of our sensations, one will encounter the skeptic (or Berkeley pretending not to be a skeptic) wondering why physical objects are a better explanation than minds (benevolent or evil). In terms of ontological simplicity, an oft–cited virtue of explanations, a world containing only minds and mental states seems to be far more economical both in terms of kinds and numbers of things and properties.

By recognizing that skeptical scenarios need not play a prominent role in the development of skeptical arguments we will also short circuit attempts to refute skepticism that focus too narrowly on ways in which one can deflect the force of such scenarios. Thus we can happily agree with Peter Klein[5] (and disagree with Robert Nozick[6]) that if we have reason to believe that there are physical objects we also have reason to believe that we are not being deceived with respect to the existence of physical objects by an evil demon. That seems quite right but we need, the skeptic argues, reason to believe that there are physical objects. We need reason to believe that the occurrence of certain sensations makes probable the existence of objects. If one thought that that hypothesis was innocent until doubt was cast on it by a skeptical scenario, one would, I suppose, argue that its epistemic innocence is transitive and yields support for the conclusion that we are not being deceived by an evil demon. But as I have already emphasized, the principle of inferential justification plays no favorites, treats no inferred belief as innocent until proven guilty. It requires that one have positive reason for supposing that the proposition from which one infers one's conclusion is true, and positive reason for supposing that it makes probable the conclusion.

EXTERNALISM AND INFERENTIAL INTERNALISM

The paradigm externalists will reject, of course, the principle of inferential justification. Indeed many will see it as the root of the evil of skepticism. It is, in fact, the *second* clause of the principle that will be viewed as most problematic. Even Goldman, for example, has something analogous to the first clause. Input *beliefs* can yield justified conclusions produced by conditionally reliable processes only if the input beliefs are themselves *justified*. What one doesn't have to know or justifiably believe is that the processes are reliable. One doesn't have to know or justifiably believe that the truth of the input beliefs *makes likely* the truth of the output beliefs. It is this feature of externalist views that changes so dramatically the approach an externalist would take to traditional skeptical problems.

If Goldman's, Armstrong's, Dretske's or Nozick's metaepistemological views are correct then it *may* turn out that our awareness of sensation (or even just the sensation) yields knowledge of the physical world, our memory yields knowledge of the past, our beliefs about the behavior of other bodies yield knowledge of other minds, and beliefs about the past yield knowledge of the future. The processes resulting in the respective conclusions might be reliable. The relevant subjunctives that define knowledge and justified belief on Nozick's analysis might be true. The relevant causal connections might obtain.

It is *tempting* to think that externalist analyses of knowledge and justified belief simply remove one *level* the traditional problems of skepticism. When one reads the well–known externalists one is surely inclined to wonder why they are so sanguine about their supposition that our commonsense beliefs are, for the most part, justified if not knowledge. When Nozick, for example, stresses that interesting feature of his account allowing us to conclude consistently that we know that we see the table even though we don't know that there is no demon deceiving us, we must surely wonder *why* he is so confident that the subjunctives which on his view are sufficient for knowledge are true. Perception, memory, and induction *may* be reliable processes (in Goldman's sense) and thus given his metaepistemological position we *may* be justified in having the beliefs they produce but, the skeptic can argue, we have no reason to believe that these processes *are* reliable and thus even if we accept reliabilism, we have no reason to think that the beliefs they produce are justified.

This frankly *seems* right to me, but one must realize that *if* we accept the externalists' metaepistemological views it *may* also be true that not only do we know what we think we know, but we know that we know these things. Similarly we may have not only all the justified beliefs we think we have, but we might also be justified in believing that we have these justified beliefs. The processes that yield beliefs about reliable processes may themselves be reliable. The beliefs about the truth of the subjunctives that Nozick uses to define first level knowledge might themselves be embedded in true subjunctive conditionals that, *given the metaepistemological view,* are sufficient for second–level knowledge.

But *how,* the skeptic asks, would one justify one's belief that, say, perception is a reliable process? The answer, of course, is that *if* reliabilism is true, and *if* perception is reliable, we could *perceive* various facts about our sense organs and the way in which they respond to the external world. How could we justify our belief that memory is reliable? Well, again, *if* reliabilism is true, and if memory is reliable, we could use memory, in part, to justify our belief that memory is reliable. And so for the other traditional skeptical problems developed with the principle of inferential justification. On most externalists' views, second level knowledge of knowledge, or justified belief about justified belief is no more problematic than first–level knowledge or justified belief. And the same is true of still higher level epistemic states. The only real difficulty precluding the possibility of the levels extending indefinitely is that eventually one will reach a point at which the propositions become so complex that it is doubtful that finite mind can entertain them.

It is also obvious that if the externalists' metaepistemological views are correct, *normative* epistemology should probably no longer be considered a branch of philosophy, and philosophers should simply no longer concern themselves with skeptical issues. Externalist metaepistemological positions render normative questions of epistemology straightforward empirical questions to be investigated by cognitive science. I suppose Goldman might convince some of us to switch fields, but the rest of us who become convinced of his metaepistemological views will probably restrict ourselves to refining our metaepistemological positions.

All this will, of course, drive the skeptic crazy. You can't *use* perception to justify the reliability of perception! You can't *use* memory to justify the reliability of memory! You can't use *induction* to justify the reliability of induction! Such attempts to respond to the skeptic's concerns involve blatant, indeed pathetic, circularity. That does seem right to *me* and I hope it sounds right to *you* but *if* it does then I would suggest that you have a powerful reason to conclude that externalism is false. For if externalism is true, there *is* no a priori objection to the possibility of using a process to justify our belief that the process is sufficient to yield knowledge and justified belief.

By this time, I suspect that the trenches are dug and the lines drawn between externalists and internalists. One can, of course, continue to attack specific views with counterexamples, and I find many of these counterexamples convincing (See, for example, Bonjour's arguments in *The Structure of Empirical Knowledge* [7]). The difficulty with argument by counterexample, however, is that it often doesn't seem to strike at the heart of the view being attacked. The main problem with all externalist accounts, it seems to me, just is the fact that such accounts reject the principle of inferential justification and in doing so develop concepts of knowledge and justified belief that are *philosophically* irrelevant. And I stress the adverb "philosophically". Most externalists have developed relatively clear concepts that may also be useful for all sorts of purposes in all sorts of contexts. Philosophy, however, has defined its own context for the use of terms like "knowledge" and "justified belief". The philosopher doesn't want just true beliefs, or reliably produced beliefs, or beliefs caused by the facts that makes them true. The philosopher wants to have the relevant features of the world directly before consciousness. Only that will satisfy the philosophical curiosity that gives rise to philosophical questions. It is that philosophical curiosity that would so obviously remain unsatisfied even if it should turn out on externalist analyses that all of our beliefs and metabeliefs are justified. But what, exactly, does the internalist want? The answer, I think, is an old one. The ideal is to have the fact that makes a belief true there directly before the mind. Such beliefs would then constitute the foundation for all other justified beliefs. In the case of inferentially justified beliefs, the fact that makes the belief true is obviously not there directly before the mind, but here the internalist wants the next best thing — the internalist wants before his mind a relation of making probable holding between the facts that he is directly acquainted with and the fact that makes true his inferred conclusion. Indeed, it seems to me that that is the only way one can hope to avoid a vicious regress given acceptance of the principle of inferential justification. In my concluding remarks let me try to expand briefly on this idea.

INFERENTIAL INTERNALISM AND SKEPTICISM:

If we accept the principle of inferential justification then our options for avoiding skepticism are brutally limited. The principle of inferential justification has long been used, of course, to argue for the necessity of *foundations* for knowledge and justified belief. If all justification were inferential and the principle of inferential justification is true, then a finite mind could achieve knowledge or justified belief only if there is a kind of knowledge and justified belief that does depend for its justification on inference. The historical emphasis in discussing this potential regress has been on ending the regress generated by the first clause of the principle of inferential justification. If I am to be justified in believing *P* on the basis of *E* I must be justified in believing *E* but if all justification were inferential then there must be something else I justifiably believe from which I infer *E* and so on. My concern here, however, is with the regress generated by the second clause of the principle of inferential justification. That states that if I am to be justified in believing *P* on the basis of *E*, I must also be justified in believing that *E* makes *P* probable. If I *infer* that *E* makes *P* probable from something else *F* then I must be justified in believing that *F* makes probable that *E* makes probable *P*, and so on. Unless one abandons inferential internalism, it is difficult to escape the conclusion that a foundationalist must include in the foundations of knowledge and justified belief *epistemic principles*. If one can justifiably believe *without inference* that E makes P probable, or that F makes it probable that *E* makes probable *P*, then one will have ended the potential regress generated by the second clause of the principle of inferential justification.

But *can* one plausibly claim that one can know or justifiably believe *without inference* that one proposition makes probable another? Well if entailment is simply the upper limit of making probable, then entailment is, of course, one plausible candidate for a relation holding between propositions that one could know directly. But virtually all foundationalists agree that one isn't going very far beyond the foundations of knowledge employing only deductive inference. In short the only way to avoid *massive* (perhaps not universal) skepticism is to find a relation weaker than entailment that holds between our foundations and the propositions we infer from them. But what would such a relation be? By far the most familiar concept of probability is that defined in terms of frequency. We say that a's being F is probable relative to its being G when most F's are G's (or when if there were a great many F's most of them would be G). The details of the account are far from unproblematic but the basic idea is clear. If we try to capture the sense of probability relevant to epistemic principles, the sense of probability involved in the principle of inferential justification, using the concept of frequency, I suppose we might suggest that in claiming that P is probable relative to E we are simply asserting that E and P constitute a pair of propositions which pair is a member of a certain class of proposition pairs such that, when the first member of the pair is true, usually the other is. Thus, in claiming that my seeming to remember eating this morning (E) makes it likely that I did eat this morning (P), I could be construed as asserting that the pair of propositions, E/P, is of the form S seems to remember X/X, such that most often when the first member of the pair is true, the second is. The most important task of normative epistemology could then be construed as the task of discovering which epistemic principles are true.

Notice how similar this old view about probability is to the reliabilist's conception of justified inference. Whereas the Russell of *Human Knowledge: Its Scope and Influence* insisted that for our conclusions to be rational our evidence must make them probable in a frequency sense of probable[8], the reliabilist claims that the belief dependent process that produces them must be reliable. The critical concepts on both views are defined in terms of frequencies. The difficulty with the frequency conception of epistemic principles for an inferential internalist is obvious. Non–deductive epistemic principles on a frequency interpretation are certain to be very complex *contingent* truths, and even the most daring foundationalist will be unwilling to claim direct or immediate awareness of the frequencies which must obtain in order to make them true. But if the foundationalist must infer *all* epistemic principles from evidence, there will be no escape from the specter of the vicious regress raised by the second clause of the principle of inferential justification.

If one accepts the conclusion that skepticism inevitably follows from understanding *epistemic* probability in terms of frequencies which render epistemic principles *contingent*, one might consider the possibility of construing epistemic principles as *analytic*. Propositions describing sensations make probable or make it rational to believe propositions about the physical world because that is how we *understand* or *define* rational belief. Propositions describing memory as evidence for the past, past correlations as evidence for the future, the behavior of bodies as evidence for minds are all analytic are all really simply assertions about concept of rationality. This approach is not new of course. It is essentially Strawson's solution to the problem of induction[9], Pollock's solution to a whole host of epistemological concepts,[10] and it bears at least a family resemblance to Wittgenstein's pervasive concept of the non–defining (but non–contingent) criterion. There are many difficulties with the view but I will here stress only two.

First, it seems to me a little difficult to suppose that the many skeptics and those who took them seriously were all simply misusing language. However implausible we might view skepticism about the physical world, are we really to maintain that such skeptics were simply contradicting themselves? Can we really dismiss the skeptical challenge by exclaiming that we just *understand* rationality in such a way that it follows from the concept alone that sensations make it rational to believe propositions about the physical world? In short, the solution seems too easy. It seems that one cannot accommodate the undeniable force of the skeptical challenge within the framework of this attempt to find epistemically reasonable epistemic principles. This complaint will no doubt fall on deaf ears, particularly when addressed to those philosophers who never have felt the force of the skeptical challenge and who have, instead, always viewed skepticism as a view gone so far wrong that it doesn't deserve to be taken seriously. To them, I would stress the second objection.

One is sorely tempted to suppose that philosophers who take epistemic principles to be analytic do normative epistemology by simply listing their pre–philosophical beliefs, deciding what they do infer those beliefs from, and proclaiming the epistemic principle sanctioning such inferences to be analytic. But what exactly do all of these inferences have *in common* that makes it plausible to claim that they fall under a single concept of rational inference. Is the concept of evidential connection simply a disjunctive concept? It is rational to believe *P* on the basis of *E means:* EITHER *P* is a proposition about the physical world inferred from sensation OR *P* is a proposition about the past inferred from memory states OR *P* is a proposition about the future correlation of properties inferred from past correlations of propositions OR (for theists only) *P* is a proposition asserting the existence of God inferred from a feeling of wonderment at the complexity and beauty of nature OR (for palm readers only) *P* is a proposition about one's future life inferred from the nature of the lines on one's palm OR ... . Of course it is possible to artificially define a disjunctive concept, but it seems to me absurd on the face of it to suppose that so pervasive and important a concept as making probable or making rational is an ad hoc disjunction defined in terms of pairs of proposition types. It surely makes sense to ask: "In virtue of what do both sensations and memory experiences make probable, respectively, propositions about the physical world and propositions about the past?" The frequency theorist has an answer, of course: it is in virtue of a high frequency with which there is truth preservation moving from a true proposition of one sort to a true proposition of the other sort. But as we have seen the frequency theorist leaves these propositions contingent and thus seems to eliminate the possibility of ending the crucial regress.

Is there a way of avoiding relatively massive skepticism for the inferential internalist? It seems to me that the answer is yes *only* if we can understand the concept of non–deductive epistemic probability as being much more like the concept of entailment, and can, subsequently, convince ourselves that epistemic principles are necessary truths knowable *a priori*. And if we reject the attempt to make epistemic principles analytic the only way to construe them as necessary truths knowable *a priori* is to accept a Keynesian concept of making probable as an internal[11] relation holding between propositions.[12] If propositions are the sorts of things we can hold directly before our mind, and making probable is a relation holding between them, it might not be that hard, dialectically, to claim that one can hold directly before one's mind the kind of fact that makes true propositions of the form *E makes probable P*. Epistemic principles will then become synthetic necessary truths.

I'll put the conclusion as starkly as I can. If you are an inferential internalist, i.e. you accept the principle of inferential justification, then you must hold that in the sense relevant to epistemology, making probable is an internal relation holding between propositions and that one can be directly and immediately acquainted with facts of the form E makes probable P. Otherwise, one must embrace massive skepticism with respect to the past, the external world, the future, and other minds. I think the principle of inferential justification captures the only concept of inferential justification that is *philosophically* interesting. If I don't know or justifiably believe that E makes probable P my skeptical concerns about the rationality of inferring P from E will not go away. The mere existence of probability relations defined in terms of frequencies (or reliable processes producing my beliefs) is neither here nor there when it comes to relieving skeptical worry. Unfortunately, I can't quite convince myself that I am aware of any internal relation of making probable holding between propositions. Dialectically, the position is fine and I could earn a living defending our commonsense beliefs against skeptical attack, but phenomenologically, I have a nagging suspicion that I would simply be disingenuous to claim acquaintance with the needed relation. Consequently, I have the nagging suspicion that skepticism may be the correct philosophical position concerning what I take to be the philosophically interesting concepts of knowledge and justified belief.

University of Iowa

NOTES

[1] Chisholm states this position in a number of places but nowhere more clearly than in Chapter 7 of *Theory of Knowledge*, Second Edition (Englewood Cliffs: Prentice Hall, 1977)

[2] David Hume, *A Treatise of Human Nature*, ed. by Selby–Bigge (London: Oxford University Press, 1888), p. 187.

[3] Richard Fumerton, "The Internalism/Externalism Controversy," *Philosophical Perspectives*, 2, Epistemology, 1899, 443–495.

[4] See, for examples, Dretske's *Seeing and Knowing* (London: Routledge and Kegan Paul, 1969); Armstrong's *Belief, Truth and Knowledge* (London: Routledge and Kegan Paul, 1968); Goldman's "What is Justified Belief?" in Pappas ed., *Justification and Knowledge* (Dordrecht: Reidel, 1979), 1–23 and *Epistemology and Cognition* (Cambridge: Harvard University Press, 1986), and Nozick's *Philosophical Explanations* (Cambridge: Harvard University Press, 1981).

[5] In *Certainty* (Minneapolis: University of Minnesota Press, 1981), Chapter 2.

[6] In *Philosophical Explanations*.

[7] Lawrence Bonjour, *The Structure of Empirical Knowledge* (Cambridge: Harvard University Press, 1985), Chapter 3.

[8] Bertrand Russell, *Human Knowledge: Its Scope and Limits* (New York: Simon and Schuster, 1948), Part V.

[9] Peter Strawson, "Dissolving the Problem of Induction" in Brody ed., *Readings in the Philosophy of Science* (Englewood Cliffs: Prentice–Hall, 1970), 590–96.

[10] John Pollock, *Knowledge and Justification* (Princeton: Princeton University Press, 1974).

[11] By an internal relation I mean a relation which necessarily obtains between relata in virtue of their non–relational properties.

[12] John Keynes, A Treatise on Probability (London: Macmillan, 1921).

RICHARD FOLEY

SKEPTICISM AND RATIONALITY

Skeptical hypotheses have been allowed to set the terms of the epistemological debate. They convince no one. Yet they have an enormous influence. It is often influence by provocation. They provoke epistemologists into endorsing metaphysical and linguistic positions that antecedently would have seemed to have had little appeal. Skeptical hypotheses, it is said, cannot even be meaningfully asserted, or if they can, the nature of God or the nature of objects or the nature of thought makes it altogether impossible for them to be true. There are those who refuse to be provoked, but even their epistemologies tend to be dominated by skeptical hypotheses. The hypotheses push them into an overly defensive posture from which it can seem that the test of an epistemology is how well it would fare in a hostile environment. There must be a third way. There must be a way to think about skeptical hypotheses that is neither dismissive nor submissive.

The kind of skeptical challenge that is most familiar to us is the kind that concerned Descartes. To be sure, the skeptical tradition is an ancient one, but the challenges of the ancient skeptics had a different aim from those discussed by Descartes. The followers of Pyrrho of Elis, for example, saw skepticism as a way of life and a desirable one at that. Suspending judgement about how things really are was thought to be a means to tranquillity. There is no hint of this in Descartes or in the Enlightenment philosophers who succeeded him. Descartes did think that skeptical doubt could be put to good use. It could help deliver us from prejudices and thereby help put our beliefs upon a secure foundation. But even for Descartes, skepticism was first and foremost a threat rather than an opportunity, and it remains so for us. However, Descartes thought that it was a threat that could be successfully met. He thought that by making rational use of our cognitive resources, we can be guaranteed of the truth. Correspondingly, he thought that error is something for which we are always responsible. We have the tools to avoid it. Knowledge is ours for the taking. We need only to be sufficiently reflective and sufficiently cautious. For if we are sufficiently reflective we will come to perceive clearly and distinctly the truth of various claims, and if we are sufficiently cautious we will refrain from believing anything else. Skeptical hypotheses were of interest for Descartes because they provided him with a dramatic way to illustrate these assumptions. They helped him to dramatize the potential power of reason. One need not rely upon tradition or authority for one's opinions. One can stand alone intellectually, deciding for oneself what to make of the world and what to make of one's tradition. And if in doing so one makes proper use of one's reason, one can be assured of knowledge.

An increasing specialization of intellectual labor has made us us sensitive, in a way in which Descartes was not, about the extent to which we rely upon the opinions of others, just as a heightened appreciation of cultural relativity has made us more sensitive about the extent to which we are shaped by our traditions. Even so, we are as reluctant to rely uncritically upon our authorities and traditions as Descartes and his Enlightenment

M. D. Roth and G. Ross (eds.), Doubting, 69–81.

successors were upon theirs. We realize how difficult it is to distance ourselves intellectually from our surroundings, but we realize also that even our best scientists can be mistaken and that even our most venerable traditions can be misguided. As a result, we too feel the need to make up our own minds. This creates for us an intellectual predicament that is much like the one that Descartes describes at the beginning of the *Meditations*. It is an egocentric predicament, prompted by a simple question, 'What am I to believe?'. I cannot simply read off from the world what is true, nor can I unproblematically rely upon the acknowledged experts or the received traditions to guide me towards the truth. I instead must marshall my own resources. I must marshall them to determine by my own lights what is true and who is reliable and what if anything is defensible about the traditions of my community. In this respect the individualism of Descartes has won the day.

What we find unacceptable in Descartes is his optimism. We think it naive. We no longer think that by properly marshalling our resources we can be assured of the truth. Being sufficiently reflective and sufficiently cautious is no guarantee that we will avoid error. It is not even an guarantee of reliability. Even so, philosophical problems come down to us through time, and today we remain under the spell of the epistemological aspirations of Descartes, Locke, Hume, Kant and others. The cure is to remind ourselves that their aims need not be ours. What they took to be an intellectual problem in need of a solution we can appreciate as part of the human condition. Given the kind of creatures that we are, we cannot help but lack guarantees of the sort that they sought. This is no more a problem for us than is that of finding a way to do without oxygen. We just are creatures who need oxygen. Similarly, the lack of intellectual guarantees just is part of the human condition. The problem is one of how to react to that condition.

The reaction need not be one of abandoning egocentric epistemology. Reliabilism, for example, constitutes such an abandonment. The egocentric question is 'What am I to believe?'. To answer this question, I must marshall my resources in an effort to determine what methods of inquiry are reliable. So, from the egocentric perspective, it is altogether unhelpful to be told that I am to have beliefs that are the products of reliable methods. Of course, no sensible reliabilist would claim otherwise. The point, rather, is that reliabilists tend to be satisfied with an epistemology that does not address the problems of the egocentric predicament, despite the fact that such problems have been at the heart of the great epistemological projects of the past. My point, in turn, is that we need not be satisfied with such an epistemology. We can do better.

But if we are to do better, we must give up an assumption that has had a hold on epistemologists from Descartes through Gettier. According to Descartes, it is rational to believe just that which is clear and distinct for you, and what is clear and distinct for you is true. So, for Descartes rational belief always results in knowledge. This means that there are no Gettier problems within Cartesian epistemology. No one can rationally infer a truth from a rational but false belief, since there are no rational false beliefs. Today we standardly construe the link between rational belief and true belief in a looser manner than did Descartes. A rational belief can be false. So, Gettier problems do arise within our epistemologies. Even so, the difference between Cartesian and contemporary epistemologies is not so great, since within the latter it still is commonly assumed that a rational true belief absent Gettier problems is always knowledge. It is this assumption that must be abandoned. More exactly, it must be abandoned if the answer to the question 'What is it rational for me to believe?' is to be relevant to the egocentric predicament. The assumption must be abandoned because it ties rational belief too closely with knowledge and, as a consequence, too closely with reliability. For if by being rational one cannot be assured of having mostly true beliefs, then, contrary to the assumption, a rational true belief need not be a good candidate for knowledge even absent Gettier problems.

Skeptical hypotheses can help illustrate this. Imagine a world in which a demon alters your environment so that you make massive errors about it. You regularly make perceptual mistakes. Even so, the demon allows you to have a few isolated true beliefs about your environment. Perhaps the demon permits the existence of only one chair and it is the one that you are now sitting upon. So, your belief that you are now sitting upon a chair is true. Yet almost all of your other beliefs about your environment are false. This true belief of yours is not a particularly good candidate for knowledge, but why not? There need not be Gettier problems here. You need not have inferred the truth that you are now sitting upon a chair from any falsehood. But then, on the assumption that rational true belief absent Gettier problems is knowledge, the explanation must be that your belief is not rational. But why isn't it rational? Again we seem to have little choice. The explanation must cite whatever it is that we think prevents you from having knowledge. So, if we think that you do not know that you are sitting upon a chair because your belief is the product of perceptual equipment that is unreliable in your current environment, this same fact must be what precludes your belief from being rational. The more closely rational belief is tied to knowledge, the more difficult it is to avoid this conclusion.

My counterproposal is that the prerequisites of rational belief are not so closely tied to the conditions of knowledge. More exactly, the proposal is that this is so for the sense of rational belief that presupposes the egocentric perspective. This is not the only sense of rational belief. On the contrary, we evaluate beliefs from a variety of perspectives, depending on the context and our purposes, and we tend to give expression to these evaluations using the language of rationality.[1] The more objective the perspective that is presupposed, the more plausible will be the idea that a rational true belief absent Gettier problems is always an instance of knowledge. However, this is not so for egocentrically rational belief. The evil demon or the scientist who envats your brain deprive you of knowledge, but they need not deprive you of the opportunity of being egocentrically rational. This is real lesson of the evil demon and the brain in the vat. By hypothesis these are situations that you could not distinguish from what you take to be your current situation. From your skin in, everything about these situations is as it is now. And yet, from your skin out, things are drastically different from what you take them to be in the current situation. Still, you would have egocentric reasons in such situations to believe exactly what you do now. The demon does not deprive you of these reasons. Rather, he alters your environment so that these reasons are no longer reliable indicators of truths. In so doing he deprives you of knowledge.

Knowledge, then, requires an element of luck, of good fortune. We cannot altogether eliminate the possibility of massive error by being egocentrically rational. We need the world to cooperate. This is what skeptical hypotheses teach us.[2] Knowledge is not within our control to the degree that egocentric rationality is. If contrary to what we think, the world or something in it conspires against us, then so much the worse for us as knowing creatures. Nothing that we can do with respect to getting our own house in order will succeed in bringing us knowledge. This is not a comforting thought. We like to think of knowledge as part of our birthright. The thought that it might not be is so discomforting that it makes an appeal to idealism in one of its many garbs attractive to some. This is an appeal to be resisted. It has all the advantages of metaphysics over a straightforward assessment of our situation. The better alternative is to give up success as a condition of egocentric rationality — to admit that this kind of rationality in and of itself is not enough to guarantee either truth or reliability.

Many of us will find it difficult to admit this, especially when doing philosophy. Among philosophers it is often taken for granted that the worst charge that we can make against others is that they are irrational. This attitude finds its way into our ethics as well as our epistemology. We resist the idea that egoists can be as rational as the rest of us. We think that we must prove that they are irrational, as if we would be at a loss as to how to criticize them if we could not do so. The remedy is to remind ourselves that not every failure need be one of rationality. There can be other explanations for moral failures. They might be the result of inadequate moral training, for example — a training that did not sufficiently develop our moral sensitivities. As a result, we might not be able to discriminate finely enough among the relevant features of morally difficult situations. Or more seriously, it may have left us with a fundamentally flawed character, one that has us caring for the wrong things.

Analogously, we may be tempted to think that someone who has massively mistaken beliefs must be irrational, as if this were the only possible explanation of their being so thoroughly misguided. But again, we need to remind ourselves that not every failure is a failure of rationality. There are other explanations for intellectual error, even widespread error. Like moral failure, it might be largely a matter of bad training. We might have been brought up in a culture whose intellectual traditions encourage error, a tradition that emphasizes magic, for example. Or more ominously, we might have inappropriate cognitive equipment. We might not be cognitively suited to detect truths in the environment in which we find ourselves. But whatever the explanation, the point is the same: Rationality in the theoretical sphere need be no more intimately tied to knowledge than it is to goodness in the practical sphere. Just as you can be rational and yet lacking in virtue, so too you can be rational and yet lacking in knowledge. Appreciating this can help cure the preoccupation with skepticism that has dominated modern epistemology. It can allow egocentric epistemology to be done non–defensively.[3]

A non–defensive epistemology is one that refuses to apologize for a lack of guarantees. There is no guarantee that by being rational you will avoid error. There is no guarantee that you will avoid massive error. It need not even be probable that you will avoid massive error. Much of the implausibility of the Cartesian project arises from its failure to recognize that this is part of our intellectual condition. It instead insists that by being rational we can be assured of success. This insistence has disastrous consequences for egocentric epistemology. For contrary to what Descartes thought, there is nothing that we can do with respect to marshalling our cognitive resources that will result in such guarantees. Marshall them as we please. We will still need the world to cooperate. Consider the trust that we place in our perceptual equipment. If unbeknownst to us there is a deceiving demon in this world, then many of our perceptual beliefs will be false. And if most other close worlds are also demon worlds, then trusting our perceptual equipment does not even make it probable that we will avoid massive error.[4] A non–defensive epistemology refuses to be intimidated by this possibility. It refuses to be intimidated into making success or likely success a prerequisite of rationality. It allows that it might be rational for us to trust our perceptual equipment even if doing so, unbeknownst to us, is likely to result in massive error.

It is a mistake for an egocentric epistemology to insist upon any kind of guarantee whatsoever between rationality and truth or likely–truth. This is the deepest flaw in the Cartesian approach to epistemology. It is not just that Descartes tried to guarantee too much, although this too is so. He unrealistically insisted that by being egocentrically rational we can be altogether assured of avoiding error. He was thus forced to regard any skeptical conjecture, no matter how far–fetched, as a *prima facie* defeater, one which itself had to be conclusively defeated before a claim could be rationally believed. But of course, if this were so, not much of anything would rational for us to believe.

It might seem that the solution is simply to weaken the guarantee, but this would still leaves us with a defensive epistemology, and one that would face exactly the same problem that plagues Cartesian epistemology. This problem arises regardless of the strength of the guarantee, and it arises in the exactly the same form as it did for Descartes. It arises if we say that by being rational we can be assured of having mostly true beliefs. It arises if we say more cautiously that by being rational we can at least be assured of avoiding the likelihood of massive error. It even arises if we say that by being rational we can be assured only that the likelihood of our avoiding error is greater than if we were not rational.[5] For regardless of the nature of the guarantee, there will be no non–question begging assurances that the way in which we are marshalling our cognitive resources generates beliefs that meet the guarantee. There will be no non-question begging assurances, in other words, that the way of we are marshalling our resources is suitable for our environment.

After all, the search for such assurances will itself require us to marshall our cognitive resources. It will itself involve the use of methods about which we can sensibly have doubts, doubts that cannot be addressed without begging the question. Any attempt to address them will employ methods either that are themselves already at issue or that can be made so. There is a close analogy with the practical realm. There too self–directed inquiry can raise doubts that cannot be addressed without begging the question. I commit myself to various projects, ones that initially seem worthwhile, but if I examine my commitments and the values implicit in them, doubts can occur to me. I can ask whether I want to be the kind of person who makes these sorts of commitments. Can I endorse my being that kind of person? And even if I answer 'yes', this does not definitively settle the doubts. I can go on and ask about the values implicit in this latest endorsement. Either they are values that were implicit in the commitments about which I originally had doubts or they are new values about which I can also raise doubts. It is hopeless to search for a non–question begging way to endorse all of our values, including the values implicit in the endorsement itself. Any search of this sort would be based on the assumption that there is a neutral position from which such endorsements can be made, but there isn't. Nor is there in epistemology. There is no neutral position from which to defend our intellectual commitments.

But if not, we must admit that egocentric epistemology cannot provide non–question begging assurances that we will avoid massive error by being rational. The search for such assurances is doomed from the start. It is one thing to insist that skeptical hypotheses are genuinely possible. It is another to insist that the rationality of our beliefs depends upon our having a non–question begging way to discharge them. We have no such way, and our rationality does not depend upon our having one.

Admitting this need not lead to quietism. One of our intellectual projects, arguably our most fundamental one, is to understand our own position in the world, including our position as inquirers. Within the context of such a project, it is natural to raise general doubts about our intellectual commitments. It is natural to entertain even radically skeptical doubts about them. Of course, making ourselves into an object of systematic inquiry is not an everyday occurrence. It requires some detachment from our ordinary concerns. You cannot with sanity raise general questions about your intellectual commitments when, say, discussing with your mechanic the problems you are having with your car.[6] Nor can you raise them when you are doing physics or biology or geometry. But in the context of an inquiry into our place in the world, they arise without force. We make ourselves into the objects of our study, and we recognize that these objects that we are studying are creatures who have a rich interaction with their environment. They have various beliefs about it and various desires for it, all of which become intertwined in their projects. The intellectual projects that find expression in their sciences, for example, are intertwined with projects that are aimed at controlling their environment. These projects, we further recognize, can be conducted more or less successfully. In wondering about the relative success of their intellectual projects, we are raising general questions about their beliefs, questions that make it natural to entertain skeptical hypotheses. We are wondering whether their cognitive equipment and their ways of employing this equipment are sufficiently well–suited for their environment as to be prone to produce true beliefs about it. Even in wondering about the success of their non–intellectual projects, these same questions arise indirectly. For even if we grant that these creatures are mostly successful in controlling their environment, it is natural to want some explanation for this success. Is it by having largely accurate beliefs about their environment that they are able to exercise this control or is there some other explanation? But in wondering whether there might not be another explanation, we are once again taking skeptical possibilities seriously. It is perfectly natural for us to do so in this context.

So, it is not a mistaken philosophical tradition that leads us to skeptical thoughts.[7] It is our natural curiosity. We are curious about these creatures' place in the world, including their place as inquirers. We know that they take themselves to be accurately representing their world. It is natural for us to wonder whether they are right in thinking this or whether their representations might be distorted in some systematic way. The hypothesis of the evil demon and the brain in the vat are merely dramatic devices to express these kinds of thoughts in their most radical form.

There is, of course, something else that is unusual about these kinds of thoughts. They are about our beliefs, our presuppositions, our methods of inquiry. If we are to make these things the objects of concern, we must be able to distance ourselves from them in some way. This might make it seem as if the entertainment of skeptical hypotheses is inevitably an exercise in schizophrenia.

But if this be schizophrenia, it is of a common enough sort. Indeed, it is easy to come by even in the limiting case of belief, that which is indubitable for you. Such propositions are irresistible for you once you bring them clearly to mind. Clarity about them is enough to command your assent.[8] So, you cannot directly doubt the truth of such a proposition. I may be able to do that, but you cannot. Otherwise, it would not be genuinely indubitable for you. Even so, you can do the next best thing. You can raise questions about its truth indirectly. You can do so by considering in a general way whether that which is indubitable for you is really true. You can wonder whether you might not be the kind of creature who finds certain falsehoods impossible to doubt. Your wondering this does not prove that nothing is really indubitable for you. It does not prove that you really are capable of doubting that you exist and that 2+1= 3. These propositions can still be irresistible for you whenever you directly consider them. However, you can refuse to do this. You can refuse to bring them fully to mind, and by so refusing you gain the ability to suspend belief in them hypothetically. You need not cease believing them. You merely cease focusing your direct attention upon them. In doing this you can distance yourself even from that which is indubitable for you, and thus you can make even these propositions an object of skeptical concern. There is nothing mysterious about your doing so.[9] Similarly, there is nothing mysterious about your entertaining serious and general skeptical worries about the other propositions that you believe. You can doubt in a general way whether much of what of you believe is true, and you can do so without actually giving up those beliefs. It is enough for you to suspend them hypothetically.

To think that there is something inevitably puzzling about entertaining general skeptical doubts is to make human thought into something far less flexible than it is. Atheists can debate even theological questions with theists and they can do so without altering their beliefs. They hypothetically suspend for the duration of the discussion a good portion of what they believe. Similarly, the morally upright can appreciate, ad—mire, and even enjoy the ingenuity and resourcefulness of literary villains even when that ingenuity and resourcefulness is put to repugnant purposes. They can do so by hypothetically suspending their moral scruples. There may be limits as to how much of our beliefs and values we can put into suspension, but the limits are at best distant ones. They are not so constraining as to prevent sensible discussion between atheists and the—ists, and they are not such as to preclude appreciation of the great literary villains. Nor are they so stringent as to rule out worries about the general reliability of our beliefs. We need not abandon our beliefs in order to entertain such worries. It is enough for us to suspend them hypothetically.[10]

The way to respond to skeptical doubts is not to legislate against them meta—physically, and it is not to dismiss them as meaningless, self—defeating, or even odd. It is rather to live with them. It is to recognize that what makes epistemology possible also makes skeptical worries inevitable — namely, our ability to make our methods of inquiry themselves into an object of inquiry. Within the context of such an inquiry, the worry that we might possibly have widely mistaken beliefs is as natural as it is inerad—icable. If this illustrates our whimsical condition, then so be it,[11] but it is, after all, not so surprising. We want to be able to defend or at least explain the reliability of our methods of inquiry, but the only way to do so is within our own system of inquiry. We seek to use our methods to show that these same methods are to be trusted. This leaves us vulnerable to the charge that we are begging the question against the skeptic. If the only way to defend or to explain our general way of proceeding is by using that way of proceeding, then we will not have altogether ruled out the possibility that its products might be widely mistaken. This is no more than a generalization of the problem of the Cartesian circle, and it is a circle from which we can no more escape than could Descartes.

But if we too are caught in this circle, what's the point of inquiring into the re‑liability of our methods of inquiry? Why not relax and just assume that our fundamental methods are reliable? Why not encourage or at least tolerate intellectual complacency about these matters? Because striving to use our fundamental methods of inquiry to defend or to explain their own reliability is far from pointless. Besides, even if it were, it would not matter. We cannot help ourselves. Our curiosity compels us to seek such explanations. But in fact, it is not pointless to seek them, since they need not always be forthcoming. Not all methods of inquiry are even capable of begging the question in their own defense, even though this is the least we should expect from them. The least we should expect is that they be self‑referentially defensible. What this means, for beginners, is that they be logically coherent. It must be possible to employ them in their own defense,[12] but possibility is not enough. In addition, the circumstances have to be favorable for such a defense, and the methods themselves might indicate that this is not so. It is sometimes suggested that the collection of procedures that we call 'the scientific method' is self‑referentially indefensible in just this way. The history of science, it is argued, is largely a history of error. We look back at the theories of even the best scientists of previous times and find much in those theories that is false and even silly. Moreover, there is no reason to think that future scientists won't think the same of our best current theories. In this way, the history of science might seem to give us good inductive grounds — grounds that are themselves acceptable given the methods of science — for thinking that the scientific method is unreliable.

This is a perfectly respectable argumentative strategy. If the use of the scientific method in our environment has been proven, in accordance with canons acceptable to that method, to generate mistaken theories with regularity, then so much the worse for it as a procedure to generate true theories. The least we should expect from a proposed method of inquiry is that it be able to defend itself in its own terms. Much of recent philosophy of science can be read as trying to do just that. It can be read, that is, as trying to give a construal of the scientific method and a reading of the history of science that together constitute a response to this pessimistic induction. For example, there are those who claim that any fair look at the history of science reveals not so much a history of repudiation of past theories but rather a history in which past theories are largely incorporated into their successor theories. In addition, they claim that the immediate aim of scientific theorizing is not so much to generate theories that are strictly and thoroughly true but rather ones that are at least approximately true. The aim is verisimilitude. They then point out that the history of science, so understood, provides no basis for an in‑duction whose conclusion is that present theories are not even approximately true. On the contrary, that history is marked by ever increasing predictive success, and the best explanation of this is that those sciences are getting closer and closer to the truth. So, far from supporting a pessimistic induction, the history of science gives us good reason to think that the terms of our sciences, especially our more mature ones, typically do refer.[13]

It is tempting to dismiss arguments of this sort on the grounds that they beg the question. After all, the scientific method is a method that makes essential use of arguments to the best explanation. So, questions about its reliability are in large measure questions about the truth preservingness of such arguments. And yet, the response employs an argument to the best explanation in order to defend the scientific method. It is thus presupposing exactly that which it is trying to establish.

Even so, what I have been arguing is that some questions deserve to be begged. Questions about the reliability of our fundamental methods of inquiry are just such questions. It need not be a fault of the scientific method that it cannot be defended without begging the question. The fault would lie in there being no argument by which the method can be defended. If there is no way that the method can be defended, not even a question begging way, then it would fail even the minimum test for a method of inquiry. This is only the minimum, however. There are patently silly methods that can be used to defend themselves.[14] So, if the only thing that can be said in favor of the scientific method is that it can be used to defend itself, this is not much. It is certainly not enough to provide assurances of its reliability, as proponents of arguments to the best explanation sometimes hint. On the other hand, it is not altogether insignificant either, as their opponents sometimes hint.

Likewise, it is misguided to complain about the Cartesian circle, not because Descartes did not argue in a circle — he did — but rather because this is not the flaw in his strategy. The problem is not that he begs the question by appealing to what he takes to be clear and distinct considerations in order to show that clarity and distinctness assures us of truth. If a proposed method of rational inquiry is fundamental, it cannot help but be used in its own defense if it is to be defended at all. The problem, rather, is that Descartes thought that his strategy, if successful, could altogether extinguish serious skeptical worries. He was wrong about this. Suppose that Descartes had in fact provided a clear, distinct and hence irresistible proof of God's existence and had succeeded also in providing an irresistible proof that God would not allow that which is irresistible for us to be mistaken. This still would not have been enough to answer all of the skeptic's questions, although admittedly it perhaps would come as close as possible to doing so. In large part it is this that makes the Cartesian strategy such an appealing one. If the arguments work, would–be skeptics are forced to go to extreme lengths to keep their skeptical concerns alive, but they can do so. They will not be able to do so as long as they have Descartes' irresistible proofs clearly in mind, for as long as these proofs are clearly in mind even would–be skeptics cannot help but believe that irresistible propositions are true. But of course, they need not always have the proofs in mind. Thus, as with other propositions, they can suspend belief hypothetically in the proposition that irresistible propositions are true. They can distance themselves from the spell of the proofs' irresistibility and by so doing they can sensibly raise the question of whether irresistibility really is sufficient for truth. Descartes can urge them to recall his proofs, since by hypothesis this will dispel all of their doubts. However, and this is the most important point, while not under the influence of the irresistible proofs, the would–be skeptics can grant that recalling the proofs would have this effect upon them and yet still insist that this does not settle the issue of whether irresistibility really is sufficient for truth. And they would be right.[15]

Thus, there is nothing wrong with trying to appeal to clear and distinct and hence irresistible ideas in an attempt to argue that such ideas are true. One of the things we should expect of those proposing strategies of inquiry is that they be able to use these strategies to defend their own proposals. On the other hand, it is a mistake to think any such defense will be capable of altogether eliminating skeptical worries. Skeptical worries are ineradicable, and we might as well get ourselves used to this idea.

Doing so will involve admitting that it is alright to do epistemology, and ego–centric epistemology in particular, non–defensively. The prerequisite of egocentric rationality is not truth or even reliability but rather the absence of any internal motivation for either retraction or supplementation of our beliefs. Egocentric rationality requires that we have beliefs that are to our own deep intellectual satisfaction — ones that do not merely satisfy us in a superficial way but that would do so even with the deepest re–flection. So, to be egocentrically rational is to be invulnerable to a certain kind of self–condemnation. It is to have beliefs that in our role as truth–seekers we wouldn't criti–cize ourselves for having even if were to be deeply reflective. There are various ways of trying to say what exactly this amounts to,[16] but for the issue at hand these details are not important. What is important is that even if we are deeply satisfied with our beliefs, we cannot be assured of avoiding massive error. There are no such assurances. There are not even assurances of it being even likely that we will avoid massive error. The lack of assurances is built into us, and it is built into the nature of our inquiries. We must do epistemology with this in mind.

Even so, it is equally important to remember that being deeply satisfied with one's methods and beliefs is not everything. You might be deeply satisfied with them because you are dogmatic, for example. You might have views about your methods of inquiry that effectively protect them against self–directed challenges. You have ready explanations for any would–be oddity in your method or in the beliefs that they gener–ate. Take astrology as a case in point. Most contemporary astrologers may be impos–tors, but suppose you are not. You are deeply convinced of its truth. No amount of disinterested reflection would prompt you to be critical of your methods or of the beliefs that they produce. Are your beliefs irrational? Not necessarily. Are they dogmatic and misguided? Of course.

Most of us are not afflicted with this kind of extreme dogmatism. If we are dogmatic, we are unlikely to be so all the way down. The deepest epistemic standards of even the most dedicated astrologers are not likely to be radically different from those of the rest of us. But if so, they are likely to be vulnerable to self–criticism. They themselves would be suspicious of their methods and their beliefs were they to be suf–ficiently impartial and sufficiently reflective.

There are those, no doubt, who will find this naive. Perhaps it is. But if so, the alternative is not to make all astrologers irrational by fiat. It is rather to admit that some might be rational albeit fundamentally misguided. The impulse to inject every intellectual desirable characteristic into the theory of rationality is one to be resisted. It is not un–conceivable that someone can be dogmatic without being irrational. My approach is to explain as much dogmatism as possible internally. It is to rely upon our own characters as inquirers. Most dogmatists, I claim, are violating their own deepest standards. If there are some dogmatists left over, some who are not violating even their own deepest standards, they are to be dismissed as dogmatic and that is the end of the matter. It is a mistake to try to construct an objective theory of dogmatism and then to make the avoidance of that kind of dogmatism a prerequisite of rationality. Not every short-coming is one of rationality.

Again, there is a useful analogy between the practical and the intellectual. There is no more unity among intellectually desirable characteristics than there is among non-intellectual ones. Our actions are egocentrically rationally insofar as we lack internal motivations to be dissatisfied with them. Much immoral behavior can be criticized as being irrational in just this way. We do what we ourselves cannot sincerely endorse, given our own deepest values. But of course, this makes the irrationality of immorality contingent upon our characters. It makes it contingent upon our deepest values. If there are fanatics who lack even a deeply internal motivation to detach from their vicious behavior, then we must be content with regarding them as fanatics. Their problem, and ours, is that they have vicious characters. They need not be irrational.

This is not to say that there is not a looser kind of unity between egocentric rationality and morally desirable characteristics on the one hand and between egocentric rationality and intellectually desirable ones on the other. It may be that when we have no internal motivations, not even deep ones, to be dissatisfied with what we are doing, then in general we will be acting in a morally virtuous way, and it may be that when we are not acting virtuously, there generally will be some internal motivation for detachment that we have ignored or not noticed. Our normal psychological make-up may ensure that in general this is so. As a result, it may be that egocentric rationality and morality go hand-in-hand except in situations that are bizarre or in people who are deranged.

Similarly for egocentric rationality and intellectually desirable characteristics. It may be that when we have no internal motivations to retract what we believe, then in general we are neither dogmatic nor thoroughly misguided. It likewise may be that when we are either dogmatic or misguided, there is in general some internal motivation for retraction that we have ignored. Thus, it may be that the egocentric rationality and knowledge, like egocentric rationality and morality, go hand-in-hand except in situations that are bizarre or in people who are deranged. If so, it will also be the case that except in such situations or with such people, we can expect disagreements of opinion to be largely the result of differences of information. Or put the other way around, if our intellectual peers persist in disagreeing with our opinions despite the fact that they have access to the same information, this calls for some explanation. It won't do simply to say that they are wrong and we are right. On the contrary, unless there is some plau-sible way to explain away their opinion, the disagreement ordinarily will give us a good reason to be suspicious of our own opinions.

All these things may well be so. The mistake is to try to make these general truths, if that be what they are, into categorical ones. It is a mistake to make it a matter of necessity that being egocentrically rational is likely to bring us knowledge, and it is equally a mistake to assume that those who have fundamentally misguided beliefs — even those who are misguided to the point of being deranged — must of necessity also be irrational. Correspondingly, it is a mistake to make it a matter of necessity that ra-tional people will agree with one another if they have the same information. One the presuppositions of the Cartesian project was that rationality is what stands between us and "a chaotic disagreement in which anything goes".[17] However, this need not be our presupposition. We can say that what stands in the way of chaotic disagreement is not simply the nature of rationality but also the contingent fact that we are born with similar cognitive equipment and into similar environments, a contingent fact that makes it likely that the deep epistemic standards of one person will not be radically different from those of another.

This then is a sketch of a way to think about egocentric rationality. According to this conception, egocentric rationality brings with it no guarantees of truth or likely–truth, and as a result it brings with it no guarantees that rational people with access to the same information will agree with one another. Why, then, should we be interested in egocentric rationality? Because we are interested in having beliefs that are accurate and comprehensive and because by being egocentrically rational we will be pursuing this end in a way that by our own lights seems effective. To be sure, this involves a leap of intellectual faith. It involves our having confidence in those intellectual methods that are deeply satisfying to us despite the fact that we cannot vindicate this confidence in a non–question begging way. This may be regrettable but it is also undeniable. The reality of our intellectual lives is that we are working without nets. No procedure, no amount of reflection, no amount of evidence gathering can guarantee that we won't fall into error, perhaps even massive error. We are thus forced to choose between proceeding in a way that we on reflection would take to be effective and proceeding in a way that we would not take to be effective. If we are rational, we opt for the former.

University of Notre Dame

NOTES

[1] See Richard Foley, *The Theory of Epistemic Rationality* (Cambridge: Harvard University Press, 1987), especially sec. 2.8.

[2] In his book *Philosophical Explanations* (Cambridge: Harvard University Press, 1981), Robert Nozick insists that for a belief to constitute knowledge, it must be non–accidentally true. At first glance this might seem to be at odds with what I am claiming, but in fact it isn't. Knowledge may very well require that truth and belief be non–accidentally related, so that given the belief that P it is not matter of luck that P is true, and vice–versa. Even so, we need an element of luck — we need the world to cooperate — in order for there to be this non–accidental relationship between truth and belief.

[3] I have borrowed the phrase 'defensive epistemology' from Bas van Fraassen.

[4] I assume here that if p is probable given q, then it cannot be the case that p is false in most close situations in which q is true.

[5] Socrates argued that one never acts for the worse by having a virtue. The claim here is analogous; one never believes for the worse by being rational, where believing for the worse is a matter of believing in a way that is more likely to lead to error. Rationality, it is claimed, guarantees at least this much.

[6] Descartes himself emphasized this, insisting that his method of doubt is not appropriate for use in ordinary life. See his *Discourse on Method*, in Descartes, *Philosophical Writings*, vol. I, eds. Haldane and Ross (Cambridge" Cambridge University Press, 1911), especially pp. 100–101.

[7] See Richard Rorty, *Philosophy and the Mirror of Nature* (Princeton: Princeton University Press, 1979).

[8] In the *Fifth Meditation*, Descartes says " . . . the nature of my mind is such that I would be unable not to assent to these things (which I clearly and distinctly perceive) so long as I clearly perceive them . . . " See Haldane and Ross, vol. I, 180.

9 Compare with Bernard Williams, *Descartes: The Project of Pure Inquiry* (Harmondsworth: Penguin Books, 1978), and "Descartes' Use of Skepticism", in M. Burnyeat, ed., *The Skeptical Tradition* (Berkeley: University of California Press, 1983), 337–352. See also Anthony Kenny's discussion of first–order doubt and second–order doubt in "The Cartesian Circle and the Eternal Truths," *The Journal of Philosophy* 67(1970), 685–700; and James van Cleve, "Foundationalism, Epistemic Principles, and the Cartesian Circle," *The Philosophical Review* LXXXVIII (1979), 55–91.

10 Contrast this with Hume, whose position does hint of schizophrenia. Hume reported that while engaged in philosophical reflection he found himself forced to give up his ordinary beliefs about material objects, the future and the self, but that as soon as he left his study these reflections appeared strained to him and his ordinary beliefs returned. So, according to Hume, his beliefs changed dramatically depending upon which of his personalities was engaged, his philosophical one or his everyday one. The potential for schizophrenia here is made even more dramatic if we assume not only that the philosophical Hume knew that were he to quit reflecting he would begin believing but also that the everyday Hume knew (at least tacitly) that were he to begin reflecting he would cease believing.

11 "When [a Pyrrhonian] awakes from his dream, he will be the first to join in the laugh against himself, and to confess, that all his objections are mere amusement, and can have no other tendency than to show the whimsical condition of mankind, who must act and reason and believe; though they are not able, by their most diligent enquiry, to satisfy themselves concerning the foundations of these operations, or to remove the objections, which may be raised against them." David Hume, *An Enquiry Concerning Human Understanding*, ed. L.A. Selby–Bigge with text revised by P.H. Nidditch (Oxford: Oxford University Press, 1975), Sec. XII, 128.

12 Alvin Plantinga claims that certain versions of classical foundationalism cannot possibly be used to defend themselves. See Plantinga, "Is Belief in God Rational?" in *Rationality and Religious Belief*, ed. C.F. Delaney (Notre Dame: University of Notre Dame Press, 1979), 7–27.

13 See, e.g. Hilary Putnam, *Reason, Truth and History* (Cambridge: Cambridge University Press, 1986); William Newton–Smith, *The Rationality of Science* (London: Routledge & Kegan Paul, 1981); Ernan McMullin, "The fertility of theory and the unity of appraisal in science," in R.S. Cohen *et al.*, eds., Boston Studies, 39 pp. 395–432.

14 Ernest Sosa gives the following example: "If a rule or principle contains the proposition that the earth is flat, then it is acceptable, as is the proposition that the earth is flat." See Sosa, "Methodology and Apt Belief," *Synthese* 74 (1988), 418.

15 Contrast with Bernard Williams: " So the believer can always recall the skeptic, unless the skeptic is willfully obstinate, to considering the existence and benevolence of God, and if the skeptic concentrates on those proofs, he will believe not only those propositions themselves but also something that follows from them — namely, that clear and distinct perceptions are reliable, and hence skepticism unjustified." Williams, "Descartes' Uses of Skepticism", 349. My position, in turn, is that in this context, where the issue is precisely whether irresistible proofs might be mistaken, it is not mere obstinace to refuse to recall the proofs. The skeptic's refusal to recall them is not unlike the alcoholic's refusal to enter the bar. In each case the refusal is motivated by a fear that one's weaknesses will be exploited.

16 For my suggestions, see *The Theory of Epistemic Rationality*.

17 The phrase is from Bernard Williams. See Williams, "Descartes' Use of Skepticism", 344.

JONATHAN E. ADLER

EPISTEMIC UNIVERSALIZABILITY: FROM SKEPTICISM TO INFALLIBILISM*

I. THE WAY DOWN

1. In his recent book[1], Barry Stroud imagines circumstances in which $Bill_1$ is in an excellent position to assert that he knows that his friend $John_1$ will be at a party. But Stroud supposes that $John_1$ doesn't show up. Stroud's claim is that $Bill_1$ did not know that $John_1$ would show up, even though he is warranted in asserting this.[2] I have no quarrel with that claim. However, I do want to question the implicit, and widely shared, assumption that had $John_1$ shown up (and shown up for the right reasons) then $Bill_1$ does know.

It is easy to imagine that there is another pair of friends — $Bill_2$ and $John_2$ — who are in a similar situation as $Bill_1$ and $John_1$. $Bill_2$ assures his host that his reliable friend $John_2$ will show up at the party, and $Bill_2$ has done as thorough a check as $Bill_1$. $John_2$ does show up. Nonetheless, with qualifications pending, $Bill_2$ does not know that $John_2$ will show up because $Bill_1$ failed to know that $John_1$ will show up in similar circumstances. $Bill_1$'s failure demonstrates that the standards which $Bill_2$ satisfied (and hence $Bill_1$) are too low. One must rule out those factors that interfered with $John_1$'s showing up, and so provided one of the reasons that $John_2$'s knowing is defeated.[3] Consequently, and contrary to a plausible initial supposition, $Bill_1$ was not justified either. He may have been warranted in asserting that $John_1$ would come to the party, but he was not really justified (for knowledge) in believing this.

The reasoning generalizes into a skeptical argument. Knowledge entails certainty or the absence of any reasonable ground for doubt.

(A) X is justified in believing that p only if there is no possibility of serious counterevidence (or defeater) to that justification.

A further condition on knowledge and justification (for knowledge) is that it be "universalizable":

(B) If some agent is justified (for knowledge) in believing p, then anyone in epistemically indistinguishable circumstances (*e.i.c.*), is justified in believing that P (where P is a placeholder for statements that are the correlates of p in e.i.c. In our example, p_1 = $John_1$ will come to the party, the replacement for P is p_2 = $John_2$ will come to the party.).

It follows from the level of justification required for knowledge (A) and given the requirement of universalizability (B), that

83

M. D. Roth and G. Ross (eds.), Doubting, 83–98.
© 1990 Kluwer Academic Publishers. Printed in the Netherlands.

(C) If someone is justified in believing p, then no serious counterevidence (no reasonable ground for doubt) to P is possible for anyone in e.i.c. to that agent.[4]

But there is (or it is easy to imagine that there is) an enormous number of varied instances of others in e.i.c. for any or almost any putatively justified (empirical) belief q_i. Given the vast and varied number of instances it is likely or a serious possibility that among some of them, where the relevant internal epistemic relationship holds, the correlative to q_i (in e.i.c.) q_j is, in fact, false. This failure duly observed or easily envisaged shows that compatible with the level of justification reached for q_i there is the serious possibility that q_i is false. For q_j is believed false, on no worse grounds than q_i. Since then the present claim and the one(s) that failed are for agents in e.i.c., we have disconfirmed the claim that these standards are adequate — that meeting the standard that was in fact met is sufficient to rule out all reasonable doubts. So the agent does not know that q_i.[5]

Some comments: (1) The requirement of certainty (A) is an objective condition. When we speak of "no reasonable ground for doubt", this should not be taken as "no one at that time could have a good reason to doubt" but rather "there is no good reason to doubt." Knowledge is an "achievement" term, for which it is not enough that one did the best one can. It is not enough that the agent is not culpable for having overlooked any evidence. Even if the agent has ruled out all possibilities for doubt that are considered relevant, that is still not enough. There must actually be no real room for error. His justification must take account of potential sources for error, even if knowledge of these sources only surfaces much later than the time for which justification is being assessed.[6]

(2) The argument is stated in terms of an "internalist" (justificationist) model, rather than an "externalist" model as in the "causal" or "reliability" analyses of knowledge. For the issues discussed in this paper, the internalist model is more amenable to considerations of universalizability. But no judgment is intended as to which model is correct nor even, whether a choice is necessary.[7]

(3) The argument attempts to avoid direct appeal to radical skeptical scenarios such as the Descartes' Evil Genius or the brain–in–the–vat. The assumption that justification (of empirical statements) never yields logically conclusive evidence implies that it is possible for the grounds to hold without the claim being true. If we place no restrictions on how we are to imagine that the claim is false, the appeal to universalizability does little work. One might just as well declare that knowledge requires logically conclusive grounds, which it cannot have, and be done with it.

But the usual admissions of the possibility of error can be shown to reveal a serious possibility, once we take account of the enormous and varied instances that we are legislating as warranted for knowledge. That is why we limit ourselves to actual cases or ones that are easy to imagine. (Alternatively, and less subjectively, we could speak of plausible or probable scenarios, or near–by possible worlds.) One target of this argument is those who readily admit that there are lots of ways one could be wrong, but also believe that skepticism is avoided, if none of those ways are actually realized in the case at hand. The skeptical argument challenges the assumption that these ways aren't realized (once we properly universalize).

(4) The argument has been centered on raising the standards for justification ((A) and (C) above) rather than distinguishing one's situation from others. There is no real difference, since the higher level is just what is required to distinguish the situations. However, a number of philosophers have read universalizability narrowly in a way that too quickly renders it impotent for skeptical purposes. If we assert that $Bill_1$ is justified and his justification defeated, then anyone in e.i.c. like $Bill_2$ will thereby be granted justification. Consequently, $Bill_2$ will have knowledge (also) if $John_2$ shows up. On the version just put forward it is clear that the granting of justification to $Bill_1$ is provisional, a reflection of the surface of our practices. Since justification is an objective condition, if $Bill_2$ hasn't reached the proper level, neither has $Bill_1$.[8]

(5) What factors are relevant to determining whether agents are in e.i.c.? As with ethics, we begin with a good sense of relevance (e.g. evidence) and irrelevance (e.g. the name of the agent), but improvement and systematization is the job of sub-stantive theory that I cannot offer here. Yet I don't want to deny that there aren't special difficulties which adopting the internalist point of view allows me to sweep under the rug. From that point of view, it is easy to elicit the intuition that two agents cannot differ in their epistemic circumstances by virtue merely of a fact that neither has access to. The pertinence of this intuition is much less obvious if we analyze knowledge externally as a matter of a lawful, causal or reliable connection, regardless of the agent's access to it. However these analyses then face parallel difficulties (not yet solved) of offering a criterion for distinguishing accidental from non–accidental connections; or of specifying when an alternative is genuinely relevant or not.

2. Prior to discussion of the epistemic universalizability principle (B), it will be illuminating to consider the above skeptical argument in terms of Robert Nozick's [9] account. Our argument seems immune to his already well known criticism of skepticism, for it is a straightforward skeptical argument from the real possibility of error. It does not assume that knowledge is closed under known entailments. In Nozick's terms, it denies that his third condition is satisfied: Were p not true, it *might easily* be the case that S would believe p. For example, were $John_2$ not to come to the party, $Bill_2$ might easily believe otherwise (as $Bill_1$ did).

In his discussion of skeptical strategies, Nozick observes that skeptics tradi-tionally have tried to prove a stronger thesis than they need. Skepticism holds if

I. For almost all p, there exists a q such that q entails not–p and q might be true if p were false, and we do not know that not–q.[10]

Yet what skeptics actually try to establish is the stronger thesis that reverses the quanti-fiers in I:

II. There is a q such that for almost every p, q entails not–p and q might be true if p were false, and we do not know that not–q.[11]

The attempt to establish II founders on Nozick's view because

...in specifying one possibility SK [a skeptical possibility] to do the job for almost every p, he has specified one so remote that it would not hold even if p did not...[12]

But Nozick finds little hope in arguing for I directly

> ...It is not clear what such a general argument would be like — one almost would have to believe there was an actual demon who strewed the world with different pitfalls q_i, for each p_i we believe.[13]

Nonetheless, the skeptical argument from universalizability does aim at strategy I, not II. The q_i is the particular counterinstance to the universalization of the p_i in question. The universalizability argument proposes a method, rather than one over-arching SK, for generating the appropriate q_i without having to look in detail at each different p_i. For we make the empirical assumption that there is such a q_i for each p_i, even if we cannot state ahead of time what that q_i is.

3. I turn to discussion of (B) — the epistemic universalizability principle. Extended defense of (B) is apparently not called for since reactions to epistemic universalizability, in general, has been favorable, unlike reactions to their role in drawing skeptical conclusions. The former response is unsurprising since epistemic universalizability should be primarily defended on grounds analogous to that for the requirement of *ethical* universalizability, which enjoys widespread, although certainly not unanimous, support.

Explicit recognition of the role of universalizability in epistemology is valuable not primarily as a substantive principle. In the broad terms in which it must be stated it is easy for those holding different views to accept it. Their disagreement will then be shifted to whether the conditions for its application hold (i.e. whether agents are indeed in e.i.c.). But with universalizability firmly in mind we are forced to recognize that most claims to knowledge, however narrowly conceived, imply similar claims about a vast number of actual and plausible cases. As we will see below (sections 4 and 5), it is in pushing us to explore the consequences of ascribing knowledge beyond the specific case at hand that we can gain a critical perspective on our practices. What we learn is that these practices look mainly to local circumstances in ascribing knowledge.

Universalizability, at the level likely to receive nearly unanimous support, reflects simply a commitment to the proper justificatory reasons appealing to types or kinds of features. I know that there is a vase in front of me, let's assume, because I am looking at it in good lighting conditions, well within the capabilities of my reliable perceptual mechanisms, and.... (where the "..." are filled in by further conditions for perceptual reliability). Nothing in what follows the "because" depends essentially on its being me — anyone else could be in that relationship to the vase (as I am), with as good perceptual mechanisms (as me), etc. It would be (blatantly) inconsistent to deny that someone knows something who does fulfill the same conditions that were adequate reasons for my knowing that same thing.

Knowledge making features of a situation, like right making features, are not particulars (such as who the knower is). The lowest level of such universalizability is an abstraction from individual constants and other features of formally singular reference. These must be replaceable by variables governed by universal quantifier(s). In our example, we can abstract from Bill$_1$'s claim about *John$_1$'s* coming to the party, in particular. What is truth–indicative in Bill$_1$'s grounds are general features — e.g. how reliable anyone is in carrying out their intention to go to a party with a similar record as $Bill_1$ has of $John_1$; the extent to which interfering conditions can be ruled out in similar situations and so on.

But just as there are levels of abstraction possible for universalizing putative ethical maxims, so too for epistemic ones. (Unlike some readings of the requirement of ethical universalizability, I assume that uniqueness of universalizability is not a requirement.)

At a slightly more abstract level, one can characterize $Bill_1$'s grounds–claim relationship as that of a so far highly reliable agent's authority for accurately judging their near future actions. At a very high level of abstraction, the epistemic relationship can be characterized as reaching a certain level of confirmation as a basis for judging the next case. At the most abstract level, the internal relationship is simply an inductive one.

Descartes[14] indicated an abstractness akin to the first of these more abstract levels, when he argues that we should not trust — assuming certainty as the standard — a source that has once deceived us. Russell provides an example that suggests skeptical worries at our very high level of abstraction. In *Human Knowledge: Its Scope and Limits*[15], he observes that Gauss made a conjecture that a certain inequality holds always. "It has been tested for all primes up to 10^7 and for a good many beyond this, and no particular case of its falsity has been discovered." Russell then observes that: "...Gauss' conjecture, though it turned out to be false, had in its favor vastly better inductive evidence than exists for even our most firmly rooted empirical generalizations."[16]

Each more abstract level, increases the range of vulnerability of an epistemic relationship, thereby rendering failures more likely. Initially, vulnerability is restricted to failures in cases epistemically indistinguishable except on particulars. Eventually, though, empirical claims turn out to be vulnerable merely from the defeat of knowledge at the same level of confirmation.

However, the more abstract the level, the more likely it is that information at more specific levels will render the findings at the abstract level less relevant. For we often do have, in fact, good grounds for distinguishing the cases. Thus, for example, a standard case of perceptual illusion such as the bent stick in water would be of little bearing on X's knowing by perception that there is a vase in front of him. For the medium in which X is observing the vase — sunlight and air — does not, we believe, distort perception as the water does. Indeed, Descartes precisely must move beyond his first level of doubt — doubt concerning the senses — because the examples of sensory illusions and errors do not impugn perception when limited to objects very near by.[17] Greater abstractness expands the range of vulnerability, but not as much as first appears. As the range expands, the depth or extent of vulnerability diminishes. Thus we have to be cautious in drawing skeptical conclusions from reasoning at so abstract a level as Russell's. Abstraction from particulars, the minimal condition for universalizability, is compatible with the epistemic relationship being highly specific.[18]

4. Epistemic universalizability principles accord with our practices in that a convincing way to show someone that they do not know is to point out that someone in similar circumstances turned out to be wrong about the analogous claim. But not all failures in e.i.c. call for a raising of standards for knowledge.

The reliable newspaper that prints a story giving an erroneous date for an event is not thereby judged unreliable. But a lot of these errors would lead us to question the newspaper's reliability. So why not count each small error as (epistemically) significant though we only take notice of these errors above a certain threshold? Such a response does help generate skeptical conclusions. However, it does so only by tacitly invoking a broader skeptical challenge inherent in the *Sorites*.

Sorites reasoning applied here relies on the vagueness in where to draw the line between errors that lead us to alter our standards and errors that don't. It analyzes the former as indistinguishable from the latter except for amount. Without questioning the powerful force of the Sorites, I want to try to pursue an independent line, one more in keeping with our practices, where lines are drawn despite some degree of arbitrariness.[19]

Consider now the following report by Fred Dretske[20] of a feature of our practices that appears to go against reasoning to skeptical conclusions via universalizability principles:

> It is a mistake, however, to conclude that because *your* watch is slow, *my* watch cannot be trusted, that because *some* gauges are unreliable, *all* gauges are unreliable, that if *some* people lie, *no one* is dependable, that if *any* newspaper (book, document) has ever been in error, no newspaper (book, document) conveys information of the sort required for knowledge.[21]

While I do not believe that this feature of our practice noted by Dretske is fully generalizable to anti–skeptical ends, it does suggest a valuable insight. Our resources for justification go well beyond what we have accessible to us. *X*'s watch made in Timbuktu stops working. *Y* is not aware of any feature of his watch made in Canarsie that would distinguish it from *X*'s. Still *X*'s set of beliefs may contain members that distinguish these cases, even if he is unaware of it, or they may contain a belief referring to the inherited knowledge of his community, that may contain a distinguishing belief. For example, his set of beliefs may contain the belief, or point to the community's belief, that the reliability of watches made in Canarsie is quite high, while this is not true for Timbuktu. Or, it may contain (or point to) the belief that failures of otherwise reliable watches is largely due to local environmental conditions, which could be very different in Canarsie and Timbuktu. The requirement to distinguish one's own position from the one that failed must then be read as a requirement on one's total set of (justified) beliefs, and not on the agent to produce those distinguishing features. What these reflections show, supportive of the probative force of this practice, is that an agent's resources go well beyond what he has access to.[22]

But it is equally a mistake to conclude that our practices — specifically treating failures in (seemingly) similar situations as irrelevant — are always or largely epistemically grounded. There is no good reason to assume that the implicit distinguishing grounds exist for *all* the cases where we are inclined to ignore a failure in a similar situation. In comparing Bill$_1$ and Bill$_2$'s situations I have, in fact, assumed that there is no real distinguishing grounds, and so the failure in the one case does undermine knowing in the other case. Nothing in Dretske's report leads me to believe that this assumption must be wrong or fantastic. I do, however, agree with Dretske that many such attempts to transfer between cases are illicit. (Nor do I believe that the lack of transferability in these cases is incompatible with universalizability. Dretske does not claim otherwise.)

The practice Dretske observes is partly nurtured by contingencies of questionable epistemic relevance in the context of discussions of skepticism. For example, it is gen— erally not *feasible* to learn what actually did occur to others in similar situations. It is hardly typical that $Bill_1$ would know of the outcome for an agent in China who as a matter of fact is in e.i.c. from him (Bill1). Mild science fiction helps support the claim that our practice would alter were it more feasible to learn of these failings. Imagine an *Error Computer* that kept records of noted failures. One can access the record of suc— cess or failure for anyone in e.i.c. — across all accidental distances of space and time — merely by hitting the search key on one's PC (hooked by modem to the main Error Computer). I leave it as a thought experiment for the reader whether transferability be— tween cases would be as restricted as Dretske implies, if we had the Error Computer on–line.

5. What tests are feasible to perform is also pertinent to the crucial distinction between a serious counterpossibility or real doubt, one that an agent has to eliminate and a skeptical doubt, one that the agent can ignore though its truth is incompatible with what he claims to know. The question is whether it is illuminating to conceive this dis— tinction as exhaustive.

From within Stroud's story, our (initial) attitude toward $John_1$'s not showing up, given $Bill_1$'s grounds, is that there is no serious (as contrasted to skeptical) possibility of error. What reveals this attitude as pretense is just that we so readily admit to error when we discover that $John_1$ doesn't show up. There is surprise perhaps, but there is no resistance to accepting that $John_1$ did not show up. (Compare to what our attitude would be to "evidence" for Russell's hypothesis that the universe came into existence five minutes ago with our current memories, history books, etc. in place.) A bit shocking is the reason Stroud hypothesizes for $John_1$'s not showing up — a meteor struck in his path. However, for all its fantastic nature, the possibility of the meteor striking, which we dismiss, is distinguishable from radical skeptical scenarios. For first, it is vastly more probable than the indefinite number of coincidences and wild science fiction that would have to hold for a brain in the vat scenario. Second, and a corollary, we can clearly tell in the meteor case both that $John_1$ did not show up and why he didn't show up. Neither applies to the brain in the vat case.

Moreover, we can readily tell the story differently, so that a more realistic (counter) possibility is realized, though one we still nevertheless dismiss: $John_1$ had a heart attack (or automobile accident). These counterpossibilities belong to a broad set of potentially interfering conditions — including car accidents and other transportation problems, medical emergencies, sudden and harsh changes in the weather, etc. — where the probability of some member occurring is not at all negligible (although we, nonetheless, neglect it).[23] Our shift in attitude — from the predictive stage to learning that $John_1$ didn't show up — has the revealing marks of our reaction to a lottery. We are sure we will lose the lottery, and would be willing to bet a lot that we will lose. Yet, once the announcement comes in that we won, and after the story is briefly checked, we quickly get over our initial surprise, readily accepting that we actually won. Both theory and practice go against the view that we can know or be completely justified in believing that we will lose the lottery, even when we will. (For a simpler example:

Imagine an urn with 3 million whites balls and 1 black ball. Can a person *know* that the next one he will randomly select will be white?) The consensus view on the lack of justification in the lottery case makes sense of our limited resistance toward discovering that we were wrong, despite the high probability, and our skeptical argument suggests that we should have a similar attitude toward "John$_1$ will come to the party."[24]

What seems to drive our practice in this case is just that there is no feasible way to overcome the openness toward the future. (However, it is the typical impracticality (not the infeasibility) of ruling out John$_1$'s having a bad heart condition, for example, that largely, I expect, shapes our practice.) We cannot look into the future, just as we cannot alter the fixed — by the nature of the lottery itself — probability of winning in the lottery. A simple way to recognize the force of feasibility here is to ask whether we would take Bill$_1$'s grounds as adequate in other situations where further evidence is available. Imagine that the host doesn't see John$_2$ at the party, though he knows that he came. He asks Bill$_2$ where John$_2$ is, to which Bill$_2$ says "John$_2$'s in the basement." When the host asks Bill$_2$ how he knows this, Bill$_2$ repeats the grounds similar to those invoked in the original description: "I spoke to John$_2$ a little earlier and he told me he planned to go to the basement around this time to shoot pool." Wouldn't the host be reasonable in saying "Don't tell me what he told you he *will* do. Please go to the basement and check"? The inference I want to draw is that were it feasible to raise standards in the original case of Bill$_2$ and John$_2$, we would do so.[25]

6. To sum up this part: First, epistemic universalizability principles have been defended and invoked in an argument to a skeptical conclusion. Second, we have noted some ways in which features of our practices that run counter to universalizability principles, at least as skeptically applied, can be explained on non–epistemic grounds. Third, our attitudes toward the discovery of counterevidence better parallels, it is argued, those for a lottery than what they should be according to a traditional understanding of knowledge as providing a "tether." Fourth, for the main example discussed, it is claimed that the failure in similar circumstances constitutes a significant, not a skeptical, realization of a counterpossibility in three ways: First, the failure in one case is verifiable. Second, there are many such failures or it is easy to imagine that there are. Third, if we could check so as to rule out these interfering factor, we would and should.

II. THE WAY UP

7. Skepticism about Bill$_2$'s knowing that John$_2$ will come to the party appears to show that we have an argument for radical skepticism which does not directly depend upon wildly skeptical scenarios. But the appearance is false. The example is not a good paradigm for all empirical knowledge. It generates a skepticism only about inductive knowledge. (Nozick, in fact, remains highly skeptical of such knowledge.)[26] If, though, a distinction between direct, immediate, or conclusive knowledge and indirect, inferential, or inductive knowledge is viable, then the argument as so far stated does not extend to the former.[27] If so, then I argue that *infallible* knowledge is realizable. Epistemic universalizability principles together with certain broad and weak empirical assumptions entail either skepticism or infallibilism.

Compare Bill$_2$'s case with knowing that the object in front of me is a vase. In the latter case we begin assuming, as we did in the former case, that I have excellent grounds for knowing that it is a vase (e.g. looking at it in good light with reliable per–ceptual mechanisms). Then we introduce familiar potential errors that are realizable and not completely wild: ingenious holograms, cleverly placed mirror images, realistic dreams, etc. It is readily imagined that these deceptions are successful in epistemically indistinguishable circumstances (e.i.c.). So far the parallel holds.

But these possibilities though real grounds for de facto skepticism — skepticism about the actual circumstances in which we do claim or are attributed knowledge — do not establish that we do not have the ability to know, and even to know with certainty. In both the vase and Bill$_1$'s case we are in the best position to know for all practical purposes. But in the vase case there are many available, though rarely demanded, ways for me to improve my situation. But that is not true in Bill$_1$'s case without seriously altering the method of knowing (e.g. by shifting from inductive to a perceptual method).

In the vase case, there are numerous other tests I could make to rule out each realizable, but not completely wild, skeptical possibility It's just that typically I don't. In a valuable article, Janet Levin[28] reasonably objects to my earlier (see note 3) assumption that it is plausible that some agent's justification that there is a vase in front of him in the best available epistemic circumstances is defeated. Levin writes...

> our commonsense beliefs about objects based upon a *variety* of sensory evidence all remain unthreatened, at least until we had reason to think that someone has actually been mistaken or defeated in those epistemic situations as well. But this claim is much harder to defend [than when we consider only a single source of sensory evidence]. It is hard to think of plausible, much less actual, circumstances in which someone would be similarly fooled when he approached an object, walked around it, reached out and tried to touch it....[29]

8. Levin's claim deserves careful scrutiny, but my main interest is the consequences to be drawn if she is correct. If she is correct, it would then follow, I believe, that along the same lines as we generated our skeptical argument, we can reach a quite opposed conclusion. It is seriously possible for us to have infallible knowledge that there is a vase in front of us. We can have knowledge such that there is no good reason to treat as credible any putative counterevidence. That is, the argument is not merely that we can reach certain knowledge, but that we can reach *incorrigible* knowl–edge.

The variation on our skeptical argument is simply this. Let p = There is a vase in front of me. Let e = the total evidence determined by performing all tests (e.g. using multiple senses, having other persons also check, having tests for whether these tests have been correctly applied), all of which support p. p, let us say, is completely, though not logically conclusively, verified . Under normal empirical assumptions and the lack of constraints on imagination, there are many instances (or it is plausible to imagine that there are many instances) where others are in e.i.c. i.e. they have evidence like e for analogues of p (substitutions for P, see (B) above sec.1). It is, moreover, plausible to imagine that these instances are independent and greatly varied. If there is some epistemically similar case where the replacement for P is defeated, it should then be easy to show. So, a failure to find or imagine plausible instances of *not–P* with evidence like e amounts, in effect, to passing a *severe test* of the claim of that there is a real counter–possibility to the justification of p by e. For if Levin is correct, there is no actual case in which *not–P* in e.i.c, and it is not even plausible that there are any such cases. So it is highly confirmed that there is no serious counter–possibility to the jus–tification of p by e, and so no good reason to ever accept any putative counterevidence to it.

We now consider the steps in the argument in detail:

(1) That there will be many instances depends upon earlier observations con–cerning the generality of the relevant epistemic relations, and just normal assumptions about the world (e.g. there are many cases where agents are attempting to judge largely by perception that there is a solid object right near them belonging to a broad category.) But we must also assume, what I didn't discuss earlier, that these other instances are independent and varied. When we apply the so–called 'law of averages' to flips of a fair coin to conclude that we will eventually get a sequence of 10 heads in a row fol–lowed by 10 tails, we not only need to assume that the trials are independent, but that the mechanism operative is random. The randomness enters not simply with the device involved — flipping the coin — but also in the many interfering conditions (e.g. fric–tions, small imperfections in the coin, slight alterations in how the coin is flipped) that will differ, in ways unknown, with each flip. Our imaginative abilities allow us to vary the random processes in e.i.c. as much as we would like. We can envisage vases anywhere at anytime with any sort of potential trickery, so long as we hold fixed epis–temic similarity in circumstances.

(2) The numbers, independence, and variety are important if we are to have a ground for moving from the de facto lack of defeat to a de jure claim that defeat is not seriously possible. Of course, nothing in the argument undermines the claim that we still could be mistaken despite our best tests, if "could" is understood as pure logical possibility.

The severity of a test, informally, is the greater as we look for implications (predictions) of a hypothesis most likely to fail, if the hypothesis is mistaken. If our best tests are inadequate to guaranteeing the truth of what is claimed, then we should easily be able to envisage that occurring. Hence we can test the claim severely. While we do not actually perform any test, the implication of universalizability is that if a claim to knowledge is false, it should be very easy to show. That is why, if the test is passed (if are not able to find a failure in e.i.c.), it gives a strong sense to the "could" in con–cluding that in this circumstance I could not be mistaken.[30]

(3) We are treating infallibilism largely as an empirical hypothesis subject to confirmation or disconfirmation. (It cannot be completely empirical because of its nor–mative component.) It isn't usually treated this way, since confirmation is only possible where we can make sense of instances, and it is generally assumed that the (in)fallibilist claim must attach to each belief separately. But universalizability principles allow us to make sense of instances. Each individual knowledge claim does not stand alone to turn out correct or incorrect regardless of other cases. Each one universalized allows many instances. So the infallibilism being embraced is not the thesis that satisfying all the criteria for being a vase necessarily, conceptually or by virtue of meaning entails its being a vase. Rather we are saying that the hypothesis of infallibilism (for some knowledge claims) passes all reasonable tests, and so, it should be accepted.[31]

(4) In denying the real possibility of error where we have engaged in the ex–tensive verification, I am restricting the kinds of errors to be considered.

First, I consider only two kinds of error — blunt error and failures of discrimination. With a blunt error, the vase in question turns out to clearly be something else e.g. a mirror image; a hallucination. In failures of discrimination, the vase is real, but it turns out to be indistinguishable by that agent in those circumstances from cleverly faked vases.

Two other ways of being in error are put aside because they will lead onto tangential issues. First, the concepts invoked e.g. "vase" may turn out to have null extension because of some semantic or conceptual change.[32] Second is the more troublesome problem that arises if even terms for such ordinary objects as vases are tacitly dispositional. Consequently, they have implications for the future that amount to essentially inductive components. Hence, the skeptical argument already accepted would apply to them.[33] Not wanting to address this issue, I'll just assume that it is possible to somehow restrict the implications of these terms e.g. by replacing these terms with technical ones where the meaning is stipulated, so as not to carry such a predictive component.

On Quinean grounds, some would claim that we cannot now rule out now how future discoveries may lead us to revise any statement. But Quine's reasoning for the possibility of thorough going revision, which is aimed at challenging the analytic–synthetic distinction, does not show that we will ever have a good reason for thorough going revision. Moreover, where revision is motivated not by conceptual (or theoretical) change, but by failed predictions, past a certain point of successful testing it becomes more reasonable to believe that the failure is due to future alterations, rather than errors in the non–inductive component. If the vase that I check thoroughly disappears five minutes from now, rather than infer that there was never a vase there in the first place, it seems more reasonable to infer that the vase was there, but now is no longer there, for whatever reason.

Second, I have already mentioned that Sorites reasoning is to be avoided, if possible. When we describe the limits of empirically plausible counter–possibilities, someone might suggest a counter–possibility similar to one at the extremes of empirical plausibility, but just a negligible degree more fantastic. By familiar reasoning, it can be argued that if the original case is empirically plausible so must this one be. But the assumption here of the transitivity of empirical plausibility involves Sorites reasoning, and so is to be ruled out.[34]

A more serious restriction arises from limiting our interest in the thesis of fallibilism or corrigibilism to its role in inquiry. For some beliefs, incorrigibilism denies that we will have a good reason to admit evidence that these beliefs are mistaken. Corrigibilists often point to ordinary examples of well founded beliefs turning out to be false as support for their position. If so, then they are claiming that support for their position comes from ordinary, non–fantastic, cases, where theories are falsified without raising widespread skeptical doubts. So I will understand the incorrigibilist's denial as tacitly restricted to alleged counterevidence that is conceivable or coherent with what we now believe. We can intelligibly describe it. (This allows that the counterevidence may be a source of great surprise and resistance e.g. the Michelson–Morley experiment).

Third, the incorrigibilism is limited to non–inductive empirical knowledge. Whether the distinction between inductive and non–inductive empirical knowledge ultimately holds is controversial. But if it does, and Levin's claim only holds if it does, then non–inductive knowledge entails a claim to a connection between knower and known that eliminates the essential openness (to the future) or fixed probability of error (e.g. lotteries) in inductive knowledge. The incorrigibilism being defended does not extend to scientific theories, which are an unfortunate source of bread and butter for corrigibilists. These cases do not permit complete verification or complete testing. I reject the idea that the way in which people didn't believe that some of these could be wrong (e.g. Newton's Theory) is at all comparable to the sureness one can have that there is a vase in front of one (if one has genuinely done the best tests we can come up with). Even granted the enormous support derived from precise, surprising predictions, consilience of inductions, and other features of coherence, the reach of theories (or laws) go well beyond what we can know without fear of serious counter–evidence. Theories extend widely across space and time, and it is easy to envisage areas in distant space and time, where little or no information has yet been received, for which these theories fail. Then again there is always the Humean possibility that the (alleged) laws in the theory will cease to work.

9. Levin's claim is extremely plausible for the case she gives. If we perform further obvious tests, we can immediately eliminate virtually all empirically realistic possibilities usually adduced to motivate the skeptical ones. It is genuinely hard to imagine, let alone actually gives instances of, reasonable scenarios where one can be mistaken about the vase, after multiple, varied and independent tests.

Still, how far can this claim be extended to include new gerrymandered deceptive possibilities without reaching the level of radical skeptical possibilities? (Levin does not discuss these extensions, and my comments below go beyond her discussion).[35] Given the above grounds rules, one reason to accept Levin's claim on a strong reading is just the usual one that as we get more agreement from independent sources, it requires positing greater and greater coincidences (or wilder scenarios) to account for that agreement otherwise than by appeal to a common reality.

Also, as we perform more tests according to our total available knowledge, it becomes harder to exclude our having detected new devices and means of deception. Deception primarily comes in two categories: deception through the sources of evidence (e.g. holograms, visual illusions, mirrors, replicas); or deceptions of the representing medium — the mind (e.g. dreams, hypnosis, mind–manipulators). Each new test to eliminate deceptions from members of these two categories, requires an additional positing of a new kind of deceptive instrument, beyond the reach of our beliefs as to where we can err. But the larger the kinds of deceptive devices posited, the much less likely it is that these will go undetected. The more elaborate the deception, the enormously greater coincidence we have to posit to keep these deceptive possibilities from having consequences that are detected. But if detected, usually we can guard against them. Even if not, perhaps because we cannot figure out the causes for these conse–quences, we remain with the option of withdrawing from rational certainty.[36]

One of the difficulties in recognizing just how radical or extreme the usual skeptical scenarios are is that we begin with quite familiar deceptions (e.g. holograms, perceptual errors, hypnosis), and then generalize, ignoring the restrictive and fragile conditions under which these operate (even when we add some science fiction). Recent variations begin with familiar differences between appearance and reality or conceptions of the world (between us and much less intelligent beings).[37] But here too the move from the examples to radical skeptical scenarios is a whopping leap. For in any of the familiar examples, the disparities (appearance–reality; conceptions of the world) are overwhelmingly likely to have effects or consequences that we can be aware of (e.g. a switch falters on a brain–in–a–vat; wrong or restricted conceptions of the world usually lead to mistaken judgments). Such disparities would be enough to clue us in that the world is not the thunderingly ordinary and lawful world that we know so well, but contains weird possibilities, as in dreams, science fiction, or cartoons. In that eventuality, we ourselves would become skeptics (at least about certain knowledge).

Playing the skepticism games gets us into a frame of mind where the suggestion of the deception being essentially undetected, appears as just one more extrapolation from the ordinary cases of deception. I have questioned whether, Sorites reasoning aside, there is any natural progression available from the familiar examples to the skeptical scenarios. Thompson Clarke, who greatly influenced recent, more sympathetic views of the skeptic, goes further. He questions the ultimate coherence of the radical skeptical worry once we introduce the need for the deception to go undetected. (A need driven by the demand that skepticism be a thesis that excludes the possibility of knowledge,and not merely the thesis that we don't in fact have knowledge.) Clarke asks rhetorically

> Does Descartes' possibility even *seem* to make sense, if we ask ourselves how the Evil Demon, or God, could know that he, too, wasn't dreaming — and allow that neither could?[38]

10. Infallibilism, especially in its virulent form of incorrigibilism, has seemed to many not just epistemologically wrong, but morally wrong. Yet the arguments for falli–bilism have never been very strong. The main empirical evidence is that humans can err. But, of course, the serious possibility of human error, often realized, is compatible with our being infallible about certain restricted matters in certain circumstances. If the argument stems from the mere logical possibility of error, then this hardly establishes fallibilism as any critical control on inquiry. It is a bad argument to reason that some–thing is worth believing (e.g. the world is flat) from the fact that it cannot be proven (logically) not to be so.

The main support for fallibilism (or more properly, our belief that we are fallible) comes from a sense of its moral urgency. Only fallibilism justifies tolerance and open mindedness. But fallibilism is unlikely to further those ends, if it takes the form of a blanket fallibilism about everything. It is just too indiscriminate, failing to distinguish between someone's belief that "The universe is not empty"and their belief that "Nuclear deterrence is a morally necessary policy."

Our infallibilism is, however, discriminate and highly restricted. We can reach infallibility only about those statements susceptible to complete verification by methods and tests presently available. It is obvious that for most of the claims that fallibilists want us to be fallibilist about, e.g. "Abortion is wrong," we lack any possibility of closing off serious counter–arguments or counter–evidence. Moreover, our infallibilism is compatible with a complete fallibilism — indeed, skepticism — about most of what we think we know. For it is not often the case that we have the opportunity for complete verification, and it is rarer still that we actually do all the tests necessary to secure complete verification.

However, our main conclusion remains that given epistemic universalizability and some weak assumptions, the only alternatives are skepticism or infallibilism. We exclude the sensible middle position of a non–skeptical fallibilism.

Brooklyn College, C.U.N.Y.

NOTES

* I am grateful to Catherine Elgin for detailed comments, leading to substantial revisions. Conversations with her and Peter Klein, though brief, proved helpful. I also thank the editors for their comments.

1 Barry Stroud *The Significance of Philosophical Scepticism* Oxford, 1984.

2 For this example, slightly altered, and discussion, see Stroud, ibid., 58–63.

3 This argument is a descendant of the skeptical reasoning offered in Jonathan E. Adler "Scepticism and Universalizability," *The Journal of Philosophy* 78 1981, 143–156.

4 A rough formalization would be the following:
　　(A)　(x) (Jx,p,e → −(∃d+)(−Jx,p, e&d+)) (where Jx,y,z = "z justifies x in believing that y"; "d" is intended as a defeater; "+" signifies that the defeater is a significant one in ways to be discussed).
　　(B)　(∃x)(Jx,p,e) → (x)(Jx,P,E)
　　So, (C)　(∃x)(Jx,p,e) → (x)(−(∃d+)(−Jx,P,E&d+).

5 The editors raise the question of whether this universalizability argument to skeptical conclusions doesn't assume that epistemic closeness of situations is symmetric. So, if X is in e.i.c. to Y, then Y is in e.i.c. to X. But, they observe, the analogous principle for similarity of possible worlds is not standardly assumed. I reply, none too confidently, as follows: Yes, that assumption is made. As I understand why symmetry does not hold for similarity measures for possible worlds it is because the respects in which world–*a* is similar to world–*b* may be different from the respects in which world–*b* is similar to world–*a*. (See David K. Lewis *Counterfactuals* Harvard University Press, 1973 sec. 2.4) Presumably, though, with judgments of when agents are in e.i.c. there is built in an implicit relativity to the single, even if complex, dimension of nearness to the truth (or some related central epistemic objective.) If we build in the "with respect to" dimension (*a* is in e.i.c. *b* to with respect to *R*), then symmetry seems right, and, at least, is not ruled out by the above reasoning.

6 For discussion related to this point, see Gilbert Harman, "Reasoning and Evidence One Does Not Possess," in *Midwest Studies in Philosophy Vol. V Studies in Epistemology* , P.A. French, T.E. Uehling, Jr., and H.K. Wettstein, eds. University of Minnesota Press, 1980, 162–182.

7 As briefly mentioned below (sec.2) the skeptical universalizability argument applies to Nozick's externalist model. Externalists define knowledge as holding when, roughly, the proper connections exist between the agent and the state of affairs leading him to the belief that is the candidate for knowledge. Consequently, they appear to escape the universalizability argument by narrowing the range of vulnerability to the circumstances of the particular case. But this is not so. Notions of relevant alternatives (or discrimination among competitors), reliability, and counterfactual analyses of the proper relation of the state of affairs to the agent's belief all require considering a wider variety of circumstances. That is the opening that could be exploited in an attempt to extend the universalizability argument. Nor can this opening be avoided without sacrificing the crucial and traditional distinction between true belief and knowledge. But much more would have to be said to make the argument stick against externalist accounts. And I am not at all convinced that there is a clear competition between internalist and externalist approaches. For example, externalist models work best for perceptual or immediate knowledge, while internalist accounts look better for inferential and complex knowledge such as knowledge as to why a group of agents engaged in a certain action. A number of philosophers have discussed critically the internal– externalist contrast see, for example, William Alston, "Internalism and Externalism in in Epistemology," *Philosophical Topics* Vol.14 1986, 179–221.

8 The narrow reading, restricting universalizability to the first and fourth conditions of knowledge, is found in Anthony Bruekner, "Epistemic Universalizability Principles," *Philosophical Studies* 46 1984 297–305. See especially the formulation from Adler, op.cit. he chooses on p.300 and elsewhere. More recently, see Bob Hale's "Epistemic Universalizability," *Analysis* 1988, 78–84. Hale is responding to Jonathan Dancy's treatment of epistemic universalizability in his book *Introduction to Contemporary Epistemology* Blackwell, 1985.

9 Robert Nozick *Philosophical Explanations* Harvard University Press, 1981

10 ibid., p.244.

11 ibid., p.244.

12 ibid., p.244.

13 ibid., p.245.

14 *Meditations on First Philosophy* in *The Philosophical Works of Descartes* E.S. Haldane and G.R.T. Ross, trans., Cambridge University Press, 1911. *Meditation I*

15 Bertrand Russell *Human Knowledge: Its Scope and Limits* Simon and Schuster 1948.

16 ibid., p.403.

17 See Descartes *Meditation I*, op.cit.; see also Stroud,op.cit. 8–9.

18 On this point see R.M. Hare, *Moral Thinking: Its Levels, Method and Point* Oxford University Press, 1981 p.41.

19 See section 4 in Roy A. Sorensen "The Vagueness of Knowledge," *Canadian Journal of Philosophy* 17 No.4 1987 767–804. Sorensen is right that the argument as first proposed in Adler, op.cit. appealed to a Sorites (unintentionally). For a positive view of combining a Sorites with universalizability see Peter Klein, "Epistemic Compatibilism and Canonical Beliefs," (this volume).

20 Fred I. Dretske, *Knowledge and the Flow of Information* The MIT Press, 1981.

21 Dretske, ibid. p.126. See also Stroud op.cit., p.61–63 and Hale, op.cit., p.80.

22 For this reason I do not find convincing arguments on behalf of internalism that emphasize the connection between the agent's justification and the grounds he can offer in defense. The agent may even deny justificatory beliefs that he nonetheless does have a right too. See Lawrence Bonjour, "Externalist Theories of Empirical Knowledge," in *Midwest Studies in Philosophy Vol.V* op.cit. 53–73. Alston, op.cit. is an extended critique of Bonjour's arguments.

23 The third point recalls the Sorites: Each of these possibilities are insignificant in themselves, but their sum total is significant (merely by virtue of their being independent and the probability being over a large disjunction). But the claim is that this "existential" set is significantly probable in itself. It is true that one can analyze it away into the sum of insignificant probabilities, but that is just not, in fact, the form of reasoning used. The application of any ordinary substantive term, so it seems, is capable of refutation by a Sorites. So then, at least until the Sorites problem is solved, the only way we have to predicate a term of anything is to refuse to allow such reductionist analyses as relevant to challenging a particular predication (without special reason).

24 The connection between our epistemic attitudes and the lottery paradox is explored further in Jonathan E. Adler "Knowing, Betting, and Cohering," *Philosophical Topics* Vol.14 1986 243–257. Gilbert Harman has argued from the lottery paradox, and for related reasons, against probabilistic accounts of knowledge or acceptance see his *Thought* Princeton University Press, 1973.

25 Michael Williams ("Epistemological Realism and the Basis of Scepticism," *Mind* Vol. XCVII 1988 415–439) would call such restrictions "structural constraints," rather than practical restrictions. But he does not tell us what motivates these constraints; what principled grounds there are within the context of discussing skepticism for calling restrictions due to feasibility, structural rather than practical. See ibid., p.429.

26 See Nozick, op.cit. Ch.3 sec.III. His schemata I and II for skeptical arguments, discussed above, comes before the section on evidence.

[27] Many hold to such a distinction. For one notable example see D.M. Armstrong, *Belief, Truth, and Knowledge* Cambridge University Press, 1973. There is also, of course, a powerful neo–Humean tradition that denies this distinction, conceiving all empirical knowledge as essentially fallible and inductive.

[28] Janet Levin, "Skepticism, Objectivity, and Invulnerability" *Philosophy and Phenomenological Research* Vol.XLVIII 1987. 63–78, especially section II.

[29] ibid., p.69.

[30] For the formal account and defense of "severe tests" in the corroboration of hypotheses, see Karl Popper, *Logic of Scientific Discovery* Harper, 1959. In arguing from corroboration to the denial that I *could* be mistaken about there being a vase in front of me, I am tempted to say that the "could" is of the same strength as Hume might hold for his denial that there (epistemically) could be miracles. Roughly, we have the best of reasons for thinking that there can never be good evidence for miracles (and not just that we could never be given evidence sufficient to make it rational to believe that there have been miracles). But Hume's argument is sufficiently disputed so that appeal to his authority doesn't help me much. See David Hume, *An Enquiry Concerning Human Understanding* Eric Steinberg, ed. Hackett Publishing Co., 1977 sec. X.

[31] Is the hypothesis of infallibilism itself fallible? The universalizability argument for infallibilism assumes that the world is such that given enough opportunities, errors will be revealed. This is an inductive component that could turn out wrong. But until it (and related assumptions) do infallibilism remains the best hypothesis. On a related point, see Hilary Putnam, "The Analytic and the Synthetic," in his *Mind, Language and Reality Philosophical Papers Vol.2* Cambridge University Press, 1975, especially pp. 56–62.

[32] For a skeptical argument generated along these lines see Keith Lehrer, "Skepticism and Conceptual Change," in *Empirical Knowledge* R.M. Chisholm and R.J. Swartz, eds. Prentice–Hall, 1973 47–58.

[33] The dispositional view is taken by Popper, op.cit. But the relevance to rational certainty of an implicit predictive component in ordinary concepts is made especially forcefully by Hans Reichenbach in "Are Phenomenal Reports Absolutely Certain?" in *Empirical Knowledge* op.cit. 348–359.

[34] Often the Sorites creeps in without notice. That is why I qualified my restriction at the beginning of this paragraph, excluding Sorites, by "if possible." For an instance see Roderick Firth, "The Anatomy of Certainty," in *Empirical Knowledge* op.cit. 203–223. See p.215.

[35] It is unclear how far Levin would want to take her claim. She does extend it to include the consideration of failures in other epistemic communities, and to "meta–inductions" from failures in the history of science. But she does not go any further (nor need she for her purposes of objecting to my assumptions). Moreover, she explicitly denies any infallibilistic implications (ibid., p.74, 77), albeit (a) she doesn't, at those points, consider epistemic universalizability principles and (b) she doesn't give specific reasons for these denials.

[36] In regard to specifying what similarities are pertinent to the similarity of possible worlds, David Lewis observes that it is extremely unlikely that worlds could diverge and then later perfectly converge. The convergence is unlikely because of the multitude of consequences even the smallest divergence will have. See his "Counterfactual Dependence and Time's Arrow," *Nous* Vol. XIII 1979 455–476.

[37] Those who offer such motivators are not themselves taken in. They quickly demand that the skeptical possibility go essentially undetected.

[38] Thompson Clarke, "The Legacy of Skepticism," *Journal of Philosophy* p.766. See also Levin's op.cit. discussion in section III and IV.

PETER KLEIN

EPISTEMIC COMPATIBILISM AND CANONICAL BELIEFS

INTRODUCTION

Sceptics believe that knowledge is *not* possible, because knowledge entails certainty, and certainty is not possible. Most nousists[1] believe that knowledge is possible precisely because they believe, in part, that knowledge does *not* entail certainty. For they, too, believe that certainty is not possible.[2] Thus, sceptics and most nousists agree that certainty is not possible.

I think that is a mistake. I want to argue for a compatibilist epistemic theory by showing that certainty is possible. In other words, I want to show that the nousist is right in holding that knowledge is possible and that the sceptic is right in holding that knowledge entails certainty; but that both are wrong in holding that certainty is not possible.

There is an obvious analogy with the compatibilist position in the freedom/determinism debates. Roughly, both the "hard determinist" and the "libertarians" believe that an act is free only if it is uncaused. They disagree about whether an act can be uncaused. The compatibilist in this dispute holds that they are both wrong in thinking that freedom requires uncaused acts and proposes an account of free action, namely action that is not compelled, which is such that acts can be free. The compatibilist suggests that freedom construed in that manner vouchsafes moral responsibility. Briefly put, the ethical compatibilist proposes to substitute an account of "free acts" which makes moral responsibility possible for an account of "free acts" which eliminates that possibility.

In a parallel fashion, I will be arguing that there is an appropriate sense of "certainty" available which vouchsafes the possibility of knowledge. I want to suggest that "certainty" should be taken to mean, roughly, that a belief is certain if and only if it is absolutely immune from doubt. I grant, at the outset, that if "certainty" is understood to require, roughly, that a belief is certain only if the evidence for it absolutely warrants its truth, then knowledge about matters of fact is not possible. Thus, my proposal is to substitute "absolutely indubitable beliefs" for "absolutely warranted beliefs" in the account of certainty.

I want to show (1) that absolute indubitability is a plausible rendering of what sceptics have required of beliefs and (2) that a very important belief can be absolutely indubitable. (From now on when I use "indubitable" I will mean absolutely indubitable.) To accomplish the first task, I want to appeal to what I take to be the source of most contemporary scepticism — Descartes' arguments in "Meditation I." I merely want to show that Descartes took a belief to be certain if it was indubitable. To accomplish the second task, I will develop an account of indubitability and show that there need be nothing which prohibits a very important belief from being indubitable. Of course, there is a clear relationship between the first and second task. For the account of indubitability that I wish to develop is one that was suggested by Descartes.

M. D. Roth and G. Ross (eds.), Doubting, 99–117.
© 1990 *Kluwer Academic Publishers. Printed in the Netherlands.*

There is one further parallel between epistemic and ethical compatibilism which should be mentioned at this point if a possible misunderstanding is to be avoided. Just as the ethical compatibilist cannot show by an *a priori* argument that there are free acts, because no *a priori* argument could show that there are uncompelled acts, I cannot show that any belief is certain. That might seem disappointing. For it may be thought that the most interesting question is this: Is there any knowledge? And, I will not be answering, much less, addressing that question directly. But, I suppose that the most interesting question in the free will/determinism dispute may also seem to be this: Is there free will? No argument can show that there is. For it is certainly possible that we never act freely because we always act under some compulsion or other. I believe that there is ample empirical evidence which supports the claim that we sometimes act without being compelled to act. But that claim cannot be substantiated by *a priori* arguments alone.

The same limitation applies here. I cannot show by *a priori* arguments that, in fact, any belief about contingent matters is indubitable. Again, it is possible that there is some basis for legitimate doubt for each such belief. I can show, I think, that there is no *a priori* reason to believe that there is always such a basis for doubt. However, I cannot prove that we have knowledge. But neither can anyone else.[3] I will return to this point later.

Another preliminary comment is in order. I will be considering cases of putative knowledge which are among the most problematic. Many sceptics might be willing to grant that we do have knowledge of such propositions as "there is a pain, here and now." Many nousists might be willing to grant that we do not have knowledge of very distant past or very distant future events. The disagreement seems to focus most clearly on beliefs I have in the existence of the ordinary objects in the world and their properties — tables, animals, rainbows and colors, textures and shapes. In other words, the dispute concerns beliefs about those things I typically take for granted. Let us use the expression "canonical beliefs" to refer to all of the those beliefs which seems so obviously true about the existence of objects in the world and their properties that I would find it odd that such a belief needed to be defended[4]. Of course, you have a set of canonical beliefs, too.

The status of a belief may change. At one time it may be part of the canon and later it can be dropped from the canon. And new beliefs can be added to the canon. Also, it is clear, I think, that my set of canonical beliefs may not overlap precisely with that of anyone else.

A central claim in this paper is that a meta–proposition about our canonical beliefs, namely, *the preponderance of canonical beliefs is true*, can be certain for each of us. I use the expression "preponderance of canonical beliefs" to refer to the vast majority of canonical beliefs. I don't know how many beliefs that is if only because I have no way of determining how many canonical beliefs there are or the exact proportion of them which is true. Suffice it to say that it is a very, very large number — like the number of stars in the sky — and that my claim is that I can be certain that the vast majority of them is true. More specifically, I will argue (i) that there is no belief in the canon of beliefs that is certain, but nevertheless, (ii) that we can be certain that the preponderance of them is true. No doubt, it might seem initially implausible that both (i) and (ii) can be true together. For it may appear that (i) implies the denial of (ii). That it doesn't, is one of the crucial steps in my defense of epistemic compatibilism.

One final preliminary comment is required. I will be using many terms like "belief,""proposition," and "epistemic warrant" without hesitation. That will appear foolhardy to many readers because the pedigree of those terms is somewhat suspicious, to say the least. Nevertheless, I do not believe that either my characterization of the debate between the nousist and sceptic or my suggested compatibilist reconciliation depends upon a particular account of any of those somewhat suspect notions. Thus, I will use those terms unabashedly.

ABSOLUTE WARRANT AND INDUBITABILITY

One area of agreement between a sceptic and a nousist is that there are beliefs which *apparently* are true and for which we *seem* to have considerable evidence but which *seem* to fall short of knowledge. But that agreement provides the wedge in the door which leads to scepticism. Take a simple case, but one which has a somewhat jaded history: Suppose that there is a lottery with ten tickets and only one ticket will win[5]. Surely it is much more reasonable to believe about any single ticket, t_i, that it will lose than to deny it. But neither the nousist nor the sceptic will claim that a person knows about her ticket that it will lose, even though she has a true and highly warranted belief that her ticket will lose. In fact, the sceptic will rightly point out that the probability assigned to the proposition that t_i will lose can be raised to whatever degree one pleases but it is clear that the belief will still fall short of knowledge. On that the nousist and sceptic will agree, at least initially.

But then the sceptic can point out that this case shares a common feature with *every* belief in the canon. For, after all, this is a case in which (1) the belief *ticket t_i will lose* falls short of knowledge and (2) the evidence for that belief does not absolutely warrant its truth. The sceptic will point out that it is clear that the evidence we have for canonical beliefs is such that it does not guarantee their truth.

Put another way, once it is pointed out that in such cases our evidence does not absolutely warrant the truth of our beliefs, typical arguments for scepticism become easy to formulate. It can be pointed out, correctly, that a person who apparently has knowledge can have exactly the same evidence as another person who lacks knowledge. Thus, it is claimed that in spite of the initial appearance, the first person's evidence is inadequate to produce knowledge because it is not "universalizable."[6] For example, a person who appears to know that she is looking at a book has no more reason to believe that she is looking at a book than does the infamous brain–in–a–vat for a similar belief. In fact, it is easy to construct a sceptical scenario such that the person in that scenario has exactly the same evidence as does the person in the "normal" circumstance. Thus, canonical beliefs always seem to fall short of knowledge.

The argument can be generalized even further. Since no contingent proposition is such that it is absolutely warranted by its evidence, no contingent proposition can be certain and, hence, known. That would apply even to the proposition that the preponderance of my canonical beliefs is true. For that is a contingent proposition.

Now, suppose that a nousist attempts to reply by suggesting that there is some confidence level which is necessary for knowledge and that a true belief at or above that confidence level which is the best "competitor" is knowledge.[7] The nousist could even add that the required confidence level is "context dependent." That certainly has a "pragmatic" ring of truth about it.

But, whatever characterization of competition the nousist adopts, she must reject the well–founded intuition that underlies the Lottery Case, namely, if I know that a proposition is only probably true, then I don't know that it is true. That intuition seems undeniably correct to me. For example, if I believed that it is only .99999 likely that p, and even if I knew that p had a higher probability than any of its competitors and even if the context were such that a belief with that probability is acceptable, I would not claim that I knew that p. The sceptic is correct about that. No doubt, I would bet the ranch on it; but I would not claim to know that it is true.

At this point, it might appear that the debate between the sceptic and the nousist is over. For the sceptic seems to have forced the nousist either to grant that knowledge cannot entail certainty, for if it did, there would be no knowledge or to accept a pale imitation of real knowledge as the best we can attain — namely, highly probable, true belief. But has the nousist been persuaded too easily?

In the Lottery Case it is true that (1) the belief that *ticket t ᵢ will lose* falls short of knowledge and (2) the evidence for that belief does not guarantee its truth. We can grant that both (1) and (2) are true without granting that (1) is true because (2) is true. In fact, I grant immediately that if certainty is such that a belief is certain only if the evidence for it guarantees its truth, then no contingent proposition will be certain including the proposition that *the preponderance of canonical beliefs is true.*

To return to the analogy mentioned earlier, if freedom is taken to require the absence of causal determination, then the compatibilist will grant immediately that there is no freedom. It is a particular kind of causal determination that is sufficient for freedom. Similarly, I wish to suggest that it is a particular kind of belief based on less than truth–guaranteeing evidence which is certain. I will return to the Lottery Case latter in order to give an analysis of it that employs my suggested account of certainty. Of course, we will also have to deal with the power of the sceptical scenarios. But that is getting ahead of the story. The next step is to make clear what would make a proposition certain if that is taken to mean that it is beyond all doubt.

DESCARTES' VIEW ABOUT DOUBT

A very brief discussion of Descartes' account of methodological doubt in "Meditation I" will help to clarify the desiderata of an acceptable account of certainty as immunity to an important form of doubt. Recall that Descartes is seeking an acceptable basis for doubting what I have called the canonical beliefs. By the end of the *Meditations* and after the various grounds for doubting those beliefs have been examined carefully, it turns out that the proposition that the preponderance of them is true becomes beyond doubt. Although I am not going to argue that the meta–proposition can be certain for exactly the same reasons which Descartes gave, it is crucial to note that at one point in the *Meditations*, Descartes presents what he takes to be a basis for doubting canonical beliefs, and later he presents what he takes to be an answer to those doubts. The doubt is both created and removed by "internal" means. It is through examining his beliefs and their consequences that both the potential grounds for doubt are developed *and* removed. That is *the* important feature of internal doubt — grounds for doubt can be created and removed by careful thought alone. The doubt is neither brought about nor removed by discovering new truths about the world.

Before examining that process a bit more carefully, it is important to note two other general points about internally generated and removed doubt. *First*, that type of doubt is a species of epistemological doubt. In the "Synopsis of the Six Following Meditations" while discussing the reinstatement of canonical beliefs, Descartes wrote:

> All the errors which proceed from the senses are then surveyed, while means of avoiding them are demonstrated, and finally all the reasons from which we may deduce the existence of material things are set forth. Not that I judge them to be very useful in establishing that which they prove, to wit, *that there is in truth a world, that men possess bodies, and other such things which never have been doubted by anyone of sense*...[Emphasis mine].[8]

In other words, the doubt which both arises in the earlier stages of the *Meditations* about the preponderance of canonical beliefs and is removed in the final stages is not psycho–logical. For a person to *feel* doubts that there is a world in which people have bodies would be insane. Put another way, beliefs can be epistemically doubtful even though they "never have been doubted by anyone of sense." It will be a main task of this paper to make clear what epistemic doubt is; but it should be noted at the outset what it isn't. It isn't a feeling of doubt. In fact, it is clear that the evil demon hypothesis is introduced as a heuristic device to remind Descartes that he has found a basis for rendering canonical beliefs epistemically doubtful. It is a way of reminding himself that beliefs about which no sane person would *feel* any doubt are, nevertheless, at least at that point in the *Meditations*, doubtful in the relevant, epistemic sense. Similarly, a belief may be epis–temically certain for a person, that is, completely free of epistemic doubt, and yet that person may *feel* some doubt about it.[9]

The *second* general point is one that might be overlooked, but it is important for my account of certainty. Even *after* Descartes has given the grounds which he believes make canonical beliefs temporarily doubtful, he says that they remain much more rea–sonable to believe than deny. He says of those beliefs that they are "in some measure doubtful, as I have just shown, and at the same time highly probable, so that there is much more reason to believe in than to deny them."[10] In other words, although the beliefs do not have the highest degree of epistemic warrant, i.e., certainty, nevertheless they remain much more reasonable to believe than to deny. That, presumably, is one reason, perhaps even a sufficient one, for thinking that it would be insane to harbor any psychological doubts about them. For it may be thought that a person who "lacks sense" is one who holds beliefs or doubts regardless of the weight of the relevant evidence. But my point is that even after beliefs have been temporarily classified as doubtful, they might still remain much more reasonable to believe than to deny. The question one is asking oneself is something like this: Are there any legitimate grounds for lowering the epistemic status of my beliefs? If such grounds can be found, then the beliefs are epis–temically doubtful even if they remain highly probable.

It is clear that for Descartes a belief is certain only if it is free from doubt. He says:

> ...Now for this object it is not necessary that I should show that all of these are false — I shall perhaps never arrive at this end. But inasmuch as reason already persuades me that I ought no less

> carefully withhold my assent from matters which are not entirely certain and indubitable than from
> those which appear to me to be manifestly false, if I am able to find in each one some reason to
> doubt, this will suffice to justify rejecting the whole.[11]

This is not the place to rehearse his argument which finally lead to the temporary basis for doubting that the preponderance of his canonical beliefs is true, although I will discuss it at the end of the next section. Our task, at this point, is merely to make clear what the standard of certainty was which he employed. But it is important to note what he wrote immediately after giving that general argument. He said:

> To these reasons I have certainly nothing to reply, but at the end I feel constrained to confess that
> there is nothing in all that I formerly believed to be true, of which I cannot in some measure doubt,
> and that not merely through want of thought or levity, but for reasons which are very powerful and
> maturely considered; so that henceforth I ought not the less carefully to refrain from giving credence
> to these opinions than to that which is manifestly false, if I desire to arrive at any certainty in the
> sciences.[12]

He repeats this requirement in many places, namely that beliefs should be indubitable in order to be certain. In the *Discourse on Method*, he says that he will "reject as absolutely false everything as to which I could imagine the least ground of doubt, in order to see if afterwards there remained anything in my belief that was entirely certain."[13] In the *Principles of Philosophy*, he says, "It will even be useful to reject as false all these things as to which we can imagine the least doubt to exist, so that we may discover with greater clearness which are absolutely true, and most easy to know."[14]

To generalize: (1) Descartes took beliefs to be certain just in case they were indubitable and (2) roughly, what makes a belief doubtful is that there is some carefully examined proposition which cannot be justifiably rejected and which lowers the degree of epistemic warrant of the belief.

We are now in a position to describe the *desiderata* for giving an adequate account of epistemic doubt of the Cartesian variety:

1. The account must make clear what counts as a grounds for Cartesian doubt.
2. The account must result in it being possible for a belief to be doubtful but nevertheless "much more reasonable to believe" than to deny.
3. The account of Cartesian doubt must be such that it possible to consider, accept and later reject various potential grounds for doubt on the basis of examining our belief systems.

After giving that account, we must ask this question: Is Cartesian doubt the only form of epistemic doubt? To look ahead a bit, we will see that Cartesian doubt, though an extremely important form of epistemic doubt, is not the only relevant form. But the major task of this paper is to delineate Cartesian, internal doubt. Let us turn to that task.

CARTESIAN, INTERNAL DOUBT

Recalling a passage quoted earlier from the *Meditations*, let us define "justification" as follows: A belief is justified if and only if it is much more reasonable to believe it than to deny it. That may not coincide with an ordinary notion of justification, if there is one, and it is certainly far from clear just what would make a belief much more reasonable to believe than to deny. But I think that we can safely assume that some account of reasonable belief, and hence, justification, can be developed which is acceptable to both the sceptic and nousist. For our purposes there are two important constraints on that account of justification which should be noted:

(1)   A belief can be justified even if the evidence for it does not guarantee its truth. The reason for that has already been presented, namely, if it is required that the evidence for a belief must guarantee its truth, then there is no question but that we fail to have knowledge of every contingent proposition.

(2)   Beliefs in the canon are initially justified.

That (2) is a reasonable assumption may not be immediately obvious. In fact, it may seem that we have already assumed enough to prejudice the case so strongly in favor of the nousist that the sceptic will be bound to demur. Thus, some defense of that assumption seems called for.[15]

I take it that *the* issue between the sceptic and the nousist is whether there are any beliefs that can be certain. In the Lottery Case, for example, it is clear that it is much more reasonable to believe that one's ticket will lose than to believe that the ticket will win. The sceptic and nousist agree on that. But that is to agree that the proposition that the ticket will lose is justified, given the definition of "justification" stipulated above. In addition, it is the sceptic who points to the analogy between the beliefs held in the Lottery Case and the beliefs in the canonical set. Thus, the sceptic does not weaken her case in any way by granting that those propositions are justified. The issue is not whether those propositions are justified, *the* issue is whether those propositions can be certain.

In fact, if it is not assumed that canonical beliefs are justified, the interest in scepticism immediately disappears. For the sceptical puzzle is just this: What more needs to be added to true, justified belief to make it knowledge? The answer suggested by the sceptic is "certainty."

We have already seen that Descartes holds that beliefs based upon the senses are justified, as stipulatively defined above, even after he has given the argument which he believes shows them to be less than certain. Thus, as long as it is clear that knowledge is not mere justified, true belief, then it can safely be assumed that canonical beliefs are justified. Of course, it cannot be assumed that there are no legitimate grounds which may be discovered for lowering their epistemic status. For that would, indeed, beg the question against the sceptic.

So, let us assume that we have a corpus of justified beliefs and that it includes, but is not limited to, the canonical beliefs. What would it mean for them to be doubtful in a Cartesian, internal sense? *First*, it is possible that within the corpus of beliefs there already exist grounds for doubt.[17]   That is, it may be the case that a belief, say *p*, is justified for *S* but there is some proposition, say *d*, such that (1.a) *S* believes *d* and (2.a) *d* lowers the level of epistemic warrant of *p* for *S*. This is a species of internal doubt in a full–blown sense because the grounds for doubt actually exist within the corpus of beliefs. Our account should incorporate this form of internal doubt.

But, *second*, there is another type of internal doubt — a more potent form — to which Descartes apparently appeals.   For a proposition may be doubtful even if the grounds for doubt are not located within *S* ' s belief system. This type of doubt is still a form of "internal doubt" because whether *p* is subject to it depends primarily upon features of *S*'s current corpus of beliefs, and it parallels the first type just mentioned in significant ways. We can say that a belief is internally doubtful in this sense if there is a proposition which *S* cannot justifiably deny and which is such that it would make *S* ' s belief *p* less warranted.   In other words, *p* would be subject to this type of internal doubt if there is a proposition, *d*, which is such that (1.b) *S* is not justified in denying *d* and (2.b) if *d* is added to *S* ' s beliefs, it lowers the level of the epistemic warrant of *p* for *S*.

This latter sense of internal doubt is the most interesting type to the sceptic precisely because it is so potent. Consequently, most of what follows will employ the latter sense.   Nevertheless, the account of Cartesian doubt should encompass both senses. Hence, let us say that a proposition, *p*, is internally doubtful for *S* if and only if there is a proposition, *d*, which is such that (1) either *S* believes *d* or *S* is not justified in denying *d* and (2) either *d* lowers the level of epistemic warrant of *p* for *S* or if *d* is added to *S* ' s beliefs, it lowers the level of the epistemic warrant of *p* for *S*. Let us call the first condition, (1), the "acceptance condition" and the second condition, (2), the "reduction condition."   The proposition, *d*, is a basis for internal doubt of *p* for *S* just in case *d* is accepted by or acceptable to *S* and *d* reduces the epistemic warrant of *p* for *S*.

Note that this account satisfies the three very general *desiderata* for an adequate account of Cartesian internal doubt mentioned at the end of the last section. For we have stated, at least in a very general way, what makes a proposition subject to internal doubt. We have also characterized that doubt in such a way that a belief may be doubtful but, nevertheless, justified. .For it should be apparent that although *d* satisfies the acceptance and reduction condition, it might not lower *p* below the threshold required for justification.[18]   Finally, the acceptance condition makes clear how potential grounds for doubt can be generated and accepted or rejected by "internal" means. For one asks oneself this question, "Is there anything that I believe or that I cannot deny which lowers the epistemic warrant of my justified beliefs?"

Several comments are in order about this characterization of internal doubt in order to show that it is a plausible rendering of the Cartesian notion and, in addition, that it should be an intuitively pleasing account to a sceptic. *First*, it is a *very* strong form of doubt because *d* need not lower the degree of warrant of *p* very much at all in order for *p* to be subject to internal doubt from *d*. All that is required is that it lower it a bit — a very small bit. *Second*, it is crucial to note that *d* need not be true. The Cartesian project was not to discover a true proposition which provided grounds for doubt. For example, Descartes did not think that his senses were inherently deceptive. His question was rather more like this: Is there any proposition that I am not in an epistemic position to reject that would lower the credibility of my currently justified beliefs? The proposition located need not be true. *Third, d* satisfies the acceptance condition even if I do not have a reason for thinking that *d* is true. *Fourth*, the scope of potential grounds for doubt is not limited either by my present corpus of beliefs or by my imagination. It may be that for certain psychological causes *I* cannot believe or think of a proposition which would satisfy the acceptance and reduction condition. But that is unimportant. What is important is whether there *is* such a proposition.

Finally, this form of doubt is a *very* strong form of doubt, indeed. Many beliefs become doubtful because of it. But, as mentioned above, it is not the only form of doubt. That is because *d* is not a grounds for internal doubt if there is a basis within the belief set for justifiably denying *d*. But even if a belief, *p*, is immune to this type of doubt, it is clear that *either* if *d* is true and would if added to *S* ' s belief set result in the lowering of epistemic warrant of *p*, or if some of *S* ' s beliefs used to deny *d* are themselves false, *p* is doubtful in some "objective" sense. *S* will not be able to determine by merely reflecting on her beliefs whether a belief is doubtful in this "external" sense; but the belief is doubtful, nonetheless. I will discuss this sense of external doubt very briefly latter, but it is worth noting at this point that this is the sense of resistance to defeat which has been extensively examined by defeasibility theorists. Internal doubt, however, has been generally ignored and it is that sense which I believe lies at the heart of the intuitive plausibility of scepticism.

Let us look a little bit more carefully at the proposed account of internal doubt, beginning with the *acceptance condition.* Whether a belief satisfies the acceptance condition depends upon what is already in a *S* ' s justified belief set. That is obviously true for (1.a). But it also applies to (1.b). For example, if some proposition, say *e* is available for *S* to use as a reason for denying *d*, then *d* is not a grounds of doubt for *S*. But if *e* were not available to *S*, *d* might provide a reason for doubt for *S*. But that is as it should be. Consider an example from "Meditation I." Descartes apparently believed that dream–images were distorted copies of images which arose in "waking" life. Thus, Descartes had a belief within *his* corpus of justified beliefs which he could use as a basis for denying that all of his images have been obtained during sleep. If the proposition that they had all been obtained during sleep were added to his belief set, it would lower the epistemic warrant of his belief that there are objects in the world about which he gains some knowledge by means of his senses. But he had a legitimate way of denying that all of his "ideas" could have been obtained while he was asleep.[19] The point is that without his belief about the origin of dream– images, *he* might not have had a way to reject the claim that all of his "ideas" could have been obtained while dreaming.

The inclusion of the *reduction condition* is designed to account for the following: Even if S does not have a basis for denying a particular proposition, *S* ' s corpus of beliefs may be such that the proposition need not create a doubt even though at first glance it may appear to provide such a basis. Recall that Descartes considered and rejected many potential grounds for doubt because they did not hold up under "mature" and "careful" reflection. In "Meditation I," Descartes considers the proposition that his senses have misled him in the past. He cannot justifiably deny that. In fact, he apparently had that belief prior to beginning his meditations about the scope of scepticism. That is, it is clear that the acceptance condition is fulfilled because both (1.a) and (1.b) are fulfilled. But he rejects that as a grounds for doubt because he believes that he has a good basis for distinguishing those times when his senses have been trustworthy from those times when they have not.[20]   He is clearly employing something like the reduction condition in the following:

> ...All that up to the present time I have accepted as most true and certain I have learned either from the senses or through the senses; but it is sometimes proved to me that these senses are deceptive, and it is wiser not to trust entirely to any thing by which we have once been deceived.
>
> But it may be that although the senses sometimes deceive us concerning things which are hardly perceptible, or very far away, there are yet many others to be met with as to which we cannot reasonably have any doubt, although we recognize them by their means. For example, that there is the fact that I am here, seated by a fire, attired in a dressing gown ...

To further clarify my suggested account of internal doubt, consider the *proposition everyone who has evidence similar to mine about the existence of a table has been wrong*. Does it provide a basis for doubting the canonical proposition that there is a table? That proposition clearly fulfills the reduction condition; but it does not fulfill the acceptance condition. Recall that we are supposing that the canonical beliefs are justified. The issue is whether such justified beliefs are certain. But if I am justified in believing that there are tables, I am justified in believing that there is at least one person who has evidence similar to mine who has not been wrong, namely me. In other words, I am justified in denying this candidate proposition as providing a basis for doubt.[22]   In fact, imagine a person who said that (i) she believed there were tables and (ii) everyone who believes that there are tables was mistaken. I think our response would be, "How can you believe (i) and (ii)?" The reason for our response is simply that the belief expressed in (i) provides an adequate basis for denying the belief expressed in (ii).

But now, consider this proposition, call it "*c*": *The number of people who have had perceptual evidence similar to mine for the existence of a particular table and who have been misled by their senses is not zero*. Is that a legitimate basis for doubting the proposition that there is a table before me? *First*, does it satisfy the acceptance condition? No doubt, I may never be in such circumstances. Further, the number of people in such circumstances may indeed be zero. In other words, *c* might be false. But as we have seen, a proposition which provides a basis for internal doubt need not be true. I certainly cannot use either the belief that there is a table before me or the belief that I am able to recognize *some* unreliable perceptual circumstances as a basis for denying *c*. In fact, it appears that I do not have any basis for denying it. Indeed, I believe *c* and, in fact, it seems justified. Have not people been taken in by various illusions that seemed as real as the table before me does? Thus, *c* fulfills the acceptance condition.

Second, what about the reduction condition? What is the effect of *c* on the epistemic warrant of my belief that there is a table before me?

That is a difficult question. The answers goes to the heart of the dispute between the sceptic and the nousist and to the heart of my suggestion for a compatibilist "solution." Consider a standard perceptual case — one in which I seem to see a table. Call it the "Table Case." Suppose that in the Table Case, I am justified in believing that there is a table before me. Now, I add *c* to my beliefs. I am still justified in believing that there is a table before me because it is still much more reasonable to believe that there is a table before me than to deny it. But *c* certainly does lower the degree of epistemic warrant of *p*. There is nothing available to me to block the power of *c*. Thus, *the belief that there is a table before me is not beyond internal doubt.* It is not certain. It is not known.

That much, I think, must be granted to the sceptic. I do not think that grants too much. After all, believing what I do about human beings and the ways in which they can be deceived, can I ever really be certain that there is a table before me when it looks just like there is. In other words, when I keep in mind what I justifiably believe about the various ways in which I could be wrong, the epistemic warrant of my belief that there is a table before me must be lowered somewhat. It isn't epistemically certain that there is a table before me because I cannot justifiably deny *c* and adding *c* to my beliefs lowers the epistemic warrant of the proposition that there is a table before me. But we must be *very careful* here to note (1)what it is that is being conceded to the sceptic at this point and (2) why it is being conceded.

(1)   What is being conceded is that my belief about any *particular* sensible object is not beyond doubt. Those beliefs are not certain.

(2)   The reason that my belief about a particular table fails to be certain is *not* because my evidence fails to guarantee its truth. It is not certain because it is doubtful. It is true that the evidence fails to guarantee its truth, but that is *obviously* true for every empirical, contingent proposition.[23] The point is that the proposition is not beyond all legitimate grounds for doubt.

Recall the Lottery Case. In that case, the belief that my ticket will lose is justified. But it is not certain because there is a clear, assignable probability that I am wrong. Thus, the suggested account of certainty captures the intuition mentioned earlier that if I believe that a proposition is only probably true, then I don't know that the proposition is true. The only significant difference between the Lottery Case and standard perceptual cases, like the Table Case, is that I can quite easily assign the degree to which I should lower the epistemic warrant of the proposition that my ticket will lose by taking account of the number of tickets in the lottery. The proposition, *the number of people who have evidence similar to mine who have been wrong is not zero,* is one which fulfills the acceptance and reduction condition in the Lottery Case. As we have seen, it also satisfies both conditions in the Table Case. In the Table Case, I do not know how to quantify the degree to which the epistemic warrant of the proposition that there is a table before me should be lowered once *c* is added to my beliefs because I do not know how many people, if any, have had my evidence for thinking that there is a table before them and been wrong. The sceptic was right that we do not possess knowledge in the Table Case for essentially the same reason that we do not possess it in the Lottery Case.[24] The beliefs, though justified, are not knowledge because they are subject to internal doubt. But the sceptic was wrong in thinking that the reason is that evidence does not guarantee the truth of the beliefs.

Now, it may be thought that my suggested analysis of the Lottery Case does not just provide a mere wedge in the door that leads to scepticism, but that I have just flung open the door after laying down the welcome mat! After all, if I don't know with certainty that there is a table before me on any particular occasion, how can I know with certainty that the preponderance of canonical beliefs is true? For it may seem that if I cannot know that there is a table before me, then I cannot know that there are tables. And, if I cannot even know that there are tables, I certainly cannot know that the preponderance of my canonical beliefs is true. Surprisingly, I want to argue that even though no particular canonical belief is certain, the meta–claim about my canonical beliefs — that most of them are true — can be certain.

The point is a simple one. It is this: Each proposition in a set of propositions may be subject to internal doubt and yet the claim that the preponderance of propositions in that set is true may not be subject to internal doubt. For the grounds for doubting each proposition may not apply to the meta–proposition about the set of propositions.

Recall Descartes' discussion concerning the possible ubiquity of dream–images. He grants that *each* image could be a dream–image. But it certainly does not follow immediately from this that *every* image could be a dream–image. In fact, given what he believes about the origin of dream–images, if any *one* of the images is a dream–image, there must have been at some previous time an image that was not a dream–image.[25] His beliefs place him in the position to reject the claim that all of his images could be dream images. In other words, by supposing that a particular image is (or was) a dream–image, he must also suppose that there is at least one waking–image. The general moral I wish to draw from this example is merely that when we add a proposition to our belief system which lowers the epistemic warrant of each belief of a particular sort in the system, it may not lower the epistemic warrant of the meta–proposition that some beliefs of that sort are true. In fact, as in the argument concerning dream–images, it may raise the epistemic warrant of the meta–proposition.

I think that is the case with regard to canonical beliefs. To see that, suppose that I am considering the canonical belief that there are tables. I think the most plausible candidate for doubting that canonical belief is a proposition like the following, call it "*b*": *There are beliefs in the current canon of beliefs which are false and which are in every relevant way similar to the belief that **there are tables**.* There are two questions to ask: (1) Do propositions of that form provide a basis for doubting each canonical belief with the appropriate substitutions in the belief clause? (2) If each canonical belief is internally dubitable, does that doubt extend to the meta–proposition that the preponderance of canonical beliefs is true?

To answer the first question, note that *b* is similar in structure to *c*, considered earlier and, for similar reasons, propositions like *b* provide a legitimate basis of internal doubt for each canonical belief. It fulfills the acceptance condition. It might not be true, but I have no basis for denying it. In fact, I can think of examples which seem to satisfy it. After all, the belief that there are witches was once part of the canonical belief set. In addition, it fulfills the reduction condition. If added to my beliefs, it would lower the epistemic warrant of the belief that there are tables. Thus, each canonical belief is doubtful because there is a proposition like *b* which could be formulated for *each* canonical belief simply by substituting it after the belief clause in *b*. In other words, no canonical belief is certain.

In answering the second question, it is absolutely crucial to note that *b* in conjunction with all of the propositions sharing the *b*–form would not make doubtful the proposition *the preponderance of beliefs in the set of canonical beliefs is true.* For just as Descartes believed that if one of his images is labelled as a dream–image, at least one other image must be labelled as a waking–image, I believe that when a canonical belief is labelled as false or its epistemic warrant is decreased, it is because we employ many other canonical beliefs whose epistemic warrant is, thereby, increased.[26] I am assuming, of course, that the epistemic warrant of a proposition is increased if its position in the web of beliefs is enhanced.

Return to the example mentioned in the previous paragraph and suppose that at one time *there are witches* was part of the canonical belief set. If we suppose that canonical belief is false, we must also suppose that there is some explanation of its having appeared to be true. Presumably, we would employ *many, many* other canonical beliefs about human behavior, the causes of disease, the societal need for developing myths, and perhaps, the need for oppressed people to ban together in secrete groups (i.e., covens) to resist oppression. In other words, accepting that a canonical belief is false or lowering its epistemic warrant strengthens the epistemic warrant of many other canonical beliefs. Thus, although *b*–form propositions do lower the epistemic warrant of each canonical belief, they do not lower the warrant of the belief that my basic picture of the world is correct. Quite the contrary, when one (or more) of my canonical beliefs is considered to be false or its warrant is lowered, many others increase in warrant because I employ them to explain how it could be that the false or doubtful one(s) appeared to be true. Thus, *b*–form propositions do not provide a basis for doubting the proposition *the preponderance of canonical beliefs is true*.

But even if the argument in the previous paragraph were correct, we have not yet considered the most often cited basis for doubting that the preponderance of our canonical beliefs is true — the appeal to the so–called sceptical scenarios. Nevertheless, I believe that this appeal is rather easily handled. Each sceptical scenario is constructed so that all, or almost all, of the canonical beliefs are false. There are no hands, no sky, no people, no earth, etc. There is, perhaps, just a disembodied ego thinking. But surely I am justified in denying that such a thing is true. After all, I am justified in believing that I have hands, that there is a sky, that there are people and that there is an earth. In other words, although such a supposition would surely fulfill the reduction condition, it just as surely fails the acceptance condition. In fact, the more bizarre the scenario, that is, the greater the number of canonical beliefs which would have to be rejected,the greater the warrant I have for denying it.

I cannot justifiably deny that some of my canonical beliefs are false. But I can justifiably deny the meta–proposition that the preponderance of my canonical beliefs is false. The reason is simple. Even if I were in one of the sceptical scenarios, let's say a brain in the vat, I would be justified in denying that I was a brain in the vat. The reason is that I would have identical evidence to that which I now have. Since I am now justified in believing that I am not a brain in a vat on the basis of that evidence, I would be justified in believing that I was not a brain in a vat on the basis of that very same evidence even if I were a brain in a vat. Of course, if I were a brain in a vat, the meta–proposition that the preponderance of my canonical beliefs is true would be doubtful in some sense — the sense I will call "external doubt." For in that case, there is a set of *facts* which if added to my beliefs would lower the epistemic warrant of the meta–proposition. I cannot give an *a priori* argument whose conclusion is that the sceptical scenarios are false, although I am justified in believing that they are false. I will return to this point in the next section.

The sceptical scenario argument is often taken to be the basic sceptical argument and it is also taken to be the one which Descartes employed in the "Meditation I." If it were, we have just found an answer to it. But that is not the suggested basis for the doubt which Descartes gives in the *Meditations*.

It seems fitting to conclude this section by looking at the grounds for doubt which Descartes actually proposed. After suggesting that it is clearly within God's power to deceive us if he wishes, he says:

> There may indeed be those who would prefer to deny the existence of a God so powerful, rather than believe that all other things are uncertain. But let us not oppose them for the present, and grant that all that is here said of a God is a fable; nevertheless in whatever way they suppose that I have arrived at the state of being that I have reached — whether they attribute it to fate or to accident, or make out that it is by a continual succession of antecedents, or by some other method — since to err and deceive oneself is a defect, it is clear that the greater will be the probability of my being so imperfect as to deceive myself ever, as is the Author to whom they assign my origin the less powerful. To these reasons I have certainly nothing to reply.[27]

Note, there is no evil spirit here. Descartes' point, I take it, is that on the assumption that his epistemic "equipment" was created by a less than perfect being, then by its very nature, the equipment is imperfect and, hence, likely to fall into deep, systematic error. He thinks that is a reasonable assumption at this point in the *Meditations* because he has yet to understand how human error is compatible with there being a perfect creator. Later in the *Meditations* he develops an answer to this doubt by showing that the creator of his epistemic equipment is, indeed, perfect and that, nevertheless, human error is possible.

My point here is twofold. *First*, Descartes' ground for doubt arose because of particular features in his set of canonical beliefs which includes the belief that the less perfect cannot cause the more perfect. Since we do not share that belief (because we — or at least most of us — believe in evolution), then this argument ought not to cause us to doubt our sensory equipment. In other words, we have a reason for believing that our senses are inherently more likely to get things right than wrong even though they are created by a "continual series of [imperfect] antecedents." So *our* canonical belief set is immune to the particular basis for internal doubt proposed by Descartes concerning the likelihood of systematic error. *Second*, it should be clear from the general structure of the *Meditations* that Descartes sought an answer to his particular grounds for doubt by carefully examining his belief system to see whether he could show that his creator was perfect and that such a being would not deceive him. In other words, he showed that the acceptance condition was not, in the end, satisfied by the proposed basis for doubt suggested in the argument. The general point I wish to make here is that just as Descartes had the makings within his belief set to eliminate an important argument for scepticism, we have the makings, though different from his, within our belief set for resisting that same argument.[28]

Let me conclude this section by summarizing what I hope has been shown. I hope this section has presented a convincing argument for the claim that there are no general reasons for supposing that the meta–proposition *the preponderance of canonical beliefs is true* is subject to internal doubt. We have examined what I think are the most plausible grounds for internal doubt and found either that we are justified in denying the candidate proposition or that the proposition, even if added to our canonical beliefs, does not lower the epistemic warrant of the meta–proposition. In other words, each candidate proposition has been shown to fail either the acceptance or the reduction condition.

NON–CARTESIAN, EXTERNAL DOUBT

Thus far, we have been considering *internal* grounds for doubt. As mentioned earlier, those grounds need not be true propositions and even if true, the belief set may have sufficient resources for rejecting them. But as also mentioned earlier, there is a sense in which a justified belief may be less than certain even if the belief is part of a set of justified beliefs which can resist internal grounds for doubt.

Take a clear case: Return to some sceptical scenario and suppose that, in fact, even thought there are tables, I have never, in fact, seen any. Clearly, if that were added to my belief set, the epistemic warrant for *there are tables* would be lowered significantly. The belief that there are tables would be objectively dubitable. External doubt can be defined by modifying the definition already given for internal doubt. Roughly, a proposition, say *p*, is externally doubtful for *S* if and only if there is some true proposition which if added to *S* s justified belief set would lower the epistemic warrant of *p*.[29] This account of external doubt merely appeals to a strong form of the defeasibility ac—count of knowledge and, consequently, it need not be defended in any detail here.[30]

Nevertheless, there are a couple of points which should be mentioned in passing. *First,* whether a proposition is a basis for external doubt remains somewhat dependent upon the belief set because the belief set may have an "answer" to the true proposition which would block its effect. To recall a famous case, suppose that I am justified in believing that Tom Grabit has stolen a book from the library and that I am also justified in believing that Tom's mother has the delusion that she has another son, John.[31] Let us suppose that she has said, with apparent sincerity, that John stole the book rather than Tom. The epistemic warrant of my belief that Tom stole the book is not lowered if I add *Mrs. Grabit said that John stole the book* to my belief set because I believe that she suffers from the delusion about another son, John. On the other hand, the belief set of a person who was ignorant of Mrs. Grabit's delusion would not be immune to external doubt on that basis.

Second, the reason for my claim at the beginning of the paper that I can not prove *a priori* that any proposition is certain should now be clear. Whether a proposition is immune to external doubt depends upon what contingent propositions are true. In particular, whether a proposition, say *p*, is immune to external doubt depends upon whether *p* is true. For if *p* were false, ~*p* would make a belief that *p* subject to external doubt. For example, if the preponderance of my canonical beliefs were false, then it would not be certain that the preponderance of my canonical beliefs is true. But it is a contingent fact that the preponderance of my canonical beliefs is true. Thus, since I cannot prove that any contingent proposition is true or that it is false by *a priori* means, I cannot prove *the preponderance of my canonical beliefs is true* is (externally) certain. But that should not be at all troublesome. Who would have expected an *a priori* proof of a contingent proposition? Put another way, whether we have any knowledge is a con—tingent matter. But, again, who would have thought otherwise?

CONCLUSION

I have discussed two types of doubt. Those two types of doubt should be joined so that a belief is certain if and only if it is neither internally nor externally doubtful. Knowledge can be defined as true, justified, certain belief. That is my proposal to be placed before the sceptic and nousist. I believe that the account should be acceptable to both of them. In addition, I have argued that the proposition *the preponderance of canonical beliefs is true* can be certain. In other words, certainty and, hence, knowledge is possible. We cannot be certain that all of our canonical beliefs are true and we cannot be certain that any one of them is true. But we can be certain that our basic picture of the world is, in the main, true. That's good enough for me.

Rutgers University

NOTES

1 Although not currently in our vocabulary, I will use "nousist" to refer to those philosophers who argue against scepticism. To call them anti–sceptics implies that I do in fact believe their fundamental views are incompatible with those of the sceptic. And, of course, I think that is wrong. On the other hand, to use terms like "dogmatist" or "cognitivist" would be misleading for various reasons. "Dogmatist" brings with it the implication of close mindedness and "cognitivism" is a particular view held in ethical theory. So, it seems preferable to make up a new term.

2 It was, of course, the hallmark of pragmatism to suppose that knowledge did not entail certainty. See for example, Dewey's The Quest for Certainty, Milton, Balch and Company, 1929. More recently, that view has been defended most notably by Roderick Chisholm and Keith Lehrer. See, Chisholm, *Theory of Knowledge*, (second edition), Prentice Hall, 1977, see especially pp. 102–119; Lehrer, *Knowledge*, Oxford University Press, 1974, especially pp. 236–239.

3 I realize that it is not obvious that an *a priori* proof of knowledge is not possible. For example, Colin McGinn argues that Davidson's account of radical interpretation has just that consequence. That is one of the reasons McGinn gives for rejecting Davidson's account. (see Colin McGinn, "Radical Interpretation and Epistemology," in *Truth and Interpretation: Perspectives on the Philosophy of Donald Davidson*, ed. Ernest LePore, Basil Blackwell, 1986). On the other hand, I have argued that Davidson's rejection of scepticism fails because he begs the very question at issue; namely do we have knowledge of the "external" world, i. e., knowledge of the properties of physical objects? (See my paper, "Radical Interpretation and Global Scepticism" in the same volume mentioned above edited by LePore.) I take it that Davidson's account of belief is such that a belief is just that state of ourselves which bears a type of causal relation to some physical event or object. (See Davidson's paper in the LePore collection entitled "A Coherence Theory of Truth and Knowledge.") Thus, to assert that we have beliefs is to assert that there are states of ourselves which are causally related to external objects or events. Thus, whether we have beliefs becomes problematic from the sceptic's viewpoint because such an assertion requires evidence for its verification that there are states of ourselves which do, in fact, bear the appropriate causal relationship with physical events or objects. Now, of course, I believe that there are such correlations. But that there are requires empirical evidence. Thus, I don't think McGinn is correct that Davidson's argument against scepticism is really an *a priori* one. In addition, it may be thought that Descartes gives an *a priori* argument designed to show that we have knowledge. I grant that the argument for God's existence and epistemic benevolence appears to be *a priori* (at least in "Meditation V") and, if successful, it would show that God exists and has certain "other" properties. Thus, there does appear to be an *a priori* argument, which if successful, would show that we have knowledge that we are "not alone in the world" as Descartes puts it in "Meditation III." But this

knowledge, if there is any, is about a necessarily existing object. The knowledge I am interested in here concerns contingent beings. Our knowledge of those depends, according to Descartes, upon whether we have a clear and distinct idea of them. Even if that were correct, it cannot be shown by a priori argument that we have clear and distinct ideas. Each one of our ideas might be obscure or confused. That they aren't is determined by inspecting them and that is an "empirical" investigation though, perhaps, nothing more than introspection. But that is "empirical" in the appropriate sense, namely, the sense in which the results of experience provide evidence for a belief.

4 For the sake of simplifying the argument in the paper, it will be useful to stipulate that canonical beliefs are "first order" beliefs. Thus, the belief there are tables is in the canon but the belief the canon of beliefs contains the belief that there are tables is not in the canon. In particular, the belief the preponderance of beliefs in the canon are true is not in the canon. Exactly how to draw the line between first order beliefs and the others is a difficult question and the specter of various paradoxes haunts the attempt to draw that line. In particular, the so–called Preface Paradox hovers near. I believe that line can be drawn without falling prey to that paradox, but delineating the solution would take us too far afield from the main concerns of this paper. (See my paper "Virtues of Inconsistency," Monist, 68, 1985, pp 105–135, for a discussion of the Preface Paradox and some related issues.)

5 For an excellent bibliography on the Lottery Paradox, see A. A. Derksen, "The Alleged Lottery Paradox Resolved," American Philosophical Quarterly, 15, (January, 1978), 67–73.

6 The clearest and best use of this argument for scepticism is given by Jonathan Adler, "Skepticism and Universalizability," Journal of Philosophy, 78 (1981), pp. 143–156.

7 Keith Lehrer has presented the most fully developed account of competition in Knowledge.

8 Descartes, "Synopsis of the Six Following Meditations," in The Philosophical Works of Descartes, edited by E. S. Haldane and G. R. T. Ross, Dover Publications, 1955, Vol. I, p. 143. All references to Descartes will be to that collection of his works, hereafter referred to as "H&R."

9 From now on in this paper, unless I explicitly indicate otherwise, I will be referring to epistemic doubt or epistemic certainty when I use the expressions "doubt" or "certainty."

10 H&R, p. 148.

11 H&R, p. 145. This is an unfortunate thing for Descartes to have said since (1) it is false and (2) it is inconsistent with his own views. It is false because, as we will soon see, doubt is not distributive. It is inconsistent with his own views because, as we will soon see, he held that there are grounds for supposing that it is doubtful that each image is a "waking–image," but it is not doubtful on that basis that every image is a "waking–image."

12 H&R, p. 148.

13 H&R, p. 101.

14 H&R, p. 219.

15 It should be clear that I am interested primarily in a Cartesian form of scepticism. Pyrrhonian Scepticism, that is, the scepticism which holds that no–nonevident proposition is known because no–nonevident proposition is more reasonable to believe than to deny is not my concern here. I have discussed the relationship between the two forms of scepticism in Certainty, University of Minnesota Press, 1981. But the crucial, relevant point is this: It is not at all clear that the class of evident propositions and the class of canonical beliefs are mutually exclusive. That is a matter of some textual interpretation. In other words, my theses here concerning canonical beliefs might be acceptable to the Pyrrhonians. But, equally important, I think that if one can show that propositions can be certain, then one will have shown that Pyrrhonian Scepticism is incorrect. In addition, Descartes, himself, appears to be examining and rejecting many of the various arguments for Pyrrhonian Scepticism in "Meditation I."

17 I wish to thank Tim Maudlin, who read a draft of this paper, for pointing out a serious problem with the definition of internal doubt contained in that draft. It had included only (1.b) and (2.b). As he pointed out, given that account, S could be certain that p even if there were grounds for doubt within S's belief system. Hence, a person who actually believed d could be certain whereas a person who did not believe d (but did not

have grounds for denying *d*) would not be certain. *S* could instantly become certain by believing *d*! I believe that by including (1.a) and (2.a) that problem can be avoided.

18 Although I will discuss some features of this account, I will not attempt in this paper to develop all of the important constituent concepts. In particular, I will not try to explain in any detail what changes in a belief set are required when a new belief is added. That can be done. I have tried to begin the task of developing rules for the modification of belief sets when new beliefs are added in my paper "Immune Belief Systems", *Philosophical Topics*, 14, 1986, pp. 259–280.

19 I use quotation marks in this sentence to make clear that I am using "ideas" in a sense which refers to Descartes' use of the term.

20 My comments here apply most clearly to the Meditations since in both the *Discourse* (H&R, p. 101) and *Rules* (H&R, p. 220) he seems to suggest that the fact that our senses have once deceived us is a good reason for doubt.

22 The issue could be generalized as follows: If *S* is justified in believing that *p*, can *S* use *p* to justify denying *q*, where *q* entails the denial of *p*? Much has been written about a related issue, i. e., the so-called Closure Principle. If it can be shown that *p* can be used as a reason for ~*q* whenever *q* entails ~*p*, then the Closure Principle would be vindicated. Space simply does not allow me to discuss this point in any great detail, here. I have discussed it elsewhere (see *Certainty*, especially pp. 26–44). For my purpose, here, it is sufficient to note that it is the sceptics who generally defend that principle and, at least for the sake of the discussion here, it would seem appropriate to assume it. For I am attempting to develop an account of certainty which is compatible with the sceptic's basic position.

23 It might be thought that there are exceptions to the general claim that the evidence for an empirical, contingent proposition never guarantees its truth. It could be suggested that if one argues that Socrates is mortal by citing the evidence that Socrates is a man and all men are mortal, then one has presented evidence which is entailing. But my point is that somewhere in the evidential ancestry of a belief there is a non-entailing step. So the existence of some entailing steps would not suffice to show that the evidence is entailing in the relevant sense.

24 At one time I thought the difference between the Lottery Case and the Table Case made a significant difference in the plausibility of scepticism. My mistake was that I had illegitimately limited the type of doubt to what I here call "external" doubt. (See Certainty, p. 195.)

25 Gilbert Ryle makes the same point in *Dilemmas* in the chapter entitled "Perception" (Cambridge University Press, 1962), pp 93–110.

26 The analogy, here, is not perfect because in the dream–image case, it is the proposition there is at least one waking–image whose epistemic warrant is increased. In this case, it is the proposition the preponderance of canonical propositions are true whose warrant is increased. Nevertheless, the analogy seems useful to me because it illustrates the basic point that doubt does not distribute over sets of propositions.

27 H&R, p. 148.

28 I am supposing that in our canon of beliefs is this one: The more perfect can come from the less perfect. Of course, if someone does not accept some account of evolution and accepted the claim that if we were created by something perfect, that something could make it such that our epistemic equipment is inherently deceptive, then it seems to me that Descartes' argument would provide grounds for doubting the relevant meta–proposition. A proof of God's epistemic benevolence would be in order if scepticism is to be avoided!

29 But this is only a rough definition. For as it stands it is subject to a type of counterexample given our ordinary intuitions governing the extent of our knowledge. (I was reminded of this example by John Bennett and Ernest Sosa at the University of Rochester conference on Skepticism in May, 1989, where I read an earlier version of this paper. My suggested solution here is an extension of my treatment of the misleading defeater cases discussed in "Knowledge, Causality and Defeasibility," *Journal of Philosophy*, 73, 1976, pp. 792–812, and in "Misleading Evidence and the Restoration of Justification," *Philosophical Studies*, 37, 1980, 81–89.) Here is a form of the counterexample: Consider any putative piece of knowledge, say *p*. Now, suppose that *S* has some false belief (any false belief), say *q*, in her belief set.

There is now a true proposition, $\sim(q \& p)$, which is such that if added to q gives some reason to lower the epistemic warrant for p. Thus, as long as there is any false proposition in S's corpus of beliefs, there will be a basis for external doubt. There are two responses. The first is to discover an intuitively satisfying way of treating these defeaters. The answer along these lines, I believe, is to appeal to the accounts mentioned above and to suggest that what defeats p essentially involves a falsehood, namely q, because it is only by combining the truth, $\sim(q \& p)$, with the false proposition, q, that defeat occurs. Hence, we could simply include this case along with other misleading and, hence, pseudo–defeaters which depend essentially upon a false proposition. In other words, a genuine defeater must not rely upon a false proposition in order to defeat. That does seem to accord with our intuitions and preserves the basic intuition that a proposition is externally doubtful on the basis of what is, in fact, true. I prefer that response. But another one is available: Given the context of the discussion here, namely the debate between the sceptic and nousist, we could grant that anyone who has a false belief fails to have knowledge without granting what the sceptic needs to prove her case. Recall that the sceptic claims that we lack knowledge because one of the necessary conditions of knowledge, i.e., certainty, cannot be fulfilled. But all that would be granted is that, as a matter of fact, it is highly unlikely that any one of us has knowledge, because it is highly likely that each one of us has at least one false belief. Nevertheless, we can have knowledge. Nothing, in principle, prevents us from satisfying all of the necessary conditions of knowledge.

30 It may seem that this account is too weak because of the existence of so–called misleading defeaters. I believe that there is an answer to those problems (See my "Misleading Evidence and the Restoration of Justification", *Philosophical Studies*, **37**, 1980, pp. 81–89.) Nevertheless, for the purposes of this paper we can grant to the sceptic that even in such misleading cases, S fails to have knowledge. The reason is that there need not be misleading defeaters in every case of putative knowledge, and hence, although the range of what is known will be less than what we would typically expect, there is no reason to suppose that there are "misleading" grounds for the general truths of the canonical belief set. For suppose that some hitherto reliable person said that there really are no tables or that no living person has seen a table. If that were added to my belief set, there are two possible responses. I think I am justified in simply believing that the hitherto reliable person is surely not reliable in this case. But even if the epistemic warrant of the proposition that there are tables would be lowered, it would occur only because I continue to be justified in believing that there are people who know things about the world. In other words, the preponderance of beliefs in the set of my canonical beliefs not only remains but I would have to employ other canonical beliefs were this proposition to lower the epistemic warrant of the proposition that there are tables.

31 I believe that the case was first introduced by Keith Lehrer and Thomas Paxson in "Knowledge: Undefeated Justified True Belief," *Journal of Philosophy*, **66**, 1969, pp. 225–237.

PART 2

DENIALS

RICHARD FELDMAN

KLEIN ON CERTAINTY AND CANONICAL BELIEFS

In "Epistemic Compatibilism and Canonical Beliefs" Peter Klein argues that we can't know much about the world around us, but we can know that most of our ordinary beliefs about the world are true.[1] He calls the set of the most obviously true common-sense beliefs about the world around us "the canon".[2] The canon includes beliefs such as that there are tables, there are dogs, and there are trees outside. According to Klein, we can't know any of the propositions in the canon. About them, skeptics are right. But, contrary to what skeptics assert, we can know a general proposition about these canonical beliefs, namely, that the preponderance of them is true. Let us call this general proposition 'the meta–proposition'. Thus, on Klein's view, although we can't know what we might call "specific facts" about the world, we can know that the meta–proposition is true, i.e., we can know that our general world view is correct.

This may at first appear to be an implausible view. How could it be that a person can know that the preponderance of a large group of propositions is true without knowing with respect to any member of that group that it is true? Let us give the name 'collectivism' to the view that one can know that the vast majority of a collection of propositions is true, without knowing any member of the collection to be true. In this paper I will argue that collectivism is indeed true, but I will argue against Klein's version of collectivism, according to which knowledge requires certainty, we do not know any of the propositions in the canon, but we do know the meta–proposition.

COLLECTIVISM WITHOUT CERTAINTY

There are lots of cases in which we are inclined to say that we know that the preponderance of a group of propositions is true but we don't know of any particular member of the group that it is true. Lottery cases provide a clear example of that. We know that the vast majority of a collection of propositions — ticket$_1$ will lose, ticket$_2$ will lose, etc. — is true, but we don't know of any one of those propositions that it is true. Here's another example. I have an aquarium in my house. Suppose that I've given the fish names: 'Molly', 'Angel', etc. From time to time a fish jumps out the tank, gets eaten by another fish, or otherwise ceases to be a living member of the community. Each morning I go down to the basement to check on the fish. Being the optimist that I am, I always believe that Molly will still be alive, Angel will be alive, etc. The mortality rate in my aquaria may well prevent me from knowing any one of these propositions to be true. But it does not prevent me from knowing that the preponderance of them is true. Depending upon how generous you are with your attributions of knowledge, you may think that I know this meta–proposition to be true before I see the fish each morning. Even if you deny that, you are likely to agree that I know the meta–proposition about the fish to be true when I see the aquarium and see that there are a whole bunch of fish there, but have not yet looked at them closely enough to identify any particular one.

M. D. Roth and G. Ross (eds.), Doubting, 121–126.

Examples like this convince me that collectivism is true. But Klein does not defend collectivism for anything like the reason I just gave. In fact, he would not accept my examples since, on his view, I don't even know that the meta–proposition about the fish is true when I am looking carefully at my fish. Indeed, on his view, I don't even know that I have an aquarium or that there are fish. Similarly, on his view I couldn't know that most of the tickets in the lottery will lose, or even that there is a lottery. This is because, on his view, knowledge requires certainty and I can't be certain of any of these things. Nevertheless, he still thinks that I can know that my general world view is correct.

A key part of Klein's view is his acceptance of the idea that knowledge requires certainty. He argues that we can't be certain of any particular proposition in the canon, but we can be certain that the preponderance of propositions in the canon is true. Hence, we can't know any particular proposition, but we can know the meta–proposition. In the remainder of this paper I will discuss three aspects of Klein's view: 1) his account of certainty; 2) his argument that, on his account of certainty, particular propositions in the canon can't be certain; and, finally, 3) his argument that the meta–proposition can be certain.

KLEIN'S ACCOUNT OF CERTAINTY

On Klein's view, knowledge does require certainty, where certainty includes absolute immunity from doubt.[3] He characterizes this notion of doubt in the following way:

> p is internally doubtful for S iff there is a proposition, d, which is such that either (1) S believes d or S is not justified in denying d and (2) either d lowers the level of epistemic warrant of p for S or if d is added to S's beliefs, it lowers the level of epistemic warrant of p for S.

The first clause of this definition is called 'the acceptance condition' and the second clause is called 'the reduction condition'.

There is one major point about the reduction condition that I'd like to see clarified. Klein does not spell out clearly what he means by 'lowers the epistemic warrant'. It could be that d lowers the level of warrant of p for S provided that either S believes d and the warrant for p would be greater than it is if S did not believe d or S does not believe d and the warrant for p would be lower if S did believe d. This seems implausible to me, since the level of warrant a proposition has is a function of a person's evidence, not the person's beliefs. So, if S has evidence for d, and d counts against p, then the warrant for p is "lower", whether S believes d or not. Another way to interpret "lowers the warrant" is vaguer, but more suitable. One proposition lowers the warrant of another when it "counts against" it, or is evidence against it. Although vague, this account will suffice for present purposes.

THE UNCERTAINTY OF PROPOSITIONS IN THE CANON

Klein argues for the uncertainty of propositions in the canon by means of what he calls 'The Table Case'. Applied to my present belief that

1. There is a table before me,

his argument is that it is rendered uncertain by the proposition

2. The number of people who have evidence (about a table) similar to mine and have been wrong (about there being a table) is not zero.

(2) satisfies clause (1), the acceptance condition, because I'm not justified in denying (2). Indeed, I may well be justified in believing (2). Klein also claims that it satisfies the second clause, the reduction condition. He writes, "[(2)] certainly does lower the degree of epistemic warrant of [(1)]. There is nothing available to me to block the power of [(2)]."(p. 16) Similar arguments establish that other propositions in my canon are also uncertain.

I will grant that (2) does "count against" (1). Propositions like (1) are uncertain and propositions like (2) do render them uncertain. Notice that Klein says that nothing "blocks the power of" (2). Apparently, the fact that I am justified in believing (1), and thus justified in believing that I am not one of the people with evidence like mine who is misled does not make (2) not a doubt–maker for (1). Keep this in mind as we turn to the alleged certainty of the meta–proposition.

THE CERTAINTY OF THE META–PROPOSITION

Perhaps the most intriguing claim in Klein's paper is the claim that the meta–proposition, the proposition that the preponderance of propositions in the canon is true, is certain. His argument for this claim is as follows: all the potential doubt–makers for the meta–proposition, that is, all the potential instances of d in the definition, fail either the acceptance condition or the reduction condition. The modest doubt makers, such as (2), don't satisfy the reduction condition relative to the meta–proposition. This is because anything that is a doubt–maker for some elements of the canon is not a doubt–maker for most elements of the canon. Other doubt makers are more global, e.g., the proposition that I am being deceived by an evil demon, but they don't satisfy the acceptance condition. We are justified in rejecting such propositions.

I want to examine the first part of this argument more carefully. Consider the proposition

3. There are tables.

Klein says that a doubt–maker for it is

4. There are beliefs in the current canon of beliefs which are false and which are in every relevant respect similar to the belief that there are tables.

With respect to a lot of propositions in the canon like (3), there are doubt makers like (4). What might render the meta–proposition doubtful, then, is the conjunction of propositions like (4). Klein says about this, "it is absolutely crucial to note that [(4)] in conjunction with all of the propositions sharing [its] form would not make doubtful the" meta–proposition.(p. 19) The reason for this is that "when a canonical belief is labelled as false or its epistemic warrant is decreased, it is because we employ many other canonical beliefs whose epistemic warrant is, thereby, increased."(p. 19) This idea is illustrated by means of an example. When the belief that there are witches was part of the canon, it wasn't certain. But, Klein says, "if we suppose that canonical belief is false, we also suppose that there is some explanation of its having appeared to be true. Presumably, we would employ *many, many* other canonical beliefs about human behavior, the causes of disease, the societal need for developing myths, and perhaps the need for oppressed people to ban together in secret groups to resist oppression. In other words, accepting that a canonical belief is false or lowering its epistemic warrant strengthens the epistemic warrant of many other canonical beliefs."(p. 20)

I will make four points about Klein's argument for the certainty of the meta–proposition.

(A) Klein's example about witches is supposed to help us see that the conjunction of propositions like (4) doesn't cast doubt on the meta–proposition. This is because, when we add this conjunction to our belief set, we would add with it an explanation of why we were misled in the relevantly similar cases. And this explanation would appeal to and strengthen other elements of our canons. Perhaps this is true. But, as I see it, the question is whether (4), conjoined with lots of other propositions of similar form, casts doubt on the meta–proposition. Even if it is true that this conjunctive doubt–maker requires the truth of many other elements of the canon, there is no reason at all to think that it requires the truth of the preponderance of the canon. So, Klein's argument that the conjunction of propositions like (4) fails to render the meta–proposition uncertain is quite unconvincing.[4]

(B) Notice that to cast doubt on the meta–proposition something need not call into question most of my beliefs. The meta–proposition is that the preponderance, the vast majority, of my canonical beliefs is true. Let us introduce a technical term, 'a bunch', to refer to that part of a collection which is just large enough to make the remainder of the collection less than a preponderance. So, to cast doubt on the meta–proposition, one must provide some support for the view that a bunch of my canonical beliefs are false. One need not undertake the much more difficult task of providing support for the view that the preponderance, or even most, of my canonical beliefs are false. It seems clear to me that the conjunction of propositions of the form of (4) does count in favor of the proposition that a bunch of my canonical beliefs are false, and thus does count against the meta–proposition.

(C) I believe that there are quite a few other propositions that do cast doubt on the meta– proposition, at least a little bit. That is, there are things I am not justified in denying that do "count against" the meta–proposition. For example, consider

5. There are canons for people of which it is not the case that the preponderance is true and which are in every relevant way similar to my canon.

I'm not sure whether I believe (5), but I am quite sure that I am not justified in denying it. That is, it seems to me that people could be relevantly like me (whatever that means) and have a canon that is not predominantly true. The criterion of relevant similarity is important here, but maybe people with deeply anti–scientific views, or deeply religious views, are relevantly similar. Perhaps people who think that contemporary science shows that people are never responsible for their behavior and that evaluative or emotional reactions to human behavior are never appropriate are relevantly similar. But not all of these world views can be predominantly correct. So, the idea is just to recognize that there are mistaken world views. And (5), it seems to me, lowers, perhaps just a tiny bit, the warrant of the view that my world view is substantially correct. Even if I am justified in believing that my world view is correct, the fact that there are mistaken ones lowers my justification. In this respect, the case is analogous to Klein's example about tables. The fact that people have been mistaken in beliefs relevantly like my belief that there are tables counts against my belief (even if it does not make it unjustified). Similarly, the fact that some people have had false meta–propositions counts against my belief in my meta–proposition (even if it does not make it unjustified).

Furthermore, there are other propositions that count against the meta–proposition for me. There is testimonial evidence against it. Some skeptics and other dissenters claim that my world view (a reasonably conventional late 20th century American world view) is significantly wrong. Thus, there is this potential doubt–maker for my meta–proposition:

6. Some intelligent people claim that a bunch of my canonical beliefs are false.

Along these lines, one might consider the arguments of those who contend that contemporary physics, which asserts that determinism is false and that everyday objects are largely empty space, counts against world–views such as mine.

It is difficult to argue convincingly for claims about what lowers the epistemic probability of what since we currently lack a precise and usable account of that notion. However, to defend his view Klein has to argue that although (2) does lower the probability of (1) and (4) does lower the probability of (3), things like (5) and (6) do not lower the probability of the meta–proposition. These cases seem perfectly analogous to me and I see no basis for an effective argument of the sort Klein needs.

(D) Finally, the conclusion that I am not certain of the meta–proposition seems exactly right to me. I am not certain that my world view is substantially correct. If knowledge requires certainty, then I don't know even that. Of course, my views about this topic are what I'd call 'compatibilist', though in a sense that differs from Klein's. I think that knowledge and uncertainty are compatible, that I'm certain of rather little, but that I do know a fair amount.

I conclude that although Klein is right in claiming that we can know that a preponderance of some collection of propositions is true without knowing of any member of the collection that it is true, he is mistaken in applying this collectivist view to the meta–proposition and the canon, especially given his view that knowledge requires certainty. In the sense of 'certain' that he characterizes, the elements of the canon and the meta–proposition are all uncertain.[5]

University of Rochester

NOTES

1 Forthcoming.

2 There are actually many different canons, one for each person and time. But these differences among our canons will be of no concern here. So, for the sake of simplicity, I will write as if there is only one canon.

3 According to Klein, certainty also requires lack of external doubt. External doubt is created by true propositions that cast doubt on a belief. I will not discuss external doubt in this paper.

4 My own reaction to the realization that (4) casts doubt on (3) is to think, "If I could be wrong about (3), then I could be wrong about a lots of things" That is, propositions like (4) do induce a kind of psycological doubt about the meta–proposition for me. But perhaps this does not show that they produce the relevant sort of epistemic doubt.

5 An earlier version of this paper was presented at a conference on skepticism at the University of Rochester in May, 1989. I benefitted from Peter Klein's response and the discussion that followed.

PAUL K. MOSER

TWO ROADS TO SKEPTICISM*

There are two main roads to skepticism about knowledge of the external world: a low road and a high road. The low road rests on a common but unconvincing philosophical ploy: redefining a key term to gain support for a controversial claim. Many skeptics advance their skepticism by redefining what knowledge is, specifically, by raising the standards for knowledge beyond plausibility. This strategy amounts to a low victory by high redefinition — really no victory at all. And it suffers from all the disadvantages of the fallacy of *ignoratio elenchi* by redefinition. Notable low–road skeptics include Descartes in the opening *Meditations*, David Hume, Peter Unger (1975), and Barry Stroud (1984). Part 1 of this paper assesses Stroud's central argument for skepticism. It shows that the low road is really a dead end, that the low road is altogether ineffective against the nonskeptic.

The high road to skepticism, in contrast, is not guilty of a fallacy. On this approach, the skeptic accepts the nonskeptic's notion of knowledge, but argues that on this very notion we cannot, or at least do not, have knowledge of the external world. Skeptics taking this road are, it seems, few and far between. And this is understandable if I'm right in thinking that travelers of the high road to skepticism can't really get there from here, where "here" is the standpoint of the sort of empirical evidence most of us have. I'll return to this matter, in Part 2, after closing down the low road to skepticism. My main conclusion overall will be that there's no safe, affordable road to knowledge skepticism that derives from considerations about justification.

I. STROUD'S LOW ROAD

Strong knowledge skepticism states that we *cannot* possess propositional knowledge about the external world. The most recent comprehensive defense of such skepticism is Barry Stroud's book, *The Significance of Philosophical Scepticism* (1984). (Subsequent parenthetical page–numbers refer to this book.) Stroud's skepticism derives mainly from Descartes's "Dreamer Hypothesis": the hypothesis that for anyone who takes himself to perceive that something is so, it is possible that he is dreaming that it is so. The Cartesian skeptic often assumes that if one is dreaming that something is so, one does not *thereby* know that it is so. But this assumption does not quite explain how the Dreamer Hypothesis, which concerns the *mere possibility* of dreaming, is actually a skeptical hypothesis. The Cartesian skeptic needs to explain what the exact connection is between one's dreaming that something is so and one's *lacking knowledge* that it is so.

Thus, Stroud relies on the following assumption to infer a skeptical lesson from the Dreamer Hypothesis: for any possibility incompatible with our knowing something, we must know that that possibility does not obtain if we are to know the thing in question (p. 26). Given this Cartesian assumption, according to Stroud, we cannot know anything about the external world, since we cannot know at any particular time

127

M. D. Roth and G. Ross (eds.), Doubting, 127–139.
© 1990 *Kluwer Academic Publishers. Printed in the Netherlands.*

that we are not dreaming. (Stroud's notion of one's dreaming apparently is not intended to be equivalent to the notion of one's *merely* dreaming; it evidently is intended to allow for causal overdetermination of one's experience.)

Stroud's argument that we cannot know at any time that we are not dreaming runs in outline as follows (pp. 20–22):

1. One knows that one is not dreaming only if one has a test enabling one to determine that one is not dreaming.

2. One has a test enabling one to determine that one is not dreaming only if one knows (a) that the test in question is reliable, and (b) that one is not dreaming that one has such a reliable test.

3. But one cannot know that one has, and is not dreaming that one has, the reliable test in question.

4. Hence, one cannot know that one is not dreaming.

Premises 2 and 3 obviously invite questions, and premise 1 is far from compelling without independent argument. Let's begin with a brief consideration of premises 2 and 3.

Stroud supports premise 3 with this claim: "a person would have to have known at some time that he was not dreaming in order to get the information he needs to tell at *any* time that he is not dreaming — and that cannot be done" (p. 21). But we are left wondering just *why* this can't be done. Stroud's remarks in support of premise 3 fail to show that we can't tell that we are not dreaming; at most they raise the question of *how* we can tell this. But of course the mere raising of this question lends no credibility to premise 3. As premise 3 is not self-evident, it requires support beyond that provided by Stroud's question of how we can tell that we aren't dreaming.

As for premise 2, Stroud owes us an explanation why it is inadequate that one's test simply *be* reliable, why one needs to know that it is reliable. Stroud's requirement here is excessive, since it generates an endless regress of required known propositions. To illustrate this, let us state the requirement explicitly:

One knows that one is not dreaming that P_1 only if one knows that P_2: one has, and is not dreaming one has, a reliable test specifying that one is not dreaming that P_1.

This requirement is perfectly general, and thus it applies to P_2 also. So we have this implication:

One knows that P_2 [=one has, and is not dreaming one has, a reliable test specifying that one is not dreaming that P_1] only if one knows that P_3: one has, and is not dreaming one has, a reliable test specifying that one is not dreaming that P_2.

The requirement in question also applies to P_3, and to each member of the ensuing endless regress of required known propositions. But surely it is implausible to hold that one's knowing any *single* proposition requires one's knowing an *infinity* of propositions. This is especially implausible if knowledge requires believing or assenting (as it evidently does). For we have no independent reason to think that one's knowing a single proposition requires one's believing, or assenting to, an infinity of propositions. Thus, premise 2 of Stroud's skeptical argument seems unacceptable.

We have here a symptom of low–road skepticism: the setting of excessively demanding, implausible requirements for knowledge. Since Stroud fails to justify his requirement or even to remove its initial implausibility, we have no reason to follow his low road.

We can further illustrate the implausibility of Stroud's skeptical argument by considering his Cartesian requirement that "there are always certain possibilities which must be known not to obtain if I am to know what I claim to know" (p. 26). The relevant possibilities, according to Stroud, are possibilities incompatible with one's knowing what one claims to know (p. 27). Thus, let's state Stroud's Cartesian requirement explicitly as follows:

> CR. For any possibility, X, necessarily if X is incompatible with S's knowing a physical–object proposition, P, then if S knows that P, then S knows that X does not obtain.

Without this principle, Stroud's case for strong knowledge skepticism is hopeless, and Stroud himself apparently recognizes as much.

Problems face not only CR itself, but also what Stroud takes to satisfy its antecedent. Regarding CR, we should ask why S is required to *know* that X does not obtain, why X's simply *not obtaining* is inadequate for the relevant necessary condition. Given this requirement, CR is excessive: it generates an endless regress of the sort arising from premise 2. To see this, consider the following requirement due to CR:

> S knows that P_1 only if S knows that P_2: possibility X incompatible with S's knowing that P_1 does not obtain.

This requirement, being perfectly general, applies to P_2 also; thus:

> S knows that P_2 only if S knows that P_3: possibility X incompatible with S's knowing that P_2 does not obtain.

The requirement at hand also applies to P_3, and to each member of the resulting endless regress of required propositions. But again it is implausible to hold that one's knowing any single proposition requires one's knowing an infinity of propositions. Stroud's low–road skepticism again rests on an excessive demand.

Regarding the satisfaction CR's antecedent, Stroud would have us believe that this proposition:

> (a) Possibly, I now am dreaming that there is a white piece of paper before me.

is incompatible with this proposition:

(b) I know that there is a white piece of paper before me.

But this seems wrong. What reason do we have to think that my knowing that there is a white piece of paper before me excludes the *mere logical possibility* that I now am dreaming that there is a white piece of paper before me? Clearly, this mere possibility of my dreaming does not entail either (i) that there is no white piece of paper before me, (ii) that I do not believe that there is a white piece of paper before me, (iii) that I am not justified in believing that there is a white piece of paper before me, or (iv) that the fourth condition for knowledge, on any plausible construal, is not satisfied. (On the relevant fourth condition, see Moser (1989, chap. 6).) Why then should we grant that *the mere possibility* of my dreaming is incompatible with my knowing? Conceivably, Stroud has in mind some notion of *epistemic* possibility that avoids this problem. But, so far as his actual account goes, it's a complete mystery what such a notion might involve. And Stroud gives no plausible argument whatsoever that shows that we can't exclude the epistemic possibility of our dreaming, i.e., the *evidential probability* of our dreaming.

Perhaps Stroud would nonetheless have his skeptical argument turn on a thesis about *justification*. Here is the best reconstruction I can offer (where *P* is any contingent physical–object proposition):

1. Necessarily, if it is logically possible that I am dreaming that *P*, while having evidence *E*, then it is logically possible that (*E* & –*P*). (Dreamer Hypothesis Assumption)

2. It is logically possible that I am dreaming that *P* while having *E*, for any of my evidence. (Assumption)

3. Necessarily, if *E* justifies *P* for me, then *E* logically entails *P*. (Assumption)

4. Necessarily, if it is logically possible that (*E* & –*P*), then *E* does not justify *P* for me. (From 3 by transposition)

5. Hence, *E* does not justify *P* for me. (From 1–4)

6. Hence, I do not know that *P*. (From 5 and the assumption that propositional knowledge requires justification)

This argument supports only weak knowledge skepticism, according to which I do not actually know that P. It does not support strong knowledge skepticism, according to which I cannot know that P. But if this is not the sort of argument underlying Stroud's skepticism, it's a complete mystery what his positive argument for skepticism actually is.

Premise 3 of the reconstructed argument is, in any case, highly implausible. Why should we accept a principle of epistemic justification that rules out the very possibility of *non*deductive justifying evidence? Stroud gives no answer to this pressing question. But once the skeptic demands that justification constitute deductive, entailing evidence, his challenge becomes uninteresting. For empirical knowledge of the external world, on virtually every nonskeptical epistemology, is *not* alleged to be based on deductive evidence. Nonskeptics widely admit that deductive evidence is not available for our justified physical–object beliefs. Here we have another illustration of the ineffectiveness, indeed the irrelevance, of low–road skepticism. I, for one, concede that deductive evidence for our physical–object beliefs is generally not to be had, but this doesn't tempt me at all with justification skepticism or knowledge skepticism. At most this consideration bears on *certainty* skepticism. But neither justification nor knowledge requires certainty.

What Stroud and other low–road skeptics owe us, then, is an argument that does not rely on premise 3. The skeptic might argue, for instance, that our being in a dream–state now is not merely possible, but is evidentially as *probable* as the physical–object propositions he calls into question. Such an argument would have to rely on intuitively plausible principles of epistemic justification. But what might these principles be? Stroud himself gives no clue whatsoever. Thus, as far as Stroud's skeptical contribution goes, the skeptic needs another, higher road to his destination.

II. THE HIGH ROAD

The high–road skeptic does not seek a shallow victory by redefining what knowledge (or justification) is. Instead, he accepts his opponent's notion of knowledge, and argues that its conditions can't be, or at least aren't, satisfied. Typically skeptics are skeptics because they have problems with the justification condition for knowledge. So, let's briefly consider high–road skepticism regarding the justification of physical–object propositions.

I shall begin with a quick outline of what I take to be the best story about noninferential empirical justification. (This outline is a sketch of the long story told in my *Knowledge and Evidence*, chaps. 2–5). A central thesis of my story is that some physical–object propositions are justifiable for one by means of their being the best explanation for one of one's sensory and perceptual contents, i.e., what one seems to sense and to perceive. My talk of *contents* of sensory and perceptual states concerns *subjective nonpropositional contents*. Such contents do not entail the existence of anything independent of the perceiver's experience of them, and they do not consist of propositions, judgments, or conceptualizations. We can characterize such contents ontologically either in the familiar adverbial manner suggested by Chisholm (1957), Cornman (1975), and others or in the equally familiar sense–datum terms proposed by Russell and Moore. But we needn't pursue that ontological matter. Nor shall I pursue psychological questions about the nature of experience itself. I shall simply assume that there can be a sort of direct experience, such as seeming to perceive or seeming to sense, that qualifies as nonconceptual experiencing. (The motivation for this assumption is explained in detail in *Knowledge and Evidence*, chaps. 2–4; see also Van Cleve (1985).)

This conditional clarifies my thesis somewhat:

> If (a) I seem to see a white piece of paper, (b) the contents of this perceptual experience are best explained for me by the physical–object proposition that there is a white piece of paper here, and (c) nothing in my overall perceptual and sensory experience indicates that there is not a white piece of paper here or that the explanatory relation of (b) does not

hold, *then* the proposition that there is a white piece of paper here is empirically epistemically justifiable for me.

This conditional states a sufficient condition for *propositional* justification, i.e., for a proposition's being justifiable for a person. It does not state conditions for *doxastic* justification, i.e., one's being justified *in believing* a proposition. I now have space to pursue only the conditions for propositional justification involving *occurrent* evidence, i.e., evidence present to one's awareness. So, for now I'll have to bracket the role of nonoccurrent phenomena in justification. I'll also be concerned only with justification as justifi*ability* rather than as justifi*edness*, where justifiability is a function just of the sort of evidence one has. Mere justifiability of a proposition, *P*, for one doesn't require one's having associated *P* with its supporting evidence in any way; it requires only that one *have* the relevant sort of evidence supporting *P* for one.

On my account, a certain notion of best explanation is partly definitive of the notion of noninferential evidential probability and empirical justification. So, let's briefly consider the conditions for a physical–object proposition's being a best explanation for one of one's perceptual contents. Regarding the notion of explanation itself, we obviously need a notion that does not presuppose the notion of epistemic justification or the notion of evidential probability. This notion is somewhat helpful: one thing explains another when and only when the former makes it, to some extent, *understandable why* the latter thing is as it is. Applying this to my story about empirical justification, we may say that a proposition *explains* certain subjective contents if and only if it makes it, to some extent, understandable why those contents are as they are, or equivalently, why those contents occur as they do. We can simplify this suggestion by characterizing the relevant notion of understandability as follows: a proposition makes certain subjective contents' occurring as they do understandable to some extent if and only if anyone who assents to that proposition as a direct result of directly experiencing those contents will thereby understand why those contents occur. This understanding will come from one's thereby *having an answer to a why–question* concerning those contents, viz., a question why those contents occur as they do. So, the relevant explanations, for my epistemological purposes, are essentially answers to why–questions of a certain sort.

A why–question is just a question why certain subjective contents are as they are, or equivalently, why such contents occur as they do. Regarding my subjective contents consisting of an apparent white piece of paper, two relevant why–questions are: why is there an apparent piece of paper here, and why is this apparent piece of paper apparently white? Any such question concerning the existence of an *actual* feature of the subjective contents of an experience is a relevant why–question for determining whether something is an explanation relative to that experience. Relevant why–questions, on my account, can't rest on false presuppositions concerning the contents in need of explanation. Incidentally, I assume that it is a job for philosophical semantics to explain the conditions for a proposition's simply being an answer to a question. Thus, I shall not pursue that general matter. (See the essays in Hiz (1978) and Kiefer (1983) for relevant discussion.)

My notion of an explanation *for one* relativizes an explanation to a person. We can understand this relativity as follows: a proposition, *P*, is an explanation for one of one's subjective contents, *C*, if and only if *P* explains *C*, and one understands *P*. This notion of an explanation for one is *not* equivalent to the notion of one's *giving* an explanation of certain contents. It allows that there can be an explanation for one that one hasn't actually given to anyone, including oneself.

Regarding conditions for a *best* explanation, we can begin with this sufficient condition: P is a best explanation of certain contents C for one if P is an explanation of C for one that is better than the explanation of C provided by any other proposition one understands. We need to introduce a key notion here: the notion of a *gratuitous entity*. A gratuitous entity, relative to explained contents C, is an item posited by an explanation of C that is not itself represented in C by means of any feature corresponding to that item, i.e., by means of any feature that represents some of the explainer's own features. Thus, a gratuitous explainer of C is an explainer of C not represented in C by means of any of its own features. In general, one explanation is better than another if, other things being equal, the first does not posit gratuitous items whereas the second does.

My current experience of an apparent white piece of paper is better explained by the physical–object proposition that there is a white piece of paper here than by the proposition that a Cartesian demon is stimulating my brain in a certain way. Even if these competing propositions answer the same why–questions about my subjective contents, only the Cartesian proposition posits a gratuitous item in answering those questions. A Cartesian demon, I'm glad to report, is *not* represented in my experience by means of any of its own features, whereas a white piece of paper is. We shun gratuitous explainers whenever possible because of an obvious multiplicity problem. Relative to the constraints of one's experiential contents, no gratuitous explainer is evidentially more supportable than any other, since every gratuitous explainer (by definition) lacks corresponding representation in one's contents. But surely not *every* gratuitous explainer is evidentially probable for one relative to one's experiential contents. Epistemic probability and justifiability don't come quite so easily.

We can now make some sense of this sufficient condition for a better explanation:

> One proposition, P, is a better explanation of subjective contents C than is another proposition, Q, if (i) P explains C, and (ii) either (a) P answers all the explanation–seeking why–questions about C answered by Q, but posits fewer gratuitous entities (and kinds of gratuitous entities) than Q does, or (b) while positing no more gratuitous entities (or kinds of gratuitous entities) than Q posits, P answers all the explanation–seeking why–questions about C answered by Q, *and still others.*

Let's try to proceed now with this condition for a better explanation, even if some minor refinements are ultimately needed.

We can now refine my story about noninferential empirical justification as follows:

> One's sensory or perceptual contents C are an epistemic justifier for one for a physical–object proposition, P, when (a) P best explains C for one without positing any gratuitous entities, and (b) there is nothing in one's overall sensory and perceptual experience indicating that P is false or that the explanatory relation of (a) does not obtain.

Clause (b) takes care of familiar cases where one's experience includes contravening, or negatively relevant, features. Suppose, for example that C is my subjective perceptual contents consisting of an apparent white piece of paper, and that P is the proposition that there is a white piece of paper before me. Suppose also that P explains C for me. But assume further that I have as part of my overall subjective contents an apparent light source generating a hologram of a white piece of paper before me. Let C^* be that part of my contents. I claim that C^* is negatively relevant to C with respect to P's explaining C for me. In such a case P is contravened as an explanation of C for me if P does not itself explain C^* and does not play an essential role in an explanation of C and C^* for me. (P would not play an essential role here if for every explanation of C and C^* for me that entails P, the proposition that P answers no why–questions about C and C^* beyond those answered when P is omitted.)

I don't have the space here to give a general characterization of negative relevance. (I have provided such a characterization in *Knowledge and Evidence*, chap. 2). But I believe one lesson emerges anyway: when one's contents C^* are negatively relevant as in the hologram example, one's explanation of one's contents C (viz., an apparent white piece of paper), if it's to be probable relative to C, must play an essential role in an explanation of C^* also. This seems to be the main lesson of the hologram case and related familiar cases.

So far I have been talking about *occurrent* justification, the sort of justification where one's supporting evidence is present to one's awareness. There can also be *non*occurrent justifiability: one can know something without currently being aware of the evidence that satisfies the justification condition for knowledge. Typically in such a case one's evidence need only be somehow stored in and retrievable from one's memory. (But the conditions for nonoccurrent justification are far from easy to specify; on some of the difficulties, see Feldman (1988).) Occurrent justification requires current awareness of supporting evidence (which shouldn't be confused with awareness of *the satisfaction* of the justification condition). But it requires more: it excludes one's having *non*occurrent as well as occurrent underminers, or contraveners, of one's relevant evidence. One's underminers are relevant to justification even if one isn't currently aware of them. Unfortunately, we can't disarm evidential underminers simply by closing our eyes to them.

But let's get back to skepticism now. My foregoing story enables us to block the high road to skepticism. Suppose I satisfy the conditions for having an epistemic justifier as follows: (i) I seem to see a white piece of paper, (ii) the physical–object proposition that there is a white piece of paper here explains the subjective contents of that experience for me better than does every other proposition I understand, and (iii) nothing in my overall experience indicates that that physical–object proposition is false or that the explanatory relation of (ii) doesn't obtain. In such a case, I claim, a physical–object proposition would be sufficiently epistemically justifiable on my evidence to satisfy the evidence condition for knowledge.

The high–road skeptic will accept my sufficient conditions for justification, but deny that they are ever satisfied. Yet how can one substantiate such a general denial? Can the skeptic show that a physical–object proposition *never* provides a best explanation for one of the subjective contents of one's experience? Consider again the proposition that there is a white piece of paper before me. We now can identify the skeptic's task as that of showing that this proposition is not a best explanation for me of my subjective contents consisting of an apparent white piece of paper. The skeptic must identify an explanation better than, or at least as good as, that provided by the proposition that there is a white piece of paper here.

Four noteworthy skeptical explanations come from the following:

> The Cartesian Evil Demon Hypothesis (=My subjective contents are best explained by the proposition that only an evil demon causes me to have such contents),

> The Hallucination Hypothesis (=My subjective contents are best explained by the proposition that I am simply hallucinating),

> The Dream Hypothesis (=My subjective contents are best explained by the proposition that I am simply dreaming),

> The Reductive Phenomenalist Hypothesis (= My subjective contents are best explained simply by the proposition that I am presented with those contents).

My foregoing story about justification enables us to challenge these skeptical views and their relevant analogues in fairly short order. When compared to such skeptical explanations, a familiar Realist Hypothesis provides an explanation that satisfies the conditions for a better explanation:

> Realist Hypothesis (=My subjective contents [e.g., those consisting of an apparent white piece of paper] are best explained by a physical–object proposition [e.g., the proposition that there is a white piece of paper before me].

We can now highlight the relative superiority of the Realist Hypothesis.

To account for my subjective contents consisting of an apparent white piece of paper, the Evil Demon Hypothesis posits something that is independent of me and is not represented, in terms of any of its own features, in the contents of my experience. The properties of being rectangular and of being paper–like, which are featured by direct analogues in my subjective contents, are not representative in *any* straightforward sense of the features of the Cartesian evil demon. And this skeptical explainer is not itself represented at all in my subjective contents. So it is gratuitous. (Directly analogous considerations apply to the familiar Berkeleyan Idealist Hypothesis.) The Realist Hypothesis, in contrast, does not posit gratuitous explainers. I am not assuming here that relative quantitative simplicity of explainers is sufficient for a better explanation. My conditions for a better explanation allow for the explanatory *inferiority* of the simpler of two explanations in cases where the simpler account fails to answer the why–questions about the relevant contents that are answered by the more complex explanation.

The Hallucination Hypothesis and the Dream Hypothesis are similar in the way they are inferior to the Realist Hypothesis. The essential features of hallucination– and dream–states are not identifiable at all in the subjective contents of my experience. That is, there is no identifiable indication in my present subjective contents of *illusive features from my hallucinating or dreaming.* I now have no indication whatsoever from my experience that I am hallucinating or dreaming. Admittedly, I *could* be hallucinating or dreaming now. But so long as there is no identifiable indication whatsoever of illusive features in my experience, the Hallucination Hypothesis and the Dream Hypothesis will be inferior, from an explanatory viewpoint, to the Realist Hypothesis. For in that case these two skeptical hypothesis will fall short of the Realist Hypothesis, as they will be guilty of positing gratuitous items. The Realist Hypothesis does not posit items unidentifiable in experience. Thus, we should prefer it to the foregoing skeptical competitors. (A similar line of argument applies to any Kantian skeptical hypothesis implying that my perceptual constitution distorts all my perceptual input.)

Let's turn finally to the Reductive Phenomenalist Hypothesis. This hypothesis is exceedingly stingy in the items it posits. Indeed, its excessiveness on this score is its downfall in the competition with the Realist Hypothesis. The Phenomenalist Hypothesis fails to be an explanation *in any sense* of the relevant subjective contents. It fails to answer any relevant why–question about those contents. If one asks, for instance, *why* there is an apparent white piece of paper before me, the Phenomenalist Hypothesis provides only the information that I am presented with an appearance of a white piece of paper. But this information is not an answer to that why–question; it simply affirms what is asked by that question. Thus, given that the features of one's subjective contents need explanation, the Realist Hypothesis is superior to Reductive Phenomenalism.

We can now challenge the high–road skeptic: he needs to provide an explanation of our subjective contents that is as good as the explanation provided by the Realist Hypothesis. In light of the foregoing considerations, I doubt that such an explanation is actually forthcoming. Thus, I also doubt that the high road really takes the skeptic to his desired destination.

If we are on the right track so far, we can challenge low–road and high–road justification skeptics with this simple but fatal dilemma: either (a) come up with plausible conditions for noninferential justification that this paper overlooks, or (b) provide an anti–realist explanatory hypothesis that improves on, or at least equals, the Realist Hypothesis. Since justification skeptics have not accomplished either task, we now have explanatory grounds for recommending the sort of physical–object realism defended above.

III. OBJECTIONS AND REPLIES

How will the skeptic object to all this? Actually I'm not sure. One line of objection (suggested to me by Dorit Bar–On) is that my challenge to the high–road skeptic succeeds only because of a questionable characterization of subjective perceptual contents. I have characterized such contents in a way that might seem to be unfairly agreeable to physical–object explainers. For instance, I have appealed to one's subjective contents consisting of an *apparent white piece of paper*. Perhaps the skeptic will object that this is question–begging, and that we need a "neutral" language to characterize subjective contents.

I find this objection quite puzzling. One problem is that it's quite unclear what a "neutral" language for subjective contents would look like. What exactly would its neutrality consist in? Another problem is that it's unclear that a neutral language is really necessary or desirable, given that one's subjective contents aren't necessarily neutral in any relevant sense. Presumably, it's meaningful to say that I seem to perceive, for instance, a white piece of paper. But if it is, my account isn't really threatened. For my account has appealed only to cases where one actually does seem to perceive a white piece of paper. Even if there are cases where one seems to perceive only "neutral" contents (e.g., odd patches and designs), these cases don't threaten my account. For I haven't said that such cases are impossible, and I haven't said that they are justification-providing regarding physical–object beliefs. On the contrary, I have focused only on cases where one's subjective contents consist of *apparent* physical–objects. Even if there are cases of "neutral" contents, there nonetheless are genuine cases of seeming to perceive physical objects. And this is all that matters for purposes of my account. So, the neutral–language proposal isn't really a threat now.

Let's turn to a more familiar line of objection. I suspect that many philosophers will balk at the epistemic role I acknowledge for nonpropositional perceptual contents. Many of these philosophers, including for instance Richard Foley (1987), seem to assume that a belief has justification for one only if one is able to defend the belief in a way that one would oneself find acceptable. Let's call this the *subjective defensibility requirement* on epistemic justification. Even if this requirement has some intuitive weight, it does not count against the role I acknowledge for nonpropositional contents. Specifically it does not favor an exclusively *doxastic* evidence basis for epistemic assessment. For the requirement does not specify *the sort* of evidence basis from which one's potential defense must derive.

As far as the subjective defensibility requirement goes, perceptual contents not represented in one's beliefs can provide basic evidential resources for the defense of a belief. That is, such contents can provide evidence pertinent to epistemic justification. One's having such evidence requires only that one have *the evidential resources enabling a defense;* it does not require that one actually use those resources to present a defense, or even that one actually formulate, describe, or articulate the components of a defense. The contrary view risks a serious confusion between *one's having evidence,* on the one hand, and one's *formulating, describing, or articulating evidence,* on the other hand. Of course one's formulating, describing, or articulating evidence may require one's forming beliefs or judgements about one's nonpropositional evidence. But this point is irrelevant to one's simply *having* evidence pertinent to justification. Having evidence doesn't entail formulating, describing, or articulating evidence.

Thus, this question arises: if an exclusively doxastic basis for epistemic assessment doesn't get its importance from the concept of knowledge or even from the subjective defensibility requirement, where does it get its importance as an 'epistemically relevant' basis? Clearly, we can assess beliefs from various standpoints, but why should we think that an exclusively doxastic standpoint has any privileged status regarding *epistemic* assessment? Why not allow instead for a broader basis of evidence from which one can epistemically assess beliefs? My account recommends a broader basis, a basis motivated in part by Aristotle's famous regress problem for inferential justification. (See Moser (1985) on the relevance of Aristotle's regress problem.)

At bottom, then, the present concern focuses on the nature of the "evidential resources enabling a defense" that are required by epistemic justification. I have a simple diagnosis of why one might accept a view of evidential resources as exclusively doxastic. One might say that since the defense pertinent to the subjective defensibility requirement is an *argument* of some sort, its components are essentially propositional, being premises or conclusions. But of course *non*propositional contents (e.g., what one seems to perceive) aren't essentially propositional, and thus aren't viable candidates for being genuine components of the pertinent defense. So, such contents aren't by themselves pertinent evidential resources. On this view, evidential resources must be propositional, as they must be candidates for being actual components (premises or conclusions) of a defense. Call this *the components view* of evidential resources.

Such a components view must face this question: why not say instead that the relevant evidential resources need only provide the (perhaps nonpropositional) raw materials on which the components of a potential defense can be based? On this contrary view, epistemic justification can supervene on such raw materials even when the actual components of a defense (its premises and conclusions) have not been formulated. Call this *the raw materials view* of evidential resources. Of course raw materials such as nonpropositional perceptual contents aren't articulated evidence, and thus don't constitute an actual, articulated defense. But such materials can enable an actual defense, at least insofar as they can provide foundational support for the premises of a defense.

One simple consideration seems to speak loudly in favor of the raw materials view over the components view: having evidence seems not to require the formulation of the premises of a defense. Most humans are able to have some justified physical–object beliefs, but few of us have actually formulated, or even are able to formulate, premises for a defense of these beliefs. For example, the typical four–year–old is able to have various justified beliefs about her favorite toys, for example, but she is quite innocent of actual premises in support of such beliefs. Instead, her justified beliefs would be based on the perceptual raw materials that support her beliefs. The components view is, in short, psychologically unrealistic. It risks making justified belief the exclusive possession of a few sophisticated epistemologists who are skilled at formulating arguments in defense of their beliefs. The raw materials view avoids this implausible risk. This is one consideration that should incline us toward the raw materials view. The present line of objection seems uncompelling, then, inasmuch as it leads to a psychologically unrealistic account of justification.

The next, and final, objection comes from philosophers who endorse a certain sort of scientific realism. These philosophers will ask about the justifiability, on my account, of atomic theory, specifically its commitment to currently unobservable electrons and quarks. On my account, electrons and quarks would seem to be gratuitous explainers, explainers that don't enjoy empirical justifiability. This doubtless will bother certain scientific realists.

Without digressing to complex issues in the philosophy of science, I want to stress that my account of justifiability fits with at least two noteworthy positions on scientific unobservables. First, we could plausibly endorse some sort of operationism about electrons and quarks, and thereby deny that explanation via electrons and quarks is gratuitous in the relevant sense. Or, second, we could simply deny that a nonoperationist commitment to electrons and quarks is now *empirically* epistemically justifiable, but grant that such a commitment may nonetheless have some sort of *non*empirical, broadly theoretical support. More specifically, we might argue that commitment to electrons and quarks may be theoretically justifiable in virtue of its being an essential part of a general physical theory that is not gratuitous in the way that the Cartesian Evil Demon Hypothesis is. We could build a plausible case for either of these options, and thus I shall not digress. For present purposes, we may rest content with my account's compatibility with either of these options.

IV. CONCLUSION

My main point has been that both the low road and the high road to skepticism are dead ends. Maybe we should take an altogether different road to skepticism. But I know of none. So, I want to recommend an altogether different destination, viz.: the nonskeptical goal of understanding (a) what exactly knowledge involves and (b) how exactly we acquire it. That is, we should replace the roads to skepticism with the projects of traditional epistemology. For skepticism itself is an exceedingly doubtful hypothesis. Or, at least, we may now doubt that it merits our assent as truth–seekers.

Loyola University of Chicago

NOTE

* A version of this paper was presented at the 1989 University of Rochester Conference on Skepticism. Dorit Bar–On was the commentator, and the paper has benefited from her comments as well as from discussion with Robert Audi. Some of this paper draws on my book, *Knowledge and Evidence* (Cambridge/New York: Cambridge University Press, 1989).

REFERENCES

Chisholm, Roderick. 1957. *Perceiving: A Philosophical Study.* Ithaca: Cornell University Press
Cornman, James. 1975. *Perception, Common Sense, and Science.* New Haven: Yale University Press.
Feldman, Richard. 1988. "Having Evidence." In David Austin, ed., *Philosophical Analysis,* pp. 83–104. Dordrecht:Kluwer.
Foley, Richard. 1987. *The Theory of Epistemic Rationality.* Cambridge, Mass.: Harvard University Press.
Hiz, Henry, ed. 1978. *Questions.* Dordrecht: Reidel.
Kiefer, Ferenc, ed. 1983. *Questions and Answers.* Dordrecht: Reidel.
Moser, Paul. 1985. *Empirical Justification.* Dordrecht: Reidel.1989. *Knowledge and Evidence.* Cambridge: Cambridge University Press.
Stroud, Barry. 1984. *The Significance of Philosophical Scepticism.* Oxford: Clarendon Press.
Unger, Peter. 1975. *Ignorance: A Case for Scepticism.* Oxford: Clarendon Press.
Van Cleve, James. 1985. "Epistemic Supervenience and the Circle of Belief." *The Monist* 68, 90–104.

DORIT BAR-ON

JUSTIFYING BELIEFS: THE DREAM HYPOTHESIS AND GRATUITOUS ENTITIES

Paul Moser distinguishes two roads leading to skepticism, the low road and the high road, both of which, he argues, are dead–ends. Travellers of the low road, among whom he identifies defenders of Cartesian skepticism like Barry Stroud, are guilty of setting excessively high and unjustified requirements for knowledge, thereby "redefining what knowledge is". At worst, they pose a threat to our claims to *shnow* things. But shnowing is not knowing. Human knowledge — as opposed to the fabricated shnowledge — may still be secure. Travellers of the high roads, on the other hand, do tell us something about *knowledge*: that our ordinary requirements for knowledge cannot or do not get met even in the cases of mundane physical–object statements. However, what they tell us is false; a proper account of the relevant requirements, which Moser outlines, would reveal that high–road skepticism, too, can be defeated. According to this ac-count, the common–sense realist belief in physical objects wins hands down over the skeptic's outlandish hypotheses.

I will begin by briefly presenting a construal of Stroud's reasoning and the diffi-culties with it which is somewhat different from Moser's. This, not by way of criti-cizing Moser's construal, but rather by way of clarifying the dialectics between Stroud and Moser and amplifying Moser's objections to Stroud. I will then turn to high–road skepticism, and argue that, until we learn quite a bit more about Moser's account of the nature of experiential contents and of what makes the Realist Hypothesis the best ex-planation of those contents, it's not clear how he can establish the superiority of the common–sense Realist Hypothesis over its skeptical competitors.

I THE LOW ROAD TO SKEPTICISM

Stroud's begins his exposition of Cartesian skepticism by citing the question which Descartes tries to answer in his Meditations: "Among all the things I believe or take to be true, what amounts to knowledge and what does not?". In the course of attempting to answer this question, Descartes makes three claims, regarding any physical object proposition p which I now believe (such as that there is a white piece of paper in front of me):

(i)   It is possible that I am now dreaming that p.
(ii) If I am now dreaming that p, then I do not *know* that p.
(iii) I do not know that I am not now dreaming that p.

The first two claims, Stroud thinks, are perfectly uncontroversial. The third one is not, but Stroud thinks Descartes can make a case for it. As I understand it, Stroud tries to use these three claims in defending the following simple and valid argument which he attributes to Descartes:

141

M. D. Roth and G. Ross (eds.), Doubting, 141–146.
© 1990 *Kluwer Academic Publishers. Printed in the Netherlands.*

(A)   I do not know that I'm not now dreaming that *p*.
(B)   If I don't know that I'm not now dreaming that *p*, then I do not know
that *p*.
Therefore,
(C)   I do not know that *p*.

(A) is the third, most controversial Cartesian claim from above. Now, Stroud makes the following two claims. First, he argues that *if* one accepts (B) as a general requirement on knowledge of at least external–world propositions, then one *has* to accept (A). Secondly, Stroud argues that it's very difficult to defeat (B), and that, in fact, (B) is embedded in our ordinary concept of knowledge. (I think Stroud believes that it somehow follows from the first two Cartesian claims.) I assess Stroud's two claims in order.

Since the proposition that I am not now dreaming something, ordinarily under–stood, is an external–world proposition, the general requirement expressed by (B) would apply to it, too. So we can obtain:

If I don't know that I'm not now dreaming that I'm not now dreaming that *p*, then I don't know that I'm not now dreaming that *p*.

And notice that the principle would apply also to the proposition that I'm not now dreaming that I'm not now dreaming that *p*, and so on. I'll spare you these further applications. This means that the principle expressed by (B) will have the consequence that to know any external–world proposition at all, one would have to know an infinity of propositions, as well as an infinitely complex proposition. (To see this, just consider the contrapositive of the above iteration.)

Now, Moser uses this observation in his criticism of Stroud. He points out, plausibly, that ordinary knowledge of external–world propositions does not involve one in knowledge of an infinity of propositions. He suggests that, insofar as Stroud must appeal to such infinite knowledge in arguing for skepticism, he is placing an excessive requirement on knowledge. But Stroud could (though he in fact doesn't) deploy this very observation to support his first claim, namely, that one cannot reject premise (A), while accepting premise (B). For, if knowing an external–world proposition *p* requires knowing an infinity of (or infinitely complex) propositions, and we do not (and perhaps even cannot) achieve such infinite knowledge, then we do not (or cannot) know any external–world proposition *p*.

But, given the devastating consequences of accepting (B), Stroud must provide independent grounds for accepting it as an intuitive requirement on knowledge. Stroud doesn't think it's enough simply to point out that we ordinarily do not expect people to rule out that they are dreaming that *p* before they can claim to know that *p*. Ordinarily, Stroud points out, we are satisfied with knowledge claims that are *reasonable*. And, he agrees, a person's claim to know that *p* could count as perfectly reasonable even when we haven't checked whether the person knows she is not dreaming that *p*. But the would–be knower's claim to know that *p*, though reasonable, may be *false*, even by ordinary lights, if the knower doesn't know she is not dreaming that *p*. And the

Cartesian project, Stroud reminds us, concerns the truth about our knowledge claims, not merely their reasonableness.

Stroud does try to provide a positive defense of premise (B). As far as I can see, the defense amounts to citing the first two Cartesian claims mentioned earlier. But I think Stroud's defense fails, for reasons discussed by Moser. Still, knowledge that one is not dreaming does seem relevant to one's knowledge of external–world propositions. And (B) seems to capture this intuitive relevance. Yet we saw that accepting (B) commits us to accepting (A) (and thus skepticism); this, on the assumption that knowledge of external–world propositions does not involve knowledge of infinitely many propositions. One way out is simply to reject this last assumption; that is, we may accept (B) as it stands, and insist that we do know we are not dreaming that p, accepting that, given (B), this means we know infinitely many (and infinitely complex) propositions.

Confronted with the dialectics presented so far, Richard Feldman suggested to me a different, much more appealing way out. He suggested that perhaps the intuition behind (B) can be better captured by the following principle:

(B´)   If I don't know that I'm not now dreaming, then I don't know that p.

That is, knowing that p requires knowing that one is not dreaming, period. It does not require that one knows one is not dreaming *that* p. The advantage of this move can be seen by considering an argument for skepticism using (B´):

(A´) I don't know that I'm not now dreaming.
(B´) If I don't know that I'm not now dreaming, then I don't know that p.
(C´) I don't know that p.

Like the argument with which I started, this argument is valid. But notice that (B´) does *not* entail (A´). If (A´) cannot be defended by appeal to (B´), then we can legitimately ask why we should accept it. After all, we all believe that we do know we're not now dreaming. And we are prepared to support our belief by citing evidence. Stroud can, of course, insist that all our evidence is logically compatible with the falsity of our belief that we're not dreaming. This just means that we may have no logically conclusive evidence that we're not dreaming. But having logically conclusive evidence for p is, on the ordinary conception of knowledge, only one way of knowing that p. The low road skeptic who relies on the claim that one cannot know an external–world proposition unless one has logical proof of it would be, as Moser maintains, relying on an excessive requirement on knowledge. Worse yet, such a skeptic would be assuming from the outset, rather than establishing by argument, that there is no such thing as non–deductive knowledge.

II THE HIGH ROAD TO SKEPTICISM

I now want to discuss briefly high road skepticism and Moser's attempt to block it. The high–road skeptic addressed by Moser maintains that ordinary physical–object propositions cannot (or at least do not) meet our normal standards of knowledge (more specif–

ically, our requirements on justification). Accepting Moser's characterization of such propositions as *hypotheses* designed to explain the subjective, nonpropositional experiential contents (which, I presume, are somehow given to us), the high–road skeptic may state her thesis as follows:

> [HS] Given a set of sensory and perceptual contents neutrally described, our common–sense physical–object theory which purports to explain the occurrence of those contents is *underdetermined*: there are alternative explanations of those contents which are *equally justified* (by our ordinary standards) and which are *incompatible* with the common–sense theory.

Various philosophers, most notably Quine[1], have maintained a version of [HS] (dubbed 'the underdetermination thesis') for our scientific theories. They have argued that, given the loose and tenuous relations between scientific theory and observation, it is highly implausible to expect that even a global "theory of the world" meeting all accepted standards of success, including simplicity, elegance and explanatory power, should turn out to be without incompatible rivals. The rivals envisaged by proponents of the underdetermination thesis, once expounded, would perhaps not seem as outlandish as the dream or evil demon hypothesis; perhaps they would compete with the accepted theory only with respect to matters concerning the high reaches of physics. But their existence should still seem threatening at least to our claims of knowledge about the fundamental nature of the external world.

Moser may argue that underdetermination in the higher reaches of physics is something we should worry about only after we have secured a respectable status to our everyday beliefs about physical objects. As long as rival physical theories will all vindicate our common–sense beliefs, we can reserve underdetermination for special treatment. But a high–minded high–road skeptic may argue that our current physics already presents a threat to our common–sense knowledge claims about physical objects. Even if current physics confirms our notion that there are external physical objects, it seems to vitiate, rather than vindicate, our common–sense ideas about the nature of those objects. Nothing in the way physics would characterize this table seems to correspond to its color or its texture ordinarily understood; though something does correspond to — and causally explains — the *appearances* of color and texture to human subjects. After motivating a general distinction between Appearances and Reality, Russell says: "The real table, if there is one, is not *immediately* known to us at all, but must be an inference from what is immediately **known**." And this raises "two very difficult questions ...; namely: (1) Is there a real table at all? (2) If so, what sort of object can it be?".[2] The general distinction, and the two questions it gives rise to, are, of course, a grist to the skeptic's mill.

Moser's suggestion is that we answer the skeptic by showing that the common–sense Realist Hypothesis is the *best explanation* of the way things appear to us. It is better than the Phenomenalist Hypothesis, because it provides *some* explanation of appearances, where the Phenomenalist Hypothesis gives us none, for it simply rests with the way things appear to us (for this reason I think we should not even regard it as a hypothesis in the first place). It is better than both the Demon and the Dream or

Hallucination Hypotheses, Moser claims, because it does not involve postulating any "gratuitous entities". This is a claim with which I want to take issue.

To remind you, a gratuitous entity, for Moser, is "an item posited by an explanation of [contents] *C* that is not itself represented in *C* by means of any feature corresponding to that item". I see the following problem with the way this notion is put to work in Moser's account of the superiority of the Realist Hypothesis. Remember what this hypothesis is supposed to explain: the way things appear to us, our sense–data. The hypothesis that there is a white table with a rectangular shape in front of me now is supposed to explain the way I am appeared to. I *posit* the table as part of my attempt to answer the question: "Why am I appeared to thusly?" But if we characterize the way I am appeared to in a completely neutral way, in a pure sense–datum language, the white rectangular table will turn out to be, by Moser's definition, a gratuitous entity. For the physical object which I posit — an enduring table of a rectangular shape and white color — is *not* represented as such in my momentary experience. From where I stand, in this light, I am appeared to rhombusly–yellowishly as of by a possibly fleeting temporal slice of something tablish (of course, for lack of a truly neutral language, I am resorting to physical–object predicates). I hypothesize, on the present account, that there is a white rectangular enduring table here. But the features I ascribe to my posit are not represented *as such* in my experience.

The features posited by the Realist Hypothesis, we want to say, do, however, correspond in some systematic way to features of my experience as described in sense–datum terms. There is a regular, causal connection between things rectangular and experiences of the sort I am now having. But such systematic connections are supposed to obtain between the evil demon's actions and my experiences as well, or between features of my nervous system when I am dreaming or hallucinating and the way things appear to me. These skeptical hypotheses are, on the present account, simply alternative causal explanations of the way things appear to me. In fact, it's misleading to talk about an *evil* or deceiving demon, about dreaming and hallucinating. We have alternative explanations of the way my experiences are in fact produced — by persisting physical objects with various properties, by a single creature's actions, by the activities of my own nervous system. Pending a further analysis of the relevant notion of representation, it's hard to see how it can be argued, as Moser does, based on the character of my experiences, neutrally (and subjectively) described, that these experiences do contain representations of physical objects but not of these alternative causes.

So I see a certain dilemma lurking here. We ordinarily tend to describe the contents of our experiences in a quasi–physical–object language. This is because we don't really have a pure sense–datum language, purged of all physical–object idiom in which to describe our inner experiences (if Wittgenstein is right, there can be no such language). If we start with our ordinary ways of characterizing the contents of our experiences, then it seems that the victory claimed for the Realist Hypothesis is bogus, for it will be built into our description of the data to be explained, and then perhaps should not really be regarded a hypothesis. If, on the other hand, we are careful not to smuggle in any physical–object talk into our characterization of subjective experiences (assuming that can be done), we are left with the task of showing how the skeptic's alternative explanations of how these experiences are produced must appeal to entities which are gratuitous in a sense in which the realist's entities are not (relative to the purely characterized experiences). The point is not that "we need a 'neutral' language to characterize subjective contents".[3] The point is that *Moser* needs to appeal to neutral characterizations, if he is to maintain (as he wants to) that the Realist Hypothesis is one among several genuine hypotheses purporting to explain one's subjective experiences, and that it wins an honest victory over its rivals by not positing any gratuitous entities. Now, in his paper, Moser characterizes subjective (nonpropositional) contents as "contents [which] do not entail the existence of anything independent of the perceiver's experience of them, and they do not consist of propositions, judgments, or conceptualizations".[4] This means that Moser's own locution for picking out one such content, viz. "an apparent white piece of paper" is just *one* way of picking out the relevant nonpropositional, unconceptualized mental object (the so–called "subjective content" of an experience). Another way could perhaps be "a demon–induced colored patch". My point is that, if Moser is to stay clear of begging the question against the skeptic, he must not assume that his way of picking out the content is privileged. The subjective content, remember, supposedly wears no conceptual labels on its sleeve; so at least *it* has to be neutral (in the way that sense–data are supposed to be[5]) with respect to different ways of picking it out. (Perhaps, to avoid misleading suggestions, one should stick to Russell's inner, non–descriptive demonstratives — the logically proper names "this" and "that" — which, however, would only be available to the subject of the experience.) But such unconceptualized content, to repeat an earlier point, would not contain representations of demons *or* physical objects.[6] So the question remains: on what grounds can the Realist Hypothesis be deemed superior to its skeptical competitors?

University of North Carolina at Chapel Hill

NOTES

[1] See, for instance *Word & Object*, The MIT Press, 1960, p. 23ff, "On the Reasons for Indeterminacy of Translation:, *Journal of Philosophy* 67, 1970, pp. 178–183, "On Empirically Equivalent Systems of the World", *Erkenntnis* 9, 1975, pp. 313–328, and "On the Nature of Natural Knowledge", in Guttenplan (ed.) *Mind and Language*, Oxford University Press, 1975, pp. 57–81.

[2] *The Problems of Philosophy*, Oxford University Press, 1959, p. 3.

[3] As Moser suggests in his reply to my comments.

[4] ms., p. 8.

[5] And Moser (ms. p. 8) accepts the sense–datum characterization as a possible characterization of his subjective experiential contents.

[6] It's very hard to see how one can ask about such a content of questions Moser presents (ms. p. 9), *viz* . "Why is there an apparent piece of paper here, and why is this apparent piece of paper apparently white?" At most, it seems to me, the subject of such a content can ask "Why is *this* (pointing inwardly to the experience) happening?" And, once again, form the subject's point of view, it's hard to see why the skeptic's hypotheses should fail to give as good a causal explanation as the Realist Hypothesis. Relevant here is the question how there can be any *epistemic* relation between Moser's purely subjective content and the hypothesis which are supposed to explain it. On this issue, see Davidson's "Coherence Theory of Truth and Knowledge", in LePore (ed.) *Truth and Interpretation*, p. 310ff.

JOHN HEIL

DOUBTS ABOUT SKEPTICISM†

We may talk of the *empiricist* way and the *absolutist* way of believing in truth. The absolutists in this matter say that we not only can attain to knowing truth, but we can *know when* we have attained to knowing it; while the empiricists think that although we may attain it, we cannot infallibly know when. To *know* is one thing, to know for certain *that* we know is another. One May hold to the first being possible without the second; hence the empiricists and the absolutists, although neither of them is a skeptic in the usual philosophic sense of the term, show very different degrees of dogmatism in their lives.

James, "The Will to Believe", sec. v.

I

Skeptics are made, not born. One is *driven* to skepticism from some non–skeptical place of origin. One may be carried by different routes, but one must be carried by some route or other. Both one's starting point and one's destination lie within the rather vague boundaries of what may be called *common sense*. The skeptic, despite appearances, does not deny common opinion. On the contrary, he abandons one platitude for the sake of others., He appeals not to arcane considerations, hidden details, but to familiar intuitions. These lead him perhaps to reject something important but, from this point of view, to do so only for the sake of the larger edifice.

I shall not attempt here to do what is almost certainly impossible: show that skepticism is or must be false — or that it is in some way incoherent. Rather I want simply to discuss certain arguments that have, from time to time, been used to buttress the skeptical conclusion. I do not say that there are not other, perhaps better, more compelling arguments to that conclusion. Still, the arguments I have in mind have been thought by some philosophers to be especially persuasive. If these are, as I suspect, flawed, then at least one well–travelled route to skepticism may be blocked. And the detours available may seem, to many of us at any rate, less attractive, certainly less direct.

II

First, I want to be clear about the sort of skepticism to be discussed: skepticism about the "external world". One skeptical in this way holds that "no one knows anything about the world around us".[1] The model for such a skeptic is the Descartes of the first Meditation, although I shall be less concerned here with the historical Descartes than with the Cartesian program as recently depicted by Barry Stroud. According to Stroud, "Descartes finds he has no good reason to believe anything about the world around him and therefore that he can know nothing of the external world" (p. 4).

This way of putting the point is, in a certain important respect, ambiguous. That is, where *p* is some empirical proposition, it might mean either that (i) unless Descartes

---

† Reprinted by permission of the author and the editors from Philosophical Studies 51 (1987) 1–17.

M. D. Roth and G. Ross (eds.), Doubting, 147–159.
Kluwer Academic Publishers. Printed in the Netherlands.

has a good reason to believe that p he does not know that p; but Descartes can never have a good reason to believe any empirical proposition; so he never know any empirical proposition; or it might mean (ii) Descartes knows that p only if he has a good reason to believe that he knows that p; but Descartes can never have a good reason to believe that he knows any empirical proposition; therefore, he never knows any empirical proposition.[2] The ambiguity here is one of epistemic *levels*, that is, it involves a conflation of (i) doxastic attitudes towards propositions (or states of affairs, or whatever), and (ii) doxastic attitudes towards doxastic attitudes — second–level attitudes. I mention this point here because, as I shall contend presently, it plays a central role in the skeptical arguments to be discussed.[3]

Consider now the Cartesian argument. Descartes reflects that he is sitting by the fire in his dressing gown gazing at a white sheet of paper that he holds in his hand. Can we say that he knows this, that he knows that he is sitting by the fire clutching a sheet of paper?

...I remind myself that on many occasions I have in sleep been deceived by similar illusions, and in dwelling carefully on this reflection I see manifestly that there are no certain indications by which we may clearly distinguish wakefulness from sleep.... .[4]

Stroud's gloss on this passage is that

...if he is to know that he is sitting by the fire he must know that he is not dreaming that he is sitting by the fire... a necessary condition of knowing something about the world around him... that condition cannot be fulfilled. (p. 12)

Let us baptize this "necessary condition of knowing something about the world", *N1*, and formulate it as follows:

> *N1.*   Where p is a proposition about the external world, S knows that p (at t) only if S knows at t that he is not dreaming that p.

That *N1* is a necessary condition for empirical knowledges is by now means obvious.[5] Indeed, it is far from clear that "S is dreaming at t" entails "S does not, at t, know that p". The dispositional character of believing evidently permits the ascription of beliefs (and, by extension, knowledge) to agents who are at the time of the ascription asleep or otherwise unconscious. Hence S may know that p at t even when, at t, S is dreaming that p. This might be so, for instance, when S has come by the belief that p earlier, when he was awake and functioning normally. Now, at t, one may feel no particular inclination to devalue S's belief.

It may, nevertheless, be possible to regard *N1* as requiring that S know (roughly) that he did not *merely* dream that p, that he came by his belief that p in circumstances in which he was not dreaming. Construed this way, *N1* appears rather more plausible, though it is still scarcely self–evident. In any case, suppose one grants some version of *N1*. Where does this take the skeptical argument?

According to Stroud, Descartes "concludes that he knows nothing about the world around him because he cannot tell that he is not dreaming; he cannot fulfill one of the conditions necessary for knowing something about the world" (p. 12). Put simply, the idea is that since "I am not dreaming" is *itself* a "proposition about the world", S can know that he is not dreaming only if he can know that he is not dreaming only if he can know that he is not dreaming that he is not dreaming — *and so on*. *This* allegedly necessary condition on knowing, however, seems to differ from *N1*. That is, whereas *N1 requires* that one *know* that one is not dreaming, this further condition seems to require that one be able to *tell* (or determine, or establish) that one is not dreaming. To stave off potential confusion, let us call this condition *N2*:

> *N2.* Where *p* is a proposition about the external world, *S* knows that *p* (at *t*) only is *S* can tell (prove, determine, establish) at *t* that he is not dreaming that *p*.

The difference between *N1* and *N2* may turn out to be insignificant, but it does, I think, represent a *move* along the path towards skepticism. We advance from the claim that empirical knowledge requires one to know that one is not dreaming, to the arguably stronger condition that one be able to *tell* that one is not dreaming. The latter seems stronger because it apparently requires the possession of a *test*, or *measure*, or *demonstration* of some sort not obviously entailed by the former.

    What, in any case, is it about the dream possibility that threatens to undermine empirical knowledge? It is not, of course, that "*S* is dreaming that *p*" implies "not–*p*". One may dream that it is raining and it may in fact be raining. The difficulty, rather, is that if one's belief that it is raining is a *result* of one's dreaming, then its truth is, in a certain way, accidental. We seem, thus, to have stumbled over another necessary condition on knowing:

> *N3.* *S* knows that *p* at *t* only if *S*;s belief that *p* nonaccidentally depends on *p*'s being the case.

This condition is, at best, necessary, since

even if Descartes' sitting by the fire with a piece of paper in his hand... is what causes him to dream that he is sitting by the fire with a piece of paper in his hand, that is still no help to him in coming to know what is going on in the world around him. He realizes that he could be dreaming that he is sitting by the fire even if he is not in fact sitting there, and that is the possibility he finds he has to rule out. (p. 15)

The dream possibility, according to Stroud, is not something "external" to Descartes' reflections.

He is led to consider how he knows that he is not dreaming at the moment by reflecting on how he knows at that moment that he is sitting by the fire with a piece of paper in his hand. If he knows that at all, he thinks, he knows it on the basis of the senses. But he realizes that his having the sensory experiences he is now having is compatible with his merely dreaming that he is sitting by the fire with a piece of paper in his hand. So he does not know on the basis of the sensory experiences that he is having at the moment that he is sitting by the fire. (p. 16)

We have here what seems to be a new condition on knowing:

> *N4.*   S knows that p at t on the basis of E only if, if E is indistinguishable from D (by S), and D is compatible with not–p, then S knows at t that not–D.

If E is a veridical "visual experience" and D is a "dream experience" that is "compatible with" – presumably indistinguishable from – E, then "knowing on the basis of E" requires ruling out D. Stroud suggests that Descartes supposed that "he could not know any... thing unless he had *established* that he was not dreaming at that time" (p. 17, emphasis added). This, however, seems to represent a strengthening of *N4*, roughly as follows.

> *N5.*   S knows that p at t on the basis of E only if, if E is indistinguishable from D (by S), and D is compatible with not–p, then S can establish at t that not–D.

The skeptical maneuver hinges on the contention that, since S can never establish that not–D, S can never know that p.

On Stroud's analysis, Descartes begins with two uncontroversial assumptions: (i) it is always possible that he is dreaming that p; and (ii) if he *is* dreaming that p, he does not know that p (p. 19). It is doubtful, however, that a skeptical conclusion follows just from this pair of assumptions. As has been noted already, one may readily grant that if an agent (merely) dreams that p, then he does not know that p (where p is some proposition about the "external world") without conceding that the agent in question must know — or prove — that he is not dreaming that p in order to know that p. Assumptions (i) and (ii), taken at face value, require only that one not *merely* be dreaming that p in order to know that p, not that one know or establish this. This much may be granted without conceding any of the conditions *N1, N2, N4,* or *N5*.

Of course, even if one wishes to move from the claim that knowledge of the external world requires that one not simply be dreaming that p to the stronger claim that one must *know* that one is not simply dreaming that p in order to have such knowledge, it is not at all obvious that knowing one has not merely dreamt that p requires one's being able to demonstrate, establish, tell, or show that one has not merely dreamt that p. The latter, it seems, is an additional assumption, one that needs additional defense. And it is the assumption, or something very like it, that, as I shall argue, generates the skeptical conclusion Stroud ascribes to Descartes.

The point is a significant one, I think, because it suggests that the skeptic may not merely be moving form simple platitudes about knowledge to his unhappy conclusion, but moving from a certain tendentious *construal* of those platitudes, one that, were we to reflect on it we should not feel compelled to embrace. One might, perhaps, wish to endorse a rather different point, namely that in order for S to know that he know that p, he must know that he has not merely dreamt that p. This , I have suggested, is not quite the same as the view that in order to know that one knows that p, one must establish (prove, show, demonstrate) that one has not merely dreamt that p. But even if one accepts *these* conditions, one is led to the brink of skepticism in the manner depicted by Stroud only if one holds the view that S's knowing that p entails that S knows (or that he can show, etc.) that he knows that p.[6]

III

One may wonder how it is that anything said thus far, however construed, might be thought to generate skepticism. It is time to examine the argument in more detail. Let us begin by conceding, for the moment, that if Descartes is to know he is sitting by the fire, he must be able to rule out by means of some test or other the possibility that he is dreaming (p. 18). The difficulty is that such a test seems on its own terms, self–defeating. suppose that it is a general condition on S's knowing that p that S know he is not dreaming that p, and suppose that *this* requires S to determine or establish via a test of some sort that he is not dreaming. Such a test "would have to be something he could know he had performed successfully" (p. 20). If it were not,

he would be in no better position for telling whether he was dreaming than he would be if he had done nothing or did not even know that there was such a test. But how is he to know that the test has been performed successfully...? Anything one can experience in one's waking life can also be dreamt about; it is possible to dream that one has performed such a test... in order to know that this test had been performed... Descartes would therefore have to establish that he is not merely dreaming that he performed the test successfully.... How could that... be known? Obviously the particular test... already in question cannot serve as a guarantee of its own authenticity since it might have been merely dreamt, so some further test... would be needed to indicate that the original test was actually performed and not merely dreamt.... But this further test is subject to the same general condition in turn. (p.22)

Stroud concludes that Descartes "can never know that he is not dreaming", hence, on his own view, never know anything at all about the external world (p 23).

If it is in general a necessary condition of our knowing something about the world around us that we know that we are not dreaming it follows that we can never know we are not dreaming... the only hopes lies in avoiding that condition. (p. 43)[7]

We may label this the *regress argument.* Such an argument seems to show that if, in order to know anything, p, one must ascertain that one is not merely dreaming that p, then knowledge is impossible. This is because one's not dreaming must itself be known to one, hence satisfy the stated requirement. That this requirement is satisfied, however, must itself be known. Schematically, the idea is this: to know that p, one must know that q (where q is the proposition that one is not dreaming that p). But to know that q, one must know that r (that one is not dreaming that q, i.e., the one is not dreaming that one is not dreaming), and so on.[8]

IV

The regress argument may be thought to provide the skeptic with a potent weapon, though only if he can somehow establish that ordinary empirical knowledge requires that agents be in a position to *rule out* the possibility that they are dreaming. If one supposes that such knowledge requires at most that this possibility not obtain (whether or not agents are capable of ruling it out), then the argument is disarmed and poses no ob–

vious threat to commonsense realism. It is crucial, then, to determine why anyone should imagine that the stronger condition is the reasonable one.

On the face of it we seem often willing to grant that a person knows something even though he is in no position to rule out countless possibilities that are or might be incompatible with his knowing what he does. I gaze out of the window and notice an automobile driving past. I may commonly be said to know this even though I may be unable to rule out the scores of possibilities — that what appears to be an automobile is in fact a papier–mâché mock–up, or that it is nothing more than a cleverly projected holographic image, and so on. To be sure, if any of these possibilities were actual, I would not know that there is an automobile driving past — for the straightforward reason that it would be false that there is an automobile driving past. But this is another matter. It is one thing to insist that certain possibilities incompatible with one's knowing not be realized, something else altogether to insist that one know — or be able to show — that these possibilities are not actual.[9] How might one support the stronger view? Stroud offers this suggestion:

> Suppose that on looking out the window I announce casually that there is a goldfinch in the garden. If I am asked how I know it is a goldfinch and I reply that it is yellow, we all recognize that in the normal case that is not enough for knowledge. "For all you've said so far", it might be replied, "the thing could be a canary, so how do you know it's a goldfinch" A certain possibility compatible with everything I have said so far has been raised, and if what I have said so far is all I have to go on and I do not know that the thing in the garden is not a canary, then I do not know that there is a goldfinch in the garden. I *must be able to rule out the possibility* that it is a canary if I am to know it is a goldfinch. (pp. 24f., emphasis added)

Such examples threaten to muddy the water, perhaps, by running together the conditions on knowing something with conditions under which we should say that someone had shown (demonstrated, established, proved) something to be the case. Although related, these conditions seem importantly different and ought, in consequence, be kept distinct.[10] I shall say more about this presently.

In any case, the moral Stroud draws from the example is that "there are always certain possibilities which must be known not to obtain if I am to know what I claim to know" (p. 26). But is this the right moral to drawn? Stroud offers it as a "familiar fact about human knowledge", but *is* it?

In the case before us there seem, on the face of it, to be at least two different ways in which the belief that there is a goldfinch in the garden can fail to qualify as knowledge. In the first place, that belief may be false (it is not a goldfinch, only a canary). Second, the agent's reasons for believing that it is a goldfinch may be, in one way or another, inadequate (that x is a yellow bird is not enough to support — epistemically — the belief that x is a goldfinch). If we exclude cases of false belief, then it seems that Stroud's example is one in which a belief fails to qualify as an instance of knowledge chiefly because it is based on epistemically insufficient reasons.

Stroud argues that "as soon as we see that a certain possibility is incompatible with our knowing such–and–such... we immediately recognize that it is a possibility that must be known not to obtain if we are to know the such–and–such in question" (p. 27). We may perhaps formulate this requirement on knowing as follows:

N6. "...[I]f I know something *p* I must know the falsity of all those things incompatible with *p*" (p. 27).

But how exactly does this requirement fall out of the goldfinch example? *There* the problem seems simply to be that an agent is basing his belief that a certain bird is a goldfinch on inadequate reasons. To elevate this belief to the status of knowledge, for all that the example shows, it need only be based on epistemically *better* reasons. What makes reasons epistemically adequate, of course, is a nice question.[11] But that is not the issue here. The problem is rather to see what it is about the goldfinch case that leads us to agree that a particular agent does not know that there is a goldfinch in the garden.

It might be imagined that tale about "adequate reasons" is nothing more than an oblique way of acknowledging Stroud's point. Thus, could a reason be adequate epistemically if it left open possibilities of the sort that trouble Stroud? Could my reasons for believing that *p* ever be adequate if they failed to rule out *all* those circumstances incompatible with *p*?

Certainly it is possible to speak of epistemic adequacy in this way. But it is not obviously necessary. One may, it seems, regard adequacy as being determined by some combination of features of the agent (his total doxastic state, the condition of his sensory systems, and the like) together with features of the world (the lighting, the presence of holograms, hologram–producing mechanisms, or papier–mâché mock–ups) whether or not these are in any sense directly accessible to the agent. Externalist views of this sort allow that an agent's belief may be supported even though the agent himself could not exhaustively spell out that support. The agent, a child perhaps, might even be incapable of understanding its nature. It seems clear, for instance, that the epistemic status of one's beliefs about one's surroundings based on vision depend (at the very least) on things going right in one's visual system. Most of us, however, would be at a loss to say how it is that this system operates. What seems to be required is that the system function properly, not that we *know* (much less, be in a position to *demonstrate*) that it is functioning properly.[12]

One may be unsympathetic towards these externalist musings. One need not be persuaded by them, however, to recognize that Stroud's account of the goldfinch case failed to establish that one's knowing that *p* requires that one be able to rule out incompatible possibilities. Stroud's reflections here are revealing.

The main difficulty in understanding [such principles] is that no principle like those I have mentioned could possibly describe the way we proceed in everyday life.... if an adherence to some such requirement were responsible for our reactions in those ordinary cases... philosophical skepticism about the external world would be true. Nobody would know anything about the world around us. If, in order to know something, we must rule out a possibility which is known to be incompatible with our knowing it, Descartes is perfectly right to insist that he must know that he is not dreaming if he is to know that he is sitting by the fire with a piece of paper in his hand. (p.30)

This *sounds* like a concession: *if* we interpret the goldfinch case as one in which knowledge is defeated because the agent cannot be said to know that a certain possibility does not obtain, *then* we shall be driven to accept skepticism. And this suggests — via *modus tollens* — that there is a flaw in our interpretation of that case. Stroud, however, is partial to the opposite line:

That conclusion [i.e., skepticism] can be avoided... only if we can find some way to avoid the requirement that we must know we are not dreaming if we are to know anything about the world around us. But that requirement cannot be avoided if it is nothing more than an instance of general procedure we recognize and insist on in making and assessing the knowledge–claims in everyday and scientific life. We have no notion of knowledge other than what is embodied in those procedures and practices. So if the requirement is a "fact" of our ordinary knowledge we will have to accept the conclusion that no one knows anything about the world around us. (pp. 30f.)

Perhaps it would be useful to step back and review the structure of Stroud's skeptic's reasoning to this point. First, we were presented with a version of the Cartesian argument purporting to show that one can not be said to know that p unless one can be said to know that one is not merely dreaming that *p*. Second, Stroud offers an explanation for the force of this argument: we instinctively recognize that one can know something only if one is in a position to rule out every possibility incompatible with that knowing. If this could be shown to be a principle that we all accept "in making and assessing knowledge–claims in everyday and scientific life", then the soundness of the Cartesian argument would be assured and skepticism vindicated. Third, Stroud provides an example — the goldfinch episode — that is intended to persuade us of the aptness of the principle in question.[13]

A great deal, then, hinges on one's understanding of the goldfinch case. If the interpretation suggested by Stroud is flawed, then the skeptical argument seems not to get off the ground. I have tried already to implant doubts about Stroud's account of why the knowledge claim about the goldfinch is defeated. I have not, admittedly, offered an exhaustive alternative explanation. I do not need to do so, however. It is enough to show that one is not *driven* to accept the interpretation favored by Stroud.

Most people would agree that a belief based on false or epistemically inadequate beliefs cannot constitute an instance of knowledge. This fact, however, if it is a fact, is compatible with many account of epistemic inadequacy other than that pressed by Stroud. True, his account may, in the end, be right, the others wrong. But, given what is at stake, this is something that must be shown, not something we should be obliged to accept at the outset.

V

Even if I am right about all this, of course, one may still feel uneasy. Thus, even supposing that Stroud has not made a convincing case for the claim that one's knowing something requires that one be able to rule out possibilities incompatible with it, he has, at the very least, offered an *explanation* of the evident force of the Cartesian dream argument. Further, I have not shown that the principle Stroud finds in that argument is false, but at most merely that it is not a necessary consequence of our ordinary reflections on the goldfinch example. The fact that one's accepting such a principle would account for the compelling character of the Cartesian argument is surely a point in its favor. In contrast, my feeble externalist homilies appear to leave Descartes in limbo. And this may be seen to count rather heavily against them.

Why *is* it that we find the Cartesian argument as formulated by Stroud so immediately and powerfully compelling? Does it perhaps turn on a subtle recharacterization of
our ordinary conception of knowledge? Stroud offers the following observation:

> One thing the skeptical philosopher can appeal to to show that he does not introduce a new or extraordinary
> conception of knowledge into his investigation... is the ease with which we all acknowledge, when pre-
> sented with the case, that Descartes ought to know that he is not dreaming if he is to know that he is sit-
> ting by the fire with a piece of paper in his hand. The force we feel in the skeptical argument when we first
> encounter it is itself evidence that the conception of knowledge employed in the argument is the very con-
> ception we have been operating with all along. (p. 71)

The idea is that the skeptic, in deploying the Cartesian argument, has touched a nerve.
We respond to the resulting irritation because it has made us starkly aware of the consequences of principles on which we implicitly and explicitly depend in our everyday
and scientific commerce with the world.

It is probably right to allow that Descartes, in speaking of knowledge, is speaking of what we should agree *is* knowledge. If we did not believe that, we should not
regard his skeptical challenge as a matter of concern. Let us concede, then, that the
Cartesian argument does indeed reveal something important about knowledge. The
question now is over precisely what it reveals.

Stroud is at pains to distinguish what he calls the "conditions of knowledge"
from the "conditions for the appropriate assessment and acceptance of *assertions* of
knowledge" (p.60). Philosophers like Austin, he thinks, in pointing our that it would
be outrageous to challenge an ordinary claim to knowledge by asking the agent making
the claim for proof that he is not dreaming or suffering from an hallucination, do not
thereby show that such proofs are not conditions on knowing. At best, these cases
demonstrate something about the conditions under which it is or is not reasonable to
assert various things.

> A necessary condition of knowledge might remain unfulfilled even though it would be inappropriate or
> outrageous for anyone to assert that it is or try to criticize my knowledge claim on that basis. (p.62)

Stroud praises Peter Unger for insisting on this very distinction, that between "the
meanings of our expressions and the conditions of their appropriate and intelligible em-
ployment" (pp.73ff.)[14]

This, too, seems a point well taken. Indeed, it is surely related in some way to
a distinction already mentioned, namely that between the conditions under which someone is entitled to *assert* (to himself or to others) that he knows something, and the
conditions under which it *is the case* that someone knows something. My suggestion is
that an argument similar to the one Stroud employs against Austin can be turned against
Stroud's skeptic. Thus, we may feel the force of the Cartesian maneuver for roughly
the same reasons that we feel the force of Austin's ironical remarks: in both cases we
are failing to make a distinction we ought to make.

Consider again Stroud's rehearsal of the Cartesian argument:

> Descartes' conclusion rests on the general requirement that we must know that we are not dreaming if we are
> to know anything at all about the world about us. That requirement is what renders inadequate any *tests* or
> *procedures for determining* that one is not dreaming: one would have to know that one was not simply

dreaming that one was performing the test, and not dreaming that one was performing any of the other tests used to determine *that*, and so on. (p.48; emphasis added)

Here a point is being made about *tests* or *procedures for determining* that something is or is not the case. But the conclusion that we are invited to draw is not simply that such tests or procedures are impossible, but that *knowledge* founded on the conditions that such tests or procedures would be used to establish is impossible. Why should we suppose, however, that knowing something entails that one has in one's possession a test or procedure for determining that the something in question obtains? Even if one feels that such things are necessary, however, the Cartesian argument, as it is construed by Stroud, seems to require much more. It seems to require that in order to know something, one must be able to demonstrate (show, establish, prove) that one knows it. And this, surely, is too strong. Or if not too strong, it seems at least to require some sort of additional defense.

If the Cartesian argument, thus interpreted, in effect equivocates in this fashion, how can we account for its force? Recall that the Cartesian project is not merely to *analyze* or to *explicate* the concept of knowledge, but rather to refute the skeptic, to demonstrate that we do in fact *possess* knowledge. Descartes is concerned not merely with the conditions under which it would be correct to say that someone *has* knowledge. He is concerned as well to show that these conditions are, on occasion, *satisfied*. *This* project does appear to require a proof or demonstration that one knows, the specification, perhaps, of a test or procedure for distinguishing cases in which the conditions on knowing are satisfied from cases in which those conditions are not met.

Stroud's discussion seems to show that such a project is doomed from the outset. It may thereby show as well that the skeptic can never be refuted — if a refutation requires the establishment of infallible tests or procedures for distinguishing instances of knowledge from instances of false belief. But from this it does not follow that the skeptic has been proved *correct*, that knowledge of the "external world" is impossible.

Consider for a moment Descartes' proposed solution to the predicament of the first *Meditation*. He argues (roughly) that a given belief counts as an instance of knowledge just in case it possesses a certain property, *clarity* and *distinctness*. Whatever one thinks of this proposal, one must not imagine that is straightforwardly equivalent to the doctrine that a belief counts as an instance of knowledge only when the agent harboring it (or anyone else, for that matter) can *show* either that it possesses the property of clarity and distinctness *or* that the possession of such a property is truth-guaranteeing. Someone might hold such a view, but it is not obvious — not to me at any rate — either that Descartes does or that he ought to. On the contrary: knowledge is, for him, constituted by one's electing to assent just to those propositions that are clear and distinct. *That* clarity and distinctness is epistemically adequate for knowledge is not something that needs to be established in order to *have* knowledge. Rather this must be established in order to prove or demonstrate that knowledge is possible or that, on a given occasion, one has knowledge. Such proofs or demonstrations, however, seem not to be necessary for ordinary knowledge. They belong, instead, to a higher-order epistemological inquiry.

In the end, for Descartes, whether we have knowledge seems to depend on the existence of a benevolent God. To *establish* that we have knowledge, we must establish

God's existence. If this turns out to be impossible, then if follows that a certain attempt to demonstrate that skepticism is false, that we *can* have knowledge of the external world, fails. It does not follow, however, that skepticism is true, at least if one takes the skeptic to be defending the claim that such considerations show that we *cannot* have such knowledge.[15]

Let C be the set of conditions necessary and sufficient for S to know that p at t. Now, we may ask, does C include among its members some condition, c^*, one requiring S to know or determine at t that the conditions in C (or perhaps those comprising a certain proper subset of C, one that includes c^*) are satisfied? If that were so, then the skeptic may be right in insisting that these conditions are, in principle, unsatisfiable, that S could never know that p. If he is right, however, it is for the altogether unremarkable reason that the envisaged conditions on knowing are either circular or lead to a regress.[16] If *all* knowledge requires knowing or establishing that c^* is satisfied, then one must in some sense know or establish that c^* is satisfied *in order* to know (or establish) that c^* is satisfied, an evident if unsurprising impossibility.

I have tried to suggest reasons for thinking that it is, in general, a mistake to include such a condition as c^* in C. c^* *belongs properly to the* conditions under which S knows or can show he knows that p, not to S's first–order knowledge that p.

A proof or demonstration that the conditions under which S knows that p are, on occasion, satisfied would constitute a refutation of skepticism. This, it seems, is what Descartes is ultimately after. But skepticism may *be* false even if it cannot be *shown* to be false. Stroud's skeptic's insistence that, in order to know that p, one must be able to *rule out* "all those things incompatible with p" seems, in effect, to constitute a denial of this point (see p.27). And, in this regard at least, his view differs crucially from that of Descartes in the *Meditations*.

VI

My account of the Cartesian argument may be found wanting, This, however, need not affect the general conclusion I wish to defend. That conclusion requires only that one distinguish two epistemological projects: (i) the specification of the conditions of empirical knowledge; and (ii) the determination of conditions under which it would be reasonable — or true — to believe or to say that those conditions are satisfied. The skeptical *arguments* to which Stroud alludes in the first two chapters of the *The Significance of Philosophical Scepticism* seem to me to apply straightforwardly to the second of these projects; the conclusions drawn, however, purport to raise questions about the first. That is, the skeptic's contention is not that we can never establish that we have knowledge of ordinary states of affairs — that would be compatible with our *having* it — but that we *do not and could not have* such knowledge.

If this is so, then Stroud's skeptic is guilty of an equivocation. And if *that* is so, we need not feel obliged to share Stroud's pessimistic moral. Still, as was noted at the outset, these considerations may pose only a minor or temporary impediment to the skeptic. We may yet be driven by some other route to accept the skeptical picture.[17]

Virginia Commonwealth University

NOTES

1 B. Stroud, *The Significance of Philosophical Scepticism*, Oxford: Oxford University Press, 1984, p. 1. Parenthetical citations refer to pages in this volume.

2 The issue with which Stroud concerns himself and, in consequence, the focus of the paper is our know ledge of the "external world", our empirical knowledge. Henceforth, then, in speaking about an agent's "knowing that p", I shall suppose that p is in every case an "empirical proposition" and not, for example, a logical or mathematical truth or a pronouncement about the agent's own state of mind. In this way the arguments discussed here do not pertain to knowledge *per se*, but only to whatever one regards as *empirical* knowledge.

3 See, e.g., W. P Alston 'Has Foundationalism Been Refuted?' *Philosophical Studies* 29 (1976): 287–305; and 'Level Confusions in Epistemology' in P. French, T. Uehling and H. Wettstein (eds.) *Midwest Studies in Philosophy*, Vol. v, Minneapolis: University of Minnesota Press, 1980, 135–140; R. Audi, 'Foundationalism, Epistemic Dependence and Defeasibility', *Synthese* 55 (1983): 597–612; A. I. Goldman, 'The Internalist Conception of Justification' in French *et al., op. cit.*, 27–51; R. Feldman, "Fallibilism and Knowing that One Knows', *Philosophical Review* 90 (1981): 266–282; and J. Heil, "Reliability and Epistemic Merit', *Australasian Journal of Philosophy* 64 (1984): 327–338.

4 E. S. Haldane and G. R. Ross, *Philosophical Works* (2 vols.), Cambridge: Cambridge University Press, 1967, Vol 1, pp. 145f., quoted in Stroud, p. 11.

5 I am indebted to Robert Audi for this observation.

6 In putting the point this way, I do not mean to suggest that knowing that one knows that p is no different from showing (demonstrating, being able to tell, etc.) that one knows that p (see Feldman, *op. cit.*). The move here, like most of those made by the skeptic, may seem inconsequential, but it is, nonetheless, a move.

7 Elsewhere, Stroud summarizes the argument in this way: "Descartes' conclusion rests on the general requirement that we must know that we are not dreaming if we are to know anything at all about the world about us. That requirement is what renders inadequate any tests or procedures for determining that one is not dreaming; one would have to know that one was not simply dreaming that one was performing the test, and not dreaming that one was performing any of the other tests used to determine *that*, and so on" (p. 48).

8 Even if one is persuaded that a regress threatens in such cases, however, one need not regard this as entailing the skeptical conclusion. It is conceivable that one does indeed know, or at least that one is justified in believing each of the required propositions. Further argument is needed if we are to rule out such a possibility. Richard Feldman convinced me of this point.

9 Knowledge may be defeated, it appears, even by non–actual possibilities, provided these are genuinely relevant. Thus, if I have reason to believe that there are hologram producing devices in the vicinity, or papier–mâché automobile mock–ups, then, even if my belief that there is an automobile driving past is true, it is not obvious that I have knowledge. Suppose that there are hologram–producing devices in the vicinity that are not at the time operating, or suppose that there are none in the vicinity, but that one such device exists hundreds of miles away in Idaho? It is far from clear that such things would constitute defeaters, they fail in some obvious sense to be *relevant* alternatives. I do not say that the determination of what constitutes relevance in such cases is a simple matter. Indeed, the vagueness of that notion may simply reflect a certain vagueness attaching to our ordinary concept of knowledge. For some interesting speculations on the matter see A. I. Goldman, "Discrimination and Perceptual Knowledge", in G. Pappas and M. Swain (eds.), *Essays on Knowledge and Justification*, Ithaca: Cornell University Press, 1978, 120–145; and H. Kornblith, "Beyond Foundationalism and the Coherence Theory', *Journal of Philosophy* 67 (1980): 597–612.

10 Indeed Stroud, in other contexts, insists that such things must be kept distinct. See, e.g., his ch. 2 *passim*, and sec. v, below.

11 See, e.g., F. I. Dretske, "Conclusive Reason', *Australasian Journal of Philosophy* 49 (1971): 1–22.

[12] This is not to say that if one has reason to suppose one's visual system *not* to be adequately function–ing — e.g., that one is myopic — even if one is wrong, that one still knows. Knowledge may be defeated either by things going wrong with the processes that generate the relevant beliefs or by the agent's beliefs about those processes. See, e.g., Kornblith, *op. cit.*, It does not follow from this, however, that in cases where the processes that generate one's belief that *p* are functioning reliably, one's knowing that *p* requires one to know (or justifiably believe) that these processes are functioning adequately. See Audi, *op. cit.*; and Heil, *op. cit.*, esp. pp. 335ff.

[13] Later, in ch. 2, he offers a second example, one involving airplane spotters borrowed from Thompson Clarke's 'The Legacy of Skepticism', *Journal of Philosophy* 69 (1972): 754–769. I shall not discuss this example, however. Its differences from the goldfinch case are, for my purposes, inessential.

[14] See P. Unger, *Ignorance*, Oxford: Oxford University Press, 1975; cf., F.I. Dretske, *Knowledge and the Flow of Information*, Cambridge, Mass.: M.I.T. Press, 1981, pp. 109f.

[15] Some of these issues are discussed in J. Van Cleve, 'Foundationalism, Epistemic Principles, and the Cartesian Circle', *Philosophical Review* 88 (1979): 55–91.

[16] Though see above, sec. iii.

[17] Work on this paper was supported by a grant from the National Institute of Mental Health (MH08406–02). The paper has benefited from discussions with Robert Audi, Jack Boyce, Richard Feldman, George Myro, Mark Overvold, and Barry Stroud.

STEWART COHEN

SKEPTICISM AND EVERYDAY KNOWLEDGE ATTRIBUTIONS

One of the more puzzling aspects of the issues concerning skepticism is the stark contrast between our everyday assertions concerning what we know and the conclusions of skeptical arguments. Skeptical arguments, which appear to be quite formidable, conclude that we know very little, whereas in everyday life we attribute a considerable amount of knowledge to ourselves.

What should we say about this contrast? Of course the skeptic must say that our everyday knowledge attributions are in some way mistaken. But if we are making a mistake when we attribute knowledge to ourselves in everyday life, exactly what kind of mistake is it?

On the other hand, most of us are not skeptics. We will then have to provide a different account of the relationship between skeptical arguments and our everyday pattern of knowledge attributions. We can claim that the skeptic is simply mistaken or we can claim that the situation is more complex — that the claims of the skeptic do not necessarily threaten our ordinary knowledge attributions.

Thus, there are a number of ways that one might construe the relationship between skepticism and ordinary life and, of course, different ways of construing that relation will have different consequences for the issues raised by skepticism. What I propose to do is to examine the feasibility of these various ways of construing the relationship between skepticism and everyday life. In particular, I want to examine the view that our everyday pattern of knowledge attributions provides the basis for a response to skeptical arguments.

Typically, skeptical arguments claim that the cases that we ordinarily think of as knowledge fall short of the standards required for knowledge. The argument proceeds by calling our attention to alternative hypotheses to what we ordinarily believe that we are unable to eliminate.[1] The skeptic then claims that our inability to eliminate these alternatives entails that we do not know what we believe. For example, the skeptic argues that we know that we see a zebra at the zoo only if we can eliminate the alternative that we see a cleverly disguised mule and we can not eliminate this alternative; or more generally that we can know anything (on the basis of our senses) only if we can eliminate the alternative[2] that we are not dreaming and that we cannot eliminate this alternative.[3]

If this is the skeptical challenge, then what exactly is the nature of the response provided by our everyday pattern of knowledge attributions? Responses of this kind enjoyed great popularity during the heyday of ordinary language philosophy. J. L. Austin and others argued vigorously that the ordinary use of instances of the schema "S knows P" shows that the skeptical arguments depend on illegitimately raising the requirements or standards that we apply in everyday life.[4] Ordinarily we do not require that someone be able to eliminate the kinds of alternatives that the skeptic raises, e.g., that we are seeing a cleverly disguised mule or that we are dreaming, in order to be able to claim correctly to know. In everyday life, we claim to know a considerable amount

161

M. D. Roth and G. Ross (eds.), Doubting, 161–169.
© 1990 Kluwer Academic Publishers. Printed in the Netherlands.

even though the skeptic's very strict standards are not met. In most ordinary contexts, a challenge to a knowledge claim based on the possibility that we are dreaming would be taken as ludicrous — as not at all relevant to the question of whether we know. As long as there is no special reason to think that you are dreaming or seeing a cleverly disguised mule, there is no requirement that you be able to rule out such a possibility. In effect, the response is that the skeptic assesses ordinary knowledge claims according to standards that are stricter than the ones that actually govern the correct use of the expression "to know". Thus the skeptic is simply mistaken when he claims that our ordinary knowledge attributions are incorrect.

Essentially, this response to skepticism underscores the rules that govern our ordinary use of the verb "to know". The skeptic is accused of objecting to knowledge attributions that are perfectly appropriate according to the rules that govern such attributions. That is, the fact that we ordinarily attribute knowledge over a wide range of cases even though the skeptic's standards are not met is alleged to show that the standards the skeptic is insisting upon are stricter than the ones we ordinarily require for a belief to be an instance of knowledge. But to deny that any beliefs are instances of knowledge on the grounds that there are no beliefs that meet the skeptics excessively strict standards would be akin, e.g., to denying that there are no physicians in New York on the grounds that there are no persons in New York who can cure any disease in twenty minutes.[5] As such, the skeptic can be accused of distorting the concept of knowledge to the point that his claims are no longer applicable to what we are claiming when we say that we know. At best he can be seen as proposing that we change the rules that govern such attributions — a proposal we may simply reject.

Unfortunately this type of response to skepticism oversimplifies matters. For one must pay attention to the distinction between appropriately applying an expression and truthfully applying that expression. Barry Stroud has recently argued this way against this appeal to ordinary language.[6] He discusses a case (which he attributes to Thompson Clarke[7]) in which airplane spotters are trained by their military manuals to perform the important task of distinguishing between planes of type E and planes of type F. The manuals tell them that planes which have features xyw are E's and planes that have features xyz are F's. It turns out that there are also a few planes of type G indistinguishable from F's which also have xyz. The manuals do not mention them because it is not important that the spotters be able to distinguish between F's and G's.

Under these conditions, it will be perfectly appropriate for one of the spotters who gets a good look at a plane with xyz to claim that he knows that it is an F. According to the rules for identifying planes, as specified in the manual, his claim would be completely justified. But clearly, because of the few G's that are around the spotter does not know that it is an F, even if it is an F. A spotter cannot know that a plane which has xyz is an F even if it is an F, unless he can rule out the possibility that it is a G. What this example shows is that it may be perfectly appropriate for someone to claim that he knows even though in fact he does not know. That is, the use of an expression may be perfectly appropriate given the rules that govern its application and yet it still be the case that the proposition expressed is false. Of course the speaker cannot be blamed for his use of the expression, but that does not mean that what he said cannot be false.

Stroud wants to assimilate the position of an airplane spotter to that of a speaker who in everyday life claims to know certain ordinary propositions. The rules that govern

the ordinary application of the expression "to know" permit us to say in a range of circumstances that we know certain things on the basis of our perceptual evidence. It is
appropriate for us to say this even though there are alternatives to what we claim to
know. The ordinary standards that govern the use of the expression "to know" do not
require that we be able to rule out the possibility that we are confronted with an alternative of the kind referred to by the skeptic. However this is consistent with it still being
the case that we in fact fail to know — that our attributions of knowledge are false —
due to the fact that we cannot rule out such possibilities.

As Stroud describes this case, he does not clearly distinguish between two features of the circumstances that could explain why, despite their falsity, attributions of
knowledge to the spotters can still be appropriate. The first is that the spotters are unaware of the existence of G's and so it can still be appropriate for them to attribute
knowledge to themselves. Because the manual tells them that the planes with xyz are F's
they are justified in claiming to know that the planes are F's. Moreover, anyone who
reads the training manual and is unaware of the omission would be justified in claiming
that someone who sees a plane with xyz knows that it is an F (provided of course that
the attributor does not have access to additional information which renders the justification of the spotter defective.) In this sense, given the rules that govern knowledge attributions, it can be appropriate to say that S knows even though it is false that S knows.
On this way of looking at matters, our everyday knowledge attributions would involve a
kind of mistake — a mistake for which we can not be faulted, but a mistake nonetheless.

There is another aspect of the case that suggests that it is not so much that our
everyday knowledge attributions involve a mistake, but rather that they perpetuate a kind
of useful fiction. As Stroud describes the case, it is very useful to the war effort to distinguish between the case where a spotter identifies a plane as an F on the basis of observing that it is xyz and the case where a spotter makes the identification on the basis of
observing merely that it is xy. In the latter case, there is no basis for thinking it is an F
rather than an E. In the former case there is a very good basis for thinking that the plane
is an F rather than an E (and there is no harm in the chance of misidentifying an F as a
G.) This is precisely the reason that it could be appropriate even for someone who
knows of the existence of the G's to claim that a spotter in the former case knows that
the plane is an F whereas it would not be appropriate in the latter case. It is appropriate
in the former case to speak in this way even though what is said is literally false because
speaking in this way marks a useful distinction and thereby subserves the war effort.

Both of these considerations could be said to apply to situations in which an attribution of knowledge might be false although perfectly appropriate given the rules of the
language. Can either of them be used to undermine the Austin–style ordinary language
response to skepticism? Of course they both illustrate that there can be no inference from
the fact that the rules of the language license an attribution of knowledge to the conclusion that such an attribution is true. It can be appropriate to say that someone knows
even when what is said is false. Surely that in itself is not surprising. But while some
anti–skeptical appeals to our everyday pattern of knowledge attributions may seem to rely
on this facile inference, in general they need not.

Let us look at each of the considerations: The first is that one can appropriately
attribute knowledge to oneself even when the attribution is false because one might have
every reason to think that it is true. As weak a point as this is, it can still be used to

undermine what was sometimes called the paradigm case argument. This argument proceeds by claiming that certain expressions can only be learned ostensively — by being shown certain cases where the term applies. It is alleged to follow that it could not meaningfully be denied that the expression applies in such cases. Anyone who questions the correctness of applying such terms in these paradigm cases shows that they have not grasped the conditions under which the term may be applied — they simply do not understand the meaning of the word. This has been held to be true for epistemic expressions like "it is certain that..."[8] According to the argument, it would follow that this expression can not meaningfully be said not to apply to those paradigm instances that are used to convey the meaning of the expression. So any skeptic who claims that nothing is certain must be confused about the meaning of "it is certain that..."

However, once we see that it does not follow from the fact that an expression is applied appropriately that it is applied truly, we can see that the paradigm case argument fails.[9] Consider an expression like "...is a miracle." In a society that firmly believes in miracles, the meaning of that expression might be taught ostensively — by having certain paradigm cases pointed out, such as a sudden and unexpected recovery from an illness, a narrow escape from an accident, etc. Someone who is brought up in such a society could be justified in believing that these events are instances of miracles and, as such, it would be perfectly appropriate for him to say that these events are miracles. Someone who denied that they were miracles might be accused of not knowing the meaning of the expression "... is a miracle." However the application of the expression to the "paradigm cases" is conditioned on the reasonable (given what the authorities of this society claim) belief that the cases fit a certain criterion, viz., being caused by supernatural intervention. Since presumably the belief that the cases fit the criterion is mistaken, the claim that the events are miraculous, while appropriate given the circumstances, is false.

Analogously while it may be true in the case of an expression like "it is certain that...", that it is taught by ostension, it could also true that the word is applied in those cases in virtue of a reasonable belief on the part of the attributors that the cases meet a certain criterion, viz., that all alternatives are eliminated.[10] So while it may be appropriate to say of beliefs like "This is a hand" that they are certain, what the skeptic calls to our attention is the falsity of our belief that these paradigm cases fit the criterion and thus to the falsity of our belief that the term "certain" applies.

So, a simple appeal to paradigm instances of application cannot undermine skeptical arguments. An attribution of knowledge that may be perfectly appropriate from the perspective of ordinary language could nonetheless turn out to be false. The sense of "appropriate" here is that such attributions may be justified for the attributor, i.e., the attributor can not be faulted.

While this kind of appeal to paradigm instances may fail for this reason, the defender of common sense can claim that the case of knowledge attributions is unlike the case of miracle attributions in a crucial respect. In the latter case, once it is conceded that the "paradigm" cases do not involve supernatural intervention, the speakers in question would presumably readily withdraw their attributions. They would agree that the cases fail to meet a necessary condition for being a miracle. But this is not necessarily true in the case of knowledge. We find it very paradoxical to concede that we fail to know anything even after the skeptic calls our attention to the skeptical alternatives. This is not to say that we do not feel the pull of the skeptical argument. The point is that we still feel the intuitive pull of saying that we know things. But unlike what would presumably be true in the miracles case, we do not, in general, simply concede the skeptical claim that our everyday knowledge attributions are false. So, the skeptic can not accuse one who appeals to our ordinary knowledge attributions of simply failing to see that an attribution can be appropriate (in the sense that the attributor is free of blame in making the attribution), while nonetheless being false.

Now the skeptic could try to dismiss the significance of our reluctance to concede the falsity of our everyday attributions by claiming that it simply reveals that our old habits are not easily shed. This persistence of our habitual ways of thinking about knowledge even after we have been confronted with skeptical arguments was noticed by Descartes ("...so insensibly of my own accord I fall back into my former opinions...")[11] and by Hume ("Nature will always maintain her rights and prevail in the end over any abstract reasoning whatsoever.")[12]

But the defender of common sense is not merely pointing out the persistence of our habitual pattern of knowledge attribution. This phenomenon would show nothing regarding the validity of the skeptical argument. What does have significance for the skeptical arguments is the fact that there are times when we find our everyday pattern of knowledge attribution compelling even while we are in the midst of sincere philosophical reflection. The fact is that when we think about skeptical arguments, we often find ourselves pulled in two directions. Often we vacillate between skepticism and common sense. So it is not just that we find that after we are confronted with skeptical arguments we continue, habitually, to attribute knowledge in our day to day lives. Rather we feel the intuitive pull of common sense even while we are considering the skeptical argument. This latter phenomenon can not be attributed merely to a kind of insensible habit.

Of course the fact that the skeptical conclusion is resisted by us does not show that the skeptic is wrong. The point is that contrary to what Stroud and others seem in part to be claiming, the appeal to our everyday knowledge attributions cannot be so easily dismissed. For these attributions can be seen as reflecting deep–seated intuitions about the concept of knowledge. Since our intuitions are a kind of data that theories of knowledge must explain, they present a formidable challenge to the skeptical position. The relation between our everyday attributions and skeptical arguments is more complex than the reply to the paradigm case argument presupposes.

There is, however, another strategy available to the skeptic that allows for an explanation of the intuitive appeal of our everyday knowledge attributions while still preserving the skeptical position that these attributions are always incorrect. As was illustrated in the spotter case, there is another way in which an attribution of knowledge could be appropriate without being true, a way that could explain the appeal of our everyday attributions even to someone who is aware of the skeptical alternatives. We noted that there is a sense in which it could still be appropriate to claim to know that a plane with characteristics xyz is an F even for someone who knows of the existence of G's (planes that are also xyz and indistinguishable from F's.) Even though strictly speaking such a person does not know that planes which are xyz are F's, there is still value in distinguishing between cases in which someone claims that a plane is an F on the basis of its being xyz and cases where the same claim is made on a weaker basis, e.g., a plane being merely xy. To say that in the former case that the spotter knows that it is an F whereas in the latter case he does not, serves to ·mark this important distinction even though strictly speaking, he does not know in either case that it is an *F*. If we were to speak strictly, we would lose this important distinction. We would have to say in every case that the spotter fails to know that he sees an *F*. By saying that he knows in the case where he observes that the plane is *xyz*, we enable ourselves to distinguish those cases that are important, even though we do so by saying something literally false. This is the sense in which it may be appropriate to say that one knows that he sees an *F* even for someone who knows of the existence of *G*'s.

The skeptic could then try to assimilate our position in everyday life to the situation of the spotter in this respect. Whereas the existence of alternatives like dreaming make it literally false that we ever know anything, nonetheless it is useful to distinguish between those cases in which we can eliminate all but the skeptical alternatives and those cases in which we can not even do this. Our ordinary use of the expression "to know" serves to mark this distinction and so is of considerable practical value. The former cases (where we can eliminate all but the skeptical alternatives) are, for all practical purposes, close enough to being instances of knowledge to make it appropriate to say that the person knows. In this way, our everyday attributions of knowledge could be considered appropriate even though strictly speaking they would always be false.[13] In the latter cases, where there are ordinary (non–skeptical) alternatives that we can not eliminate, it would not even be appropriate to say (whether correctly or not) that we know.

This pragmatic view of the role of our everyday knowledge attributions would appear to undermine their significance for skeptical arguments. It also has the advantage for the skeptic that it accounts for the intuitive appeal of our ordinary knowledge attributions, thereby avoiding the accusation that the skeptic ignores our everyday practices. Moreover, the skeptic can accuse his critic of failing to account for the appeal of skeptical arguments. For, if our everyday knowledge attributions demonstrate that the standards for knowledge are not as high as the skeptic claims, then why do skeptical arguments have any appeal to begin with? While it is true that we sometimes react to skepticism as if were preposterous, it is nonetheless true that we are often deeply troubled by the apparent threat posed by skeptical arguments. Just as the skeptic is required to explain why, if his view is correct, we find our everyday knowledge attributions so intuitively appealing, so the anti–skeptic is required to explain why, if the skeptic is wrong about those attributions, skeptical arguments appear so powerful.

Fortunately, the defender of common sense can avoid the pragmatic view and still explain the appeal of skeptical arguments by treating "knowledge" as having an indexical semantics. This would allow us to reinterpret the significance of our everyday pattern of attributing knowledge — the difference in the way we view the ordinary cases of inadequate evidence and those cases where the only uneliminated alternatives are the skeptical ones. Whereas the skeptic claims that this difference reflects the fact that under certain conditions, attributions of knowledge can be appropriate (although false), one could claim instead that it reflects the fact that in certain contexts, attributions of knowledge can be true, in less than ideal conditions. The appeal of skeptical arguments shows that there are other contexts in which similar knowledge attributions are false. By viewing "knowledge" as an indexical term, we can take our everyday attributions at face value while still giving skeptical arguments their due.[14] In everyday contexts of attribution, the standards for the truth of a knowledge attribution are such that we can truly ascribe knowledge to ourselves. This is not to deny that our standards can sometimes shift and become stricter. Skeptical arguments are effective precisely because they can have this effect on us. But the standards, once shifted, can also shift back. This explains our tendency, when confronted with skeptical arguments, to vacillate over whether we know.[15]

On this view, both our everyday claims that we know and the skeptic's claims that we fail to know can be correct. The fact that this is the case should be no more mysterious than the fact that the same surface can be truly described as flat or as not flat depending on the context in which the question is considered. There is still another alternative available to the anti-skeptic that is less charitable to the skeptic than the indexicality view.[16] This view draws an analogy between the skepticism controversy and the controversy that occurred in the first half of this century over whether physics had shown that no ordinary objects are solid. The issue concerned whether it is true that physics in discovering the atomic structure of matter, thereby demonstrating that ordinary objects contain "spaces", had shown that those objects are in fact not solid. The opposing view claimed that all that physics has shown was that, contrary to what we had believed, solid objects do contain "spaces". The resolution of this dispute hinges on subtle issues concerning the modal status of the claim that solid objects contain no spaces. The defender of the view that the solidity of ordinary objects is not threatened by physics would have to view it as a contingent claim that we had mistakenly believed to be true.

Analogously, the defender of common sense against the skeptic could hold that the same is true of the claim that our evidence in everyday cases where we attribute knowledge eliminates all the alternatives. On this view, what the skeptic has shown is not that there are no cases of knowledge but rather that our ordinary cases of knowledge are not based on as strong evidence as we thought they were. Just as physics has taught us that something we believed about solid objects is not true (that they contain no spaces), so skepticism has taught us that something we believed about our evidence in ordinary cases of knowledge is not true, viz., that it eliminates all the alternatives. The persisting appeal of skeptical arguments is to be explained analogously to the way that we might explain the persisting appeal (if there is any) of the claim that there are no solid objects — our lack of clarity over the modal status of the claim that knowledge requires evidence that eliminates all alternatives.

At this point it should be clear that the issues concerning the relationship between skepticism and everyday life are quite complex. While the defender of common sense cannot simply appeal to our everyday attributions as demonstrating that the skeptic is somehow confused about the meaning of "to know" or (equivalently) about the nature of the concept of knowledge, the skeptic can not simply accuse common sense of making a straightforward mistake. Both of these views fail to do justice to the other side.

Where does this leave us? It seems to me that what we are confronting is a burden of proof issue. Both sides of the dispute can find a way to view matters that favors their position. In this situation, it would seem that the side that has the burden of proof has to show that its way of construing matters is the correct way. One might think that this is not the case — that in fact the situation as I have described it favors the skeptic. For the fact that there are competing ways of construing the situation, one that entails skepticism and one that entails common sense, suggests that there is a standoff. And a standoff favors the skeptic. For if the skeptic has succeeded in arguing us into a standoff, then he has succeeded in undermining our right to continue to claim that we know. Until skepticism is refuted we cannot claim to know that we in fact know.

But why should the skeptic win a standoff? The situation seems to be that neither side can prove its case to the other. But this situation will favor whoever does not have the burden of proof. To say that the standoff favors the skeptic presupposes that we have the burden of proving to the skeptic that we know, — if we can not demonstrate to the skeptic that we know, then we can not claim to know. But, if the burden is on the skeptic to prove his case to us, then the fact that neither side can demonstrate its case to the other will favor common sense.

So what we need to consider is where the burden of proof lies. It seems to me that we (the non–skeptics) should view the burden of proof as lying with the skeptic. After all, the skeptic makes a claim that strikes us as intuitively outrageous. He claims that all of our everyday knowledge attributions are false — that all along when we have been saying things like, "I know what time it is." and "She knows the population of Los Angeles", we have been saying things that are literally false. Surely we should not accept such an incredible claim unless we are forced to. That is to say, it would not be rational to accept such a claim unless we were forced to. And as we have seen, we are not forced to. While the skeptic presents us with an account of our practices according to which our everyday attributions of knowledge are false, we do not have to accept that account, because we can provide a competing account according to which our knowledge attributions are true. The very fact that our account allows us to avoid the outrageous consequences of the skeptic's account constitutes a rational basis for accepting it. It does not seem to me to be a condition of our accepting an account that renders our knowledge attributions as true that we be able to show independently that the skeptic's account is incorrect. We should view the burden as being on the skeptic to demonstrate to us why we must accept his account. This would require the skeptic to show that our account is incorrect. And he does not achieve that simply by pointing out that there is an alternative account.

This is not to say that the skeptic should necessarily agree with us about where the burden of proof lies. On his view, we may be required to demonstrate to him that we do know. This would require us to show that the skeptic's account is incorrect. And, of course, we would not achieve that simply by pointing out that there is an alternative account. Where fundamental intuitions are involved, it may be impossible for either side to demonstrate the correctness of its position to the other. But that is no reason for either side to abandon its position. So for those of us who find our everyday knowledge attributions intuitively compelling, there is no reason that I can see to become skeptics.

Arizona State University

NOTES

1 There are different things that could be meant by "eliminate"here. On one view an alternative is elimi-nated just in case it is inconsistent with the evidence. A weaker view would require only that an eliminated alternative must be known to be false. Nothing I say will presuppose either of these interpretations.

2 Fred Dretske, "Epistemic Operators" Journal of Philosophy, (Dec.1970)

3 Barry Stroud, The Significance of Philosophical Skepticism (Oxford, 1974)

4 J. L. Austin, "Other Minds" Philosophical Papers, (Oxford, 1970)

5 Paul Edwards, "Bertrand Russell's Doubts About Induction", in Logic and Language, A. Flew (ed.), (Oxford,1955)

6 Stroud, op.cit., p. 57, also see John Passmore, "Arguments to Meaninglessness: Excluded Opposites and Paradigm Cases" in Philosophical Reasoning, (New York, London, 1961)

7 "The Legacy of Skepticism", Journal of Philosophy, 1972

8 Norman Malcolm, "Moore and Ordinary Language", in The Philosophy of G.E. Moore, ed. Paul A. Schilpp, (Evanston and Chicago, 1942)

9 The argument and the example that follow are from Passmore, op. cit.

10 I assume that, at least prior to an encounter with skeptical arguments, a belief to this effect would be reasonable.

11 See the end of Meditation I in Meditations on First Philosophy.

12 Enquiry Concerning Human Understanding, section 5

13 This view is discussed by Peter Unger in Philosophical Relativity, (Minneapolis, 1984)

14 I defend a view of this kind in "How to be a Fallibilist" in Philosophical Perspectives, 2, Epistemol-ogy, 1988, (J. Tomberlin,ed.); also see Fred Dretske, "The Pragmatic Dimension of Knowledge", Philo-sophical Studies, 40 (1981); G. C. Stine,"Skepticism, Relevant Alternatives, and Deductive Closure", Philosophical Studies, 29 (1976); and David Lewis, "Scorekeeping in a Language Game", Journal of Philosophical Logic, 8, (1979)

15 Since on this view, knowledge is an indexical, these points should really be expressed metalinguisti-cally, viz., the sentence"S knows p" can be true in one context and false in another. For stylistic reasons, I will not use the metalinguistic formulations. For a more precise account of how this works see "How to be a Fallibilist", ibid. Peter Unger, op. cit., argues that there is no basis for choosing between this view and, what I have called, the pragmatic view urged by the skeptic.

16 I am indebted here to conversations with Nathan Salmon

ERNEST SOSA

KNOWLEDGE IN CONTEXT, SKEPTICISM IN DOUBT:
THE VIRTUE OF OUR FACULTIES†

I KNOWLEDGE AND CONTEXT

Recent epistemology makes knowledge context–relative in many and sundry ways. According to Wittgenstein, ordinary knowledge flows on a riverbed of givens (assumptions, presumptions, background beliefs, things taken for granted), none of which amount to knowledge. Such convictions may be regarded as "beyond being *justified* or *unjustified*, as it were, as something *animal*" (*On Certainty*, par. 359). They provide me with "the *substratum* of all my enquiring and asserting (par. 162)." This substratum is not accepted on the basis of reasoning. "No: it is the inherited background against which I distinguish between true and false (par. 94)."

For J.L. Austin you know when you can rule out knowledgeably all relevant ways in which you might turn out wrong. And what is or is not relevant will vary with context; also, if you happen to consider any of the irrelevant ways in which you might turn out wrong, you must assume that it is not a way in which you do in fact turn out wrong, even if you cannot knowledgeably rule it out at the time.

> Knowing it's a 'real' goldfinch isn't in question in the ordinary case when I say I know it's a goldfinch; reasonable precautions only are taken. But when it *is* called in question, in *special* cases, then I make sure it's a real goldfinch in ways essentially similar to those in which I made sure it was a goldfinch...(J.L. Austin, "Other Minds", in his *Philosophical Papers* (Oxford: Oxford University Press, 1961), p.56). These special cases where doubts arise and require resolving, are contrasted with the normal cases which hold the field *unless* there is some special suggestion that deceit, etc., is involved, and deceit, moreover, of an intelligible kind in the circumstances, that is, of a kind that can be looked into because motive, etc., is specifically suggested. There is no suggestion that I *never* know what other people's emotions are, nor yet that in particular cases I might be wrong for no special reason or in no special way (*Ibid.*, p. 81).

Such forms of contextualism have gained many adherents in recent decades. Irrelevant alternatives (ways in which one might be wrong) are now widely thought not to require ruling out with the backing of reasons. Of those who take this approach, some view irrelevant alternatives as things one can rule out *with justification* despite the lack of any reasoned case against them. Gail Stine, for example, adopts this view — but provides no explanation of how one gets to be justified in ruling out such irrelevant alternatives, not all of which can be denied as *a priori* obviously impossible.[1]

If such "irrelevant" alternatives are contingent possibilities, how do we know them to be false? According to some, it's the community's approval that enables us legitimately to rule them out. With intellectual as with physical goods we are entitled to what "society let's us get away with," and there is nothing more to the entitlement than society's largesse. Thus Richard Rorty:

† Reprinted by permission of the author and the editors from *Philosophical Perspectives* 2, Epistemology (1988) 139–155.

M. D. Roth and G. Ross (eds.), Doubting, 171–182.
Kluwer Academic Publishers. Printed in the Netherlands.

> [We] can think of knowledge as a relation to propositions, and thus of justification as a relation between the propositions in question and other propositions from which the former may be inferred. Or we may think of both knowledge and justification as privileged relations to the objects those propositions are about. If we think in the first way, we will see no need to end the potentially infinite regress of propositions–brought–forward–in–defense–of–other–propositions. It would be foolish to keep conversation going on the subject once everyone, or the majority, or the wise, are satisfied, but of course we *can*. If we think of knowledge in the second way, we will want to get behind reasons to causes, beyond argument to compulsion from the object known, to a situation in which argument would be not just silly but impossible...To reach that point is to reach the foundations of knowledge.[2]
> Explaining rationality and epistemic authority by reference to what society lets us say rather than the latter by the former, is the essence of what I shall call "epistemological behaviorism", an attitude common to Dewey and Wittgenstein.[3]

Rorty is not alone. David Annis had indeed already published a defense of such con-textualism, including the following passage:

> Consider the case either where the objector–group does not require S to have reasons for his belief that h in order to be in a position to have knowledge and where they accept his claim. In either case there is no regress of reasons. If an appropriate objector–group, the members of which are critical truth seekers, have no real doubts in the specific issue–context, then the person's belief is justified. The belief has withstood the test of verifically motivated objectors.[4]

According to others, it is not the approval of society that enables us to deal legitimately with irrelevant alternatives. Instead, it is rather the objective improbability of impossi-bility of irrelevant alternatives that renders them negligible or rejectable, if considered at all, even in the absence of any inferential or argumentative backing.[5]

Barry Stroud agrees with the strategy of trying to "...find some way to avoid the requirement [e.g.] that we must know we are not dreaming if we are to know anything about the world around us."[6] For him a way must accordingly be found to deny that "...in order to know something, we must rule out a possibility which is known to be incompatible with our knowing it."[7] Such a strategy is in keeping with the attitude of those who would ignore or dismiss possible ways in which one might be wrong, even absent any knowledge precluding them. In particular, the approaches taken respectively by Wittgenstein, Austin, and Dretske, would permit the neglect or dismissal of various possible ways in which logically one might be wrong, without requiring that one's ne-glect or dismissal be attended by knowledge or even justification. But the approaches of that ilk taken up by Stroud, either explicitly or by implication (Austin's and, e.g., Dretske's), are all found wanting. For they ill accord with the requirements for simple knowledge commonly imposed in everyday life. Austin's work may suggest the con-trary, but that is due to confusion between the requirements for *saying* that one knows, and the requirements for *really* knowing. Reflection on simple and ordinary examples strongly promotes the conclusion that, in everyday life, one's truly attaining knowledge that *p* requires one not to leave open, not to neglect or dismiss without adequate justi-fication any possibilities known to one as incompatible with one's attaining such knowledge. Stroud does not resolve this inner tension in his book, and indeed one senses that for him the prospects are dim for any theory of knowledge that would escape skepticism about external surroundings. For such a theory would need to enable the avoidance of a very plausible requirement for the attainment of knowledge: namely, that one rule out appropriately all alternatives known by one as incompatible with one's knowledge.

Knowledge is more confidently placed in context, and skepticism hence in doubt, in recent works by Steward Cohen, who argues for the relativity of knowledge to epistemic communities.[8] "Being in a position to know" has been my own choice of expression for the requirement of *normal* cognitive equipment combined with the "social requirement" that one not lack or overlook generally known relevant information.[9] *Expert* knowledge would then require not only truth, belief, and justification, but also that one be in "in a position to know (from the *expert* point of view)," and similarly *mutatis mutandis* for a laymen's knowledge.

Where I have thus favored a *conceptual* relativity of knowledge attributions, however, Cohen favors instead a *contextual* relativity. My proposal has conceived of knowledge attributions as explicitly or implicitly relativized to an epistemic community (actual or possible) or its corresponding standards. For Cohen a knowledge attribution includes no such relativization within its *content* (explicitly or implicitly); instead of that, it includes an explicit or implicit indexical (or some kindred resource), such that the *context* of attribution determines the community or standards relative to which the attribution has truth value. I am not sure how significant this difference may turn out to be, especially in view of the emphasis placed by Cohen on the standards *intended* by the attributor. But it does seem a distinction abstractly worth making for the alternative form of relativization which it provides.[10]

Cohen compares two moves in recent epistemology: first, the relativization of knowledge attributions to an epistemic community or its correlative standards, by way of the requirement that the subject satisfy the (conceptually *or* contextually) specified standards; and, second, the appeal to relevance of alternatives in response to the skeptic. An important similarity is then found in the two moves. Just as the knowledge attributor can slide his cutoff point up or down the scale of required standards, depending on his intentions (or, perhaps, depending on other features of the context of attribution), so the relevance of an alternative can also vary depending on the context: on *how probable* that alternative is in the context.

These intriguing ideas are worth closer consideration. Knowledge is said to be twice contextual. It is said to be contextual first of all in respect of how sensitive one must be to the weight of evidence in one's possession for or against a belief that *p*. One's evidence may often provide premises for long and complex arguments that only a genius could see after long concentration. But it can be seen by examples that one's claim to know that *p*, a claim that of course could not survive a *blatant* inconsistency between one's evidence and the proposition believed (that *p*). Knowledge is thus said to be contextual in respect of how sensitive one must be to such evidence if it is to be effective in determining whether one knows that *p*. It is said to be contextual in what, for short, we shall call *the first way*. In addition, knowledge is said to be contextual in a second respect, in respect of which "alternatives" to the proposition that *p* count as *relevant*. Knowledge is thus said to be contextual in *the second way*.

Even given a fixed subject *S*, proposition that *p*, and time of utterance *t*, the attribution of knowledge that *p* to *S* at t will vary in truth value from context of attribution to context of attribution. So it is argued; but what in particular is it about the context that determines the truth value of such an utterance? Presumably it is believed that something in the context determines standards that entail whether or not one is appropriately sensitive to the weight of one's evidence. And presumably it is believed further that something in the context determines how probable an alternative must be (and relative to what factors) in order to be a relevant alternative to *P*: "relevant" in that it must be ruled out (independently of *P*) in order that one may know.

Finally, appealing to the irrelevance of skeptical alternatives is now said to be more than just an *ad hoc* response to the skeptic, since there are independent reasons why the truth of an attribution of knowledge is context–dependent. Context *also* determines, with regard to one's evidence, just how sensitive one must be to the bearing of what it contains for or against belief that *p*, in order to qualify for knowledge that *p*. (Only the most gifted could be perfectly sensitive, but knowledge is fortunately to be found as well in those less favorably endowed, depending on the context.)

Suppose now that knowledge is indeed contextual in *the first way*. This does reduce the *ad hoc* character of the claim that skeptical alternatives (evil demon, brain in a vat, etc.) are irrelevant in *ordinary* contexts and need not there be ruled out; that they need not there be ruled out for no one to know about one's surroundings, neighbors, past, etc.; though in a *philosophical* context those alternatives may yet remain relevant alternatives that do need to be ruled out. Such a claim is now less *ad hoc*, for in responding to the skeptic that knowledge is contextual in this *second* way, one is not now introducing relativity to context on the sole basis that it permits such a response to the skeptic. Relativity to context now has a further basis, one said to supplement the response to the skeptic: namely, the basis provided by the fact that knowledge is contextual in the *first* way.

That much seems quite plausible. Nevertheless, it bears mention that responding to the skeptic with the charge that skeptical alternatives are *irrelevant* may be *ad hoc* in more ways than one. For example, it may be thought to introduce contextuality of knowledge attributions in that response, and it may also be thought *ad hoc* to introduce an unexplained notion of relevance, *whether its application is contextual or not.* In order to ward off this second objection one would seek some explanatory account of relevance, no matter how partial and tentative, as is sometimes done with the suggestion that relevance of alternatives is a matter of their probability. But the explanatory account may yet in its turn leave a residue of the *ad hoc*. And that is I fear what happens with the account of relevance in terms of probability. For we are not told how to pick a reference class for the pertinent probability assignments. Suppose the skeptic presents a possibility *A* as a skeptical alternative to some proposition *P* that we believe, urging that for all we have to go on *A* might be the case rather than *P*. Now it is replied by the relevant alternatives response that *A* is *irrelevant* and needn't be ruled out, because it is too little probable relative to some factors. But too little probable relative to which factors? Or, at least, relative to factors of what sort, along what dimension?

An alternative may be said to be "relevant" relative to *S*, *P*, and *t*, in a certain context, by *definition*, iff it needs to be ruled out in that context for *S* to know *P* at *t*. Then the *concept* of relevance is relatively clear (though not transparent), but what we still need is some minimal understanding of what accounts for the relevance or irrelevance of hypotheses. If on the other hand we are told that a certain alternative is negligible (and need not be ruled out). *because* it is irrelevant, then we need some more substantial account of relevance. And if we appeal to probability at this point, then we need some minimal explication of the *sort* of reference class relative to which the relevant probabilities are to be determined.

The reference–class problem might be viewed as adequately defused by remarks like the following: "that at least there is some standard according to which the alternative that S sees a barn replica is relevant if, e.g., there are many barn replicas in the immediate area, and not relevant if there is just one barn replica in Antarctica." But that is open to doubt. For one thing, let $d =$ the information that a reliable source reports the existence of numerous barn replicas in the area. It seems plausible that S's possessing d makes it relevant (relative to the normal standards) that S sees a barn replica. But S's possessing d is compatible with there being just one barn replica in Antarctica. So it looks like the alternative that S sees a barn replica might after all be relevant even when there is just one barn replica in Antarctica. So we are back to square one with the reference–class problem. Even leaving aside the sort of problem of misinformation posed by d, moreover, it is clear *neither* that the barn–replica alternative is relevant (and must be ruled out specifically) when there are many barn replicas in the vicinity, *nor* that it is *not* relevant when there is only one barn replica in Antarctica. Suppose there are many barn replicas in the vicinity but it is part of your background knowledge that you are on the one working farm in the area. Is it then incumbent on you to come up with some specific way of ruling out the replicas alternative? Is that any more incumbent on you here than it would be when out for any ordinary drive in an ordinary countryside? As for the Antarctica case, suppose your access to the barn–like items is via TV and the transmission is alternating between the facsimile at the South Pole and a real barn. Then the existence of that facsimile would seem relevant, as it would if one knew oneself to be *either* before the facsimile at the Pole *or* before a real barn in some other wintry setting, the decision having been made by the toss of a coin. Here again the existence of that South Pole facsimile becomes relevant after all.

Suppose it is replied that these unusual contexts are not to be allowed. Take again the standard that rules the facsimile alternative irrelevant when there is only the lone South Pole facsimile. That standard, we may be told, is supposed to operate in ordinary circumstances. In that case the "standard" in question would seem not to go very deep. It would seem to depend on some deeper principle which together with the contingencies of our ordinary circumstances determines which alternatives are "relevant" and require specific ruling out. And concerning such deeper principles of "relevance" we would still be about as much in the dark as before.

So far we have considered two ways in which knowledge is said to be contextual, and a defense of the relevant alternatives response to the skeptic, a defense based on that dual contextuality of knowledge.[11]

II INTELLECTUAL VIRTUE

For further varieties of epistemic relativity, we turn next to our intellectual virtues, which might be viewed as ways of coping that are cognitively effective, a view however that would invite the question of just what might make a way of coping "cognitively effective." According to my dictionary, 'cognition' means the act or process of knowing...*also*: a product of this act." As for 'effective', it is said to mean "producing or capable of producing a result," with an emphasis on "...the actual production of or the power to produce an effect <effective thinking>." Putting all this together, it would appear that what makes a way of coping "cognitively effective" is its power to produce effects relating to or involving knowledge. But now look where that leaves us:

> What is "knowledge"? True belief that is at least justified. And what makes a true belief "justified"? That it have its source in intellectual virtue. And what is "intellectual virtue"? A skill or ability that enables one to cope in a cognitively effective way. And what makes a way of coping "cognitively effective"? That it have the power to produce effects relating to or involving knowledge.

Thus we start with knowledge and return to it in a narrow circle.

For a more illuminating account we need to escape the circle. One way to do so understands intellectual virtue not as a "cognitively effective" skill or ability, but rather as one that is truth conducive (or as the ground of such a disposition). This might elicit objections as follows.

"*First*, accepting such an account of intellectual virtue drives us back upon the question about the nature of justified belief — back, in short, to the foundationalist-coherentist dispute. For if we understand "intellectual virtues" as truth–conducive dispositions or the like, then we will want to ask how we know which dispositions are virtues, how we can know which are truth–conducive. But since, by wide agreement, our best access to truth is justified belief, this strategy leaves us with the primary notion of justification as that of justified beliefs; justified dispositions would remain secondary.

"*Second*, it is doubtful that the ordinary notion of justification can be captured by the idea of a reliable generating mechanism for beliefs. Just as there is presumably some way in which one has a say in the matter whether or not one is morally virtuous, so there should be also a way in which one has some say in the matter whether or not one is intellectually virtuous. But it is nonsense to attribute such "say" to someone regarding his reliable belief–generating mechanisms or their exercise."

Taking the two objections in reverse order, I admit first a narrow Aristotelian conception of virtue according to which a virtue is a certain disposition to make appropriate deliberate choices. And this is of course much narrower than any simple notion of a truth–conducive belief–generating mechanism. For whether or not belief is *ever* a product of deliberate choice, it surely is not *always* a product of such choice. Thus perceptual and introspective beliefs are often acquired willy–nilly. And yet even where deliberate choice is thus absent, some mechanism may yet generate one's belief. For example, it may be one's faculty of sight operating in good light that generates one's belief in the whiteness and roundness of a facing snowball. Is possession of such a faculty a "virtue"? Not in the narrow Aristotelian sense, of course, since it is no disposition to make deliberate choices. But there is a broader sense of "virtue", still Greek, in which anything with a function — natural or artificial — does have virtues. The eye does, after all, have its virtues, and so does a knife.[12]   And if we include grasping the truth about one's environment among the proper ends of a human being, then the faculty of sight would seem in a broad sense a virtue in human beings; and if grasping the truth is an intellectual matter then that virtue is also in a straightforward sense an intellectual virtue.

As for the first objection, it charged truth–conduciveness accounts of intellectual virtues with driving us "...back upon the question about the nature of justified be–lief...[and leaving] us with the primary notion of justification as that of justified beliefs." But when and how are we supposed to be thus driven back? When we try to determine the credentials of a candidate intellectual virtue, and when we ask more generally "...how we know which dispositions are virtues, how we know which are truth–con–ducive." The problem is supposed to be that to determine whether a disposition is truth–conducive we must determine whether the beliefs that manifest that disposition are mostly true. And, since "...our best access to truth is justified belief," in order to de–termine whether a belief is true we must determine whether it is a justified belief.

If that is the problem, it is apparently captured by the following argument.

A1. To determine that a disposition of one's own is truth–conducive one must de–termine that beliefs manifesting it are mostly true. (Assumption)

A2. To determine that a belief of one's own is true one must determine that it is a justified belief. (Assumption)

A3. To determine that a disposition of one's own is truth–conducive one must determine that beliefs manifesting it are mostly justified. (From 1, 2)

Even if conclusion *A3* is true, that does not immediately refute that account of justified belief as belief that manifest a truth–conducive intellectual virtue — not even if we take such an "account" to be a philosophical analysis. For how we must determine something is an epistemological question, whereas our philosophical analysis of justified belief would be something semantical or ontological, and there is no immediately ob–vious connection between the two. In particular, there is no manifest absurdity in the notion that *X* be analyzable (semantically or ontologically) as *Y* despite the fact that to determine whether *Y* applies in a certain situation you need to determine (first) whether *X* applies. Thus to be a cube may be analyzable as being a six–sided closed surface with sides all square but in a certain situation it may be easier to see that there is a cube before you than to determine that there is a closed solid that both: has six sides, and has sides all square. You may be able to see right away that it's a cube you are holding as you turn it in your hands, though you lack the time and patience to count the sides keeping track of which you have already counted; and hence you may *conclude* that it has six sides from your analysis of cubicity and from your perceptual knowledge that it is a cube.

For *some* sort of philosophical analysis or semantical analysis, however, it may perhaps turn out that if *X* has *Y* as its analysis of that sort, then it cannot in consistency turn out that to determine whether *Y* applies you must determine whether X applies. That there is such a connection between meaning and justification is of course a familiar theme of recent decades.

But the argument before us still does not rule out the account of justified belief as belief issuing from an intellectual virtue, even if this account is understood as a meaning analysis requiring the mentioned connection between meaning and justification. My objection now pertains not to what the conclusion would show even if we accepted it, but pertains rather to the truth of the second premise. Consider the following ar–gument.

B1. It rains.
B2. I (occurently) believe that it rains.
B3. It rains and I believe that it rains. (From B1, B2)
B4. If it rains and I believe that it rains, then my belief that it rains is true.
(Obvious)
B5. My belief that it rains is true. (From B3, B4)

It seems plain I can determine [B5] — that my belief that it rains is true — by means of this argument (where square brackets will function as nominalizers, so that [It rains] = that it rains). Since [B4] is obvious, since [B5] is deduced by modus ponens from [B3] and [B4], and since [B3] is deduced by conjunction from [B1] and [B2], it all goes back to the premises [B1] and [B2]. But I may just start from the following two bits of knowledge: (a) my knowledge of the fact [B1], which I have as a result (in part) of being outside and looking up and putting out my bare arms; and (b) my knowledge of the fact [B2], which I have by simple introspection. So it appears I can after all determine that a belief of my own is true without considering whether it is justified, and without considering in the course of that determination whether any particular belief of mine is or is not justified.

Accordingly, if it is true that "our best access to truth is justified belief," that is so only in a certain sense. For our best access to truth may be justified belief simply in the sense that in our search for truth we are better served by harboring beliefs that are justified rather than those that are unjustified. But it is not entailed that in order to determine that a belief of one's own is true, one must first *determine* it to be justified. Hence the sense in which indeed "our best access to truth is justified belief" is not after all one that dooms as viciously circular our account of what it is for belief to be justified: namely, our account that for a belief to be justified is for it to manifest a truthconducive faculty or intellectual virtue.

But what, again, is such a faculty or intellectual virtue? The primary meaning attributed to 'faculty' by my dictionary is "ability, power." Faculties are abilities to do certain sorts of things in certain sorts of circumstances, but how more specifically should we conceive of them? One possibility is to *define* each faculty as the ability to attain certain accomplishments. But of course an accomplishment attainable in given circumstances may be unattainable in other circumstances. Abilities correlate with accomplishments only relative to circumstances. There is for example our ability to tell (directly) the color and shape of a surface, so long as it is facing, "middle–sized", not too far, unscreened, and in enough light, and so long as one looks at it while sober, and so on. And similarly for other perceptual faculties. Compare also our ability to tell simple enough necessary truths, at least once having attained an age of reason and discernment; and our ability to retain simple enough beliefs in which we have sufficient interest. In each case our remarkably extensive species–wide accomplishments of a certain sort are explained by appeal to a corresponding ability, to a cognitive faculty; or at least we are thus provided the beginning of an explanation, an explanation sketch. But in none of these cases is there really any pretense to infallibility. All we're in a position to require is a good success ratio. Common sense is simply in no position to specify substantive circumstances in which the exercise of sight is bound to be infallible.

Of course that is not to rule out underlying abilities which are in fact infallible in speci–fiable circumstances; it is only to imply that if there are such abilities common sense is at this point unable to formulate them.

What powers or abilities do then enable a subject to achieve knowledge or at least epistemic justification? They are presumably powers or abilities to distinguish the true from the false in a certain subject field, to attain truth and avoid error in the field. One's power or ability must presumably make one such that, normally at least, in one's ordinary habitat, or at least in one's ordinary circumstances when making such judg–ments, one *would* believe what is true and *not* believe what is false, concerning matters in that field.

A faculty is, again, an ability. An ability to do *what*? To *know*? That would be circular. To believe with justification? Still circular. To believe correctly propositions of a certain sort: perceptual ones, say, or mathematical ones? That can't be enough since *every* correct belief of a proposition of the sort involved will manifest *that* ability, i.e., that *mere* ability. To tell the true from the false with a good success ratio? A similar problem arises here, since one might just through a fantastic coincidence *actually* get mostly true beliefs in a certain field, and this would manifest *that* ability, i.e., that *mere* ability.

Indeed it is probably better to think of a faculty *not* as an ability but rather as a virtue or a *competence*. One has a faculty only if there is a field *F* and there is a set of circumstances *C* such that one *would* distinguish the true from the false in *F* in *C*. But of course whenever one happens to have a belief *B*, that belief will manifest *many* such competences, for many field/circumstance pairs *F/C* will apply. How then can one rule out its turning out that just *any* true belief of one's own is automatically justified? To my mind the key is the requirement that the field *F* and the circumstances *C* must be accessible within one's epistemic perspective.[13] (Note that this requires considering servomechanic and animal so–called "knowledge" a lesser grade of knowledge, or perhaps viewing the attribution of "knowledge" to such beings as metaphorical, unless we are willing to admit them as beings endowed with their own epistemic perspectives.)

III A SOCIAL COMPONENT OF KNOWLEDGE

In earlier discussion above we took note of a certain contextual relativity in our attribu–tions of knowledge. It seems that linguistic and/or epistemic communities conceive of knowledge and, more specifically, justification, by reference to community correlated standards. Why is that so? We can now suggest an answer as follows.

All kinds of justification are a matter of the cognitive or intellectual virtue of the subject. We care about justification because it indicates a state of the subject that is important and of interest to his community. And that holds good for all sorts of epis–temic justification, from mere "animal" justification to its more sophisticated, reflective counterpart. In all cases we have a state of of interest and importance to an information–sharing species. What sort of state? Presumably, the state of being a dependable source of information over a certain field in certain circumstances. In order for this to be obtainable and to be of later use, however, the sort of field *F* and the sort of circumstances *C* must be projectible, and must have some minimal objective likelihood of being repeated in the careers of normal members of the epistemic

180 • ERNEST SOSA

community. For it is through our cognizance of such relevant F and C that we grasp the relevant faculties whose possession by us and others makes us dependable informants and cognizers.

Recall now that we are in no position to require *infallibility* for possession of a cognitive faculty or virtue. All we are in a position to require is a good success ratio. But how good a success ratio might we agree on in order to have a commonly shared standard for knowledge? A concept of knowledge requiring a perfect success ratio would not be very discriminating, and would not help us to keep track of the facts regarding epistemic dependability, our own and others'. Nor would that concept of perfect knowledge aid intercommunication of such facts amongst members of the group. It seems a reasonable conjecture that a concept of knowledge tied to virtues of approximately normal attainment would be most useful to the group. But of course what is normal in one group may be far from it in another.

The foregoing has displayed a contextual relativity of knowledge attributions to an epistemic community; and we have sketched a sort of explanation for the implied social component of knowledge. Our explanation sketch may be summed up most briefly as follows: We are social animals. One's linguistic and conceptual repertoire is heavily influenced by one's society. The society will tend to adopt concepts useful to it. A concept of epistemic justification that measures the pertinent virtues or faculties of the subject relative to the normal for the community will be useful to the community. The community will hence tend to adopt such a concept.[14]

IV SUMMARY

Concerning the relevant alternatives response to the skeptic, I have emphasized the large element of adhocness that remains even if I grant that knowledge is contextual in ways other than the way required by that response. This problem bears emphasis, I believe, because the elements of adhocness that remain beyond the question of contextuality seem to me much more serious problems of adhocness for the relevant alternatives view. Speaking for myself, at least, the main problem has been not the contextuality of relevant alternatives, but rather the obscurity of the concept (except when *defined* as alternatives that need to be ruled out), and the implausibility or adhocness or incompleteness of any explication so far offered (except possibly for Nozick's, which of course we cannot stop for at this point). The foregoing has also discussed whether knowledge is indeed contextual in the way proposed or whether the reasons adduced for considering it to be contextual cannot be taken into account with comparable overall success by the view that knowledge can vary in *content* from context to context. We next turned to intellectual virtue: the concept, its realization in humans, and its relation thereby to cognitive justification and human knowledge. Finally we considered the relativity of knowledge to epistemic communities, and offered a tentative sketch of an explanation for such relativity, whether viewed as contextual or contentual, in terms of a certain conception of intellectual virtue.[15]

Brown University

NOTES

1 "Skepticism, Relevant Alternatives, and Deductive Closure," *Philosophical Studies* 29 (1976) 249–61.
2 *Philosophy and the Mirror of Nature* (Princeton, NJ: Princeton University Press, 1979), p.159.
3 *Ibid.*, p.174.
4 "A Contextualist Theory of Epistemic Justification", *American Philosophical Quarterly* 15 (1978) 213–19. Also in Paul Moser (ed.), *Empirical Knowledge* (Totowa, NJ: Rowan & Littlefield, 1986).
5 Compare here Marshall Swain's "Revisions of 'Knowledge, Causality, and Justification'," in M. Swain and G. Pappas (eds.), *Essays on Knowledge and Justification* (Ithaca, NY: Cornell University Press, 1978). Also Fred Dretske's "The Pragmatic Dimension of Knowledge," *Philosophical Studies* 40 (1981) 363–78. For a review of the appeal to relevant alternatives, see also Palle Yourgrau's "Knowledge and Relevant Alternatives," *Synthese* 55 (1983) 175–190. We shall return to this appeal below.
6 *The Significance of Philosophical Scepticism* (Oxford: Oxford University Press, 1984).
7 *Ibid.*
8 "Knowledge and Context," *The Journal of Philosophy* 83 (1986) 574–584.
9 "How Do You Know?" *American Philosophical Quarterly* , XI, 2(April, 1974): 113–122; also in G. Pappas and M. Swain, eds. *Essays on Knowledge and Justification* (Ithaca, NY.: Cornell, 1978). esp. sec. II. According to that paper, the relativity of knowledge to an "epistemic community" is brought out most prominently by the requirement that inquirers have at least *normal* cognitive equipment (e.g., normal perceptual apparatus, where that is relevant)" (117). The reference to perception is explicitly *illustrative*, since the same sorts of consideration apply to other cognitive equipment–e.g., reason and memory –as Cohen has well made explicit.
10 Attributions of knowledge are said to vary in truth value depending on standards picked out in the context, even once we fix the subject proposition, and time. And what is it in the context that picks out the pertinent standards? This is left open, but it is mostly the intentions of the speaker that are cited and discussed. Suppose accordingly that it is really the intentions of the speaker, explicit or implicit, that determine at least sometimes the standards relative to which we must assess an attribution of knowledge. In that case, it is less than obvious that such attributions remain uniform in *content* from context to context, while nevertheless shifting in truth value. For it seems at least equally plausible to suppose that the content itself expressed by the speaker shifts from context to context, though it may do so in a regular and explicable way. Cohen's only reason against this is that it would make the concept of knowledge too shifty. But surely the contextual view for its part owes us the resources for disagreeing, arguing, and perhaps eventually agreeing about knowledge, and especially for doing so across significantly different contexts. What Cohen provides here involves the possibility of fusing one's own context with that of one's interlocutor by intending the other's standards. That being so, at present it is hard to see any very weighty reason for opting between the following two possibilities:

(1) Statements of the form "At *t*, *S* knows that *p*" vary in truth value from context to context, *without varying in content*, though it is always possible to fuse one's own context with that of another (whose own context is otherwise as different as could be), by simply intending the other's intendedstandards.

(2) Statements of the form "At *t*, *S* knows that *p*" vary in truth value from context *because they vary in content*, though it is always possible to adopt the content of another (whose situation may be quite different from one's own) by adopting a content correlated with the other's intended standards.

With option 2 we do have ambiguity of knowledge attributions. But that is quite compatible with a shared and uniformly univocal term 'knowledge', one standing for a generic sort or knowledge that spans a variety of species keyed to a corresponding variety of standards. Option 1 imposes no such ambiguity but still yields just as serious an obstacle to the meeting or clashing of minds by use of a common language. What is needed for minds to meet or clash according to the *context–intention* view is for one of the interlocutors to accommodate the other by adopting the other's standards, at least for the sake of of communication, discussion, or argument. But such explicit or implicit intending of standards can of course be equally well accommodated by the *content* view of the matter. For the *content* view, the intention of certain standards by the speaker would of course have a different bearing. Instead of determining a factor in the *context* of knowledge attributions, it would determine their content, or it would do so at least in part.

At present I see no sufficient reason for favoring either over the other of the two possible options before us.

[11] Skepticism is discussed further in my "The Skeptic's Appeal," forthcoming in *Theory of Knowledge: the State of the Art*, ed. by Marjorie Clay and Keith Lehrer.

[12] See Plato's *Republic* , Bk. I, 352.

[13] The theme of this paragraph is developed in section B4 of my "Beyond Skepticism, to the Best of Our Knowledge," *Mind* (1988).

[14] For more on the concept of epistemic justification and doubt that it can serve all the purposes which epistemology has given it, see my "Methodology and Apt Belief," forthcoming in *Synthese* (1988), a special issue on epistemology, edited by Steven Luper–Foy.

[15] This paper has benefited from the work and comments of John Greco, Stewart Cohen, and Stuart Rosenbaum, to all of whom go my appreciative thanks.

FRED I. DRETSKE

THE EPISTEMOLOGY OF BELIEF[†]

ABSTRACT. By examining the general conditions in which a structure could come to represent another state of affairs, it is argued that beliefs, a special class of representations, have their contents limited by the sort of information the system in which they occur can pick up and process. If a system—measuring instrument, animal or human being—cannot process information to the effect that something is Q, it cannot represent something as Q. From this it follows (for simple, ostensively acquired concepts at least) that if an organism that has the information–processing capabilities for knowing that something is Q.

Believing is easy, knowing is hard. Believing is easy because it is just a way of saying something in the internal language of thought. No trick at all once you have the language. Talk is cheap. The real trick is getting things right or, even harder, securing some *guarantee* that one has got things right. This is knowledge and this is hard.

Such is the conventional contrast between knowledge and belief. Underlying this contrast is the idea that knowledge, unlike belief, requires special endowments. It takes something *more* to know because knowledge requires, besides mere belief, some reliable coordination of internal belief with external reality, and this coordination, being an extremely delicate matter, requires the exercise of special skills. If, though, one takes no thought for whether they are true or false, reliable or unreliable, then believing itself is mere child's play—a form of mental doodling. Witness the fact that the ignorant believe as effortlessly as the learned—indeed it seems, with far *less* effort. According to the conventional wisdom, then, the problem, at least for epistemology (but perhaps not for the philosophy of mind), is not one of understanding how we manage to *have* beliefs, but one of understanding the sources and extent of their reliability.

This picture, I submit, dominates philosophical thinking about knowledge and belief. It is what keeps epistemology durable, if not exactly flourishing, industry. We can thank, or blame, Descartes for installing it as the centerpiece of philosophical debate about cognitive predicament. I think, though, that this picture distorts the epistemological task by grossly underestimating the cognitive demands of simple belief. Knowing is hard, but believing is no piece of cake either. In fact, or so I wish to argue, believing something requires precisely the same skills involved in knowing. Anyone who believes something *thereby* exhibits the cognitive resources for knowing. There is, as we shall see, a gap between belief and knowledge, but it is not one that provides any comfort to the philosophical skeptic. If I may, for dramatic effect, overstate my case somewhat, if you can't know it, you can't believe it either.

I. REPRESENTATION AND MISREPRESENTATION

Let me organize my defense of this thesis by discussing representations in general, and, in particular, the representational powers we typically assign to measuring instruments. I shall return to beliefs, a special kind of representation, in a moment.

Consider, first, a fairly crude altimeter, a device used for measuring altitude or height above sea level. It operates basically as a pressure gauge, responding to changes in air pressure as altitude varies. As the instrument ascends, the diminished air pressure

[†] Reprinted by permission of the author and the editors from *Synthese* 55 (1983), pp. 3–19.

M. D. Roth and G. Ross (eds.), Doubting, 183–194.
© 1990 *Kluwer Academic Publishers. Printed in the Netherlands.*

allows a diaphragm, to which a pointer is attached, to expand. The expanding diaphragm moves the pointer across a scale calibrated in feet above sea level.

We can, of course, fool this instrument. We can place it in a chamber from which air has been pumped. The partial vacuum in the chamber will cause the instrument to register, say 35,000 feet when it is, in fact, only a few hundred feet above sea level. The instrument, it seems, misrepresents its own altitude. It "says" it is at 35,000 feet when it is not. If altimeters had beliefs, this surely, would qualify as a false belief.

But have we really fooled the instrument? This depends on what we take it to be representing or saying. I said above that the instrument misrepresented its own altitude. But why suppose it is *altitude* that the instrument represents or, in this case, misrepresents? *We*, after all, are the ones who printed "feet above sea level" on the face of the instrument and called it an "altimeter". *We* are the ones making it "say" this. The instrument itself (if I may take its part for the moment) might object to this way of describing its representational efforts. It is, it might say, a device for representing pressure, and its representation of the pressure, even in a vacuum chamber, is perfectly accurate. It is making no mistake. No one is fooling it. It believes the pressure is 5 pounds per square inch and the pressure *is* 5 pounds per square inch. If anyone is making a mistake (the instrument concludes) it is we who assigned it a representational capacity beyond its actual powers. One could as well bring "Gross National Product in Dollars" on its face and then complain that it misrepresented the state of the national economy.

It seems more reasonable to say that it is the instrument's job to register the pressure and that it is *our* job (the job of those who use the instrument) to see to it that a change in pressure is reliably correlated with altitude (or whatever other quantity we any use the instrument to measure)—to see to it, in other words, that the instrument is used in conditions where alterations in pressure carry information about the magnitudes we use the instrument to measure. If this is so, then the instrument is discharging its representational responsibilities in a perfectly satisfactory way. We aren't fooling the instrument; at most we are fooling ourselves.

Is the speedometer on a car misrepresenting the vehicle's speed if we jack up the car, engage the gears and run the engine? The drive shaft and wheels will turn, and the speedometer will, accordingly, register (say) 30 m.p.h. The car, or course, is stationary. Something is amiss, and if we have to place blame, the speedometer is the likely culprit. It is saying something false. Or is it? How do we decide what the speedometer is saying? Perhaps the speedometer is representing the only thing it is capable of representing, saying the only thing it knows how to say, namely, that the wheels are turning at a certain rate. The mistake, if a mistake is being made here at all, occurs in us, in what we *infer* must be true if what the speedometer says is true.

What, then, does a measuring instrument actually represent? Or, to put it more suggestively, what does the instrument really believe? Does the altimeter have altitude beliefs or merely pressure beliefs? Does the speedometer have vehicle–speed beliefs or merely wheel–rotation beliefs? Until we are in a position to answer these questions we cannot say *how*, or even *whether*, it is possible to "fool" the instrument. We cannot say whether, in situations like those described above, the instruments are misrepresenting anything, whether it is even possible to make them "believe" something false.

It is time to stop describing instruments in such inappropriate ways. Although I think it sensible to speak of instruments representing the quantities they are designed to measure, I do not, of course, think they *say* or *believe* things. We cannot, literally, *fool* an instrument. They don't make *mistakes*. I allowed myself to speak this way in order to reveal my overall strategy. So before moving on to a discussion of creatures to which it does make sense to attribute genuine cognitive states (like belief and knowledge), let me describe an intermediate case. Some may find it more realistic, and hence more convincing, than examples involving speedometers and altimeters.

A frog in its natural habitat will flick with its tongue at small, moving dark spots. The neural mechanisms responsible for this response have, for fairly obvious reasons, been called "bug detectors". In the frog's natural habitat, all (or most) small, moving dark spots are bugs, a staple item in the frog's diet. Psychologists (with pre-sumably better intentions than I had with the altimeter) have remove frogs from their natural habitat, projected small, moving dark *shadows* on a surface in front of the frog, and observed the creature's response. Not unexpectedly, the frog "zaps" the moving shadow.

What shall we say about this situation? Has the frog mistakenly identified the shadow as a bug? Is the frog misrepresenting its surroundings? Does the frog have a false belief, a belief to the effect that *this* (small moving dark spot) is a bug? Or shall we say that the frog (assuming for the moment that it *has* beliefs) does not have "bug" beliefs at all? Instead what it has are "small–moving–dark–spot" beliefs? Since the frog *usually* operates in circumstances (swamps, ponds, etc.) where small moving dark spots *are* bugs, natural selection has favored the development of a zapping reflex to whatever the frog perceives as a small dark spot. If we take this latter view, then although psychologists can starve a frog in this artificial environment, they can't fool it. The frog never makes a mistake because it never represents, or *takes* things to be other than they are. It represents the shadow *as* a small, moving dark spot, and this repre-sentation is perfectly correct. The frog goes hungry in this situation, not because it mistakenly sees dark spots as edible bugs, but because what it correctly sees as moving spots are not, in fact, edible bugs.

If we adopt this latter strategy in describing what the frog believes, then it be-comes very hard, if not impossible, to fool the animal. If the frog has beliefs at all, it approaches infallibility in these beliefs. And this infallibility is achieved in the same way it was (or could be) achieved with the altimeter and speedometer — *viz.*, by tailoring the content of belief (representation) to *whatever* properties of the stimulus trigger the rel-evant response. If we are willing to be less ambitious in this way about what we de-scribe the frog as believing, we can be correspondingly more ambitious in what we describe the frog as knowing.

But there is, surely, a truth of the matter. The frog either believes there is a bug in front of it or it doesn't. It isn't up to *us* to determine the content of the frog's beliefs in the way it may be up to us to say what an altimeter represents.[1] Before we create, by fiat, infallible frogs we had better look to those factors, whatever they are, that de-termine the content of a creature's beliefs. Only when we are clear about this can we proceed to questions about the reliability of these beliefs — to traditional epistemological questions. This, then, brings us to the question of how belief content is determined—to the question of learning.

II. LEARNING

Dolphins have an extremely sensitive sonar system that allows them to detect, and in some cases identify, objects in the water fifty feet away. They have, for example , been taught to identify cylinders at this distance. The identification occurs whether the cylinders in question are short and squat or long and narrow, solid or hollow, metal or wood, red, yellow or blue. Regardless of the object's value along these other dimensions, the dolphin can distinguish the cylinders from the non–cylinders.

If a child of four achieved this level of discrimination, especially if its distinctive response to cylinders was the utterance of the *word* "cylinder", we would doubtless credit it (perhaps prematurely) with the concept of a cylinder and, hence, with the capacity for holding beliefs to the effect that something was a cylinder. There are those, however, who prefer to be less liberal with dolphins or, indeed, with any creature lacking a natural language. Since I do not think this issue is particularly relevant to the point I wish to make with this example, I will continue to speak of the dolphin as believing of the cylinders it picks out that they are cylinders.

Suppose, now, that when the dolphin is being taught to identify cylinders, the trainer uses *only* cylinders made of plastic. All the non–cylinders, the cubes, spheres, pyramids, etc., are made of some other material – wood, say. Since the dolphin reaches criterion (as the psychologists say) on plastic objects, responding positively to all and only plastic objects, can we say that the dolphin has learned to recognize *plastic objects*, that it now, when responding positively to X, has a belief to the effect that X is plastic? Does the dolphin now have some crude notion of *plasticity*?

Of course not. The reason we are prepared to credit the dolphin with the concept of a cylinder (and hence, with beliefs to the effect that *this* is a cylinder and *that* is not) is not *just* because it distinguishes cylinders from other shaped objects (for it does, with equal success, distinguish plastic from non–plastic objects) but because of our conviction that it was the *cylindricality* of these objects to which the creature was responding (and not their *plasticity*). The animal's sensitive sonar is capable (or so we believe) of picking up information about the shape of distant objects, and it was trained to respond in some distinctive way to *this* piece of information. There is no reason to think it was picking up, or responding to, information about the chemical constitution of these objects — to the fact that they were plastic. We could test this, of course. Merely place a wooden cylinder in the pool and observe the animal's response. A positive response would indicate that it was the cylindricality, not the plasticity, to which the animal has developed a sensitivity. It was, as I prefer to put it (more about this later), information about the object's shape, not information about its chemical structure, that guided the animal's discriminatory behavior during learning. It is this fact that lies behind our unwillingness to credit the dolphin with the concept *plastic* and our willingness (or greater willingness) to credit it with the concept of cylindricality, even though (given the restricted learning conditions) it became as successful in distinguishing plastic from non–plastic objects as it did in distinguishing cylinders from non–cylinders. Even if (cosmic coincidence) all and only cylinders were made of plastic so that our trained dolphins could infallibly detect plastic objects (or detect them as infallibly as they detected cylinders), this would not have the slightest tendency to make us say that they had acquired the concept of plastic or could now have beliefs about the plasticity of objects. The level of sophistication to which we are willing to rise in describing the belief content of the dolphin is no *higher* than the kind of information about objects to which we believe it sensitive. The dolphin can have "cylinder" beliefs but not "plastic" beliefs because, as far as we know anyway, it has a sensory system that allows it to pick up information about the shape, but not the chemical structure, of objects at a distance.

It is important to understand what is happening when we make these judgements, what kinds of considerations shape our decisions about what level of conceptual sophistication to assign an animal (whether it be a frog, a dolphin, or a human child). The decision about what concept to assign a creature, and hence the decision about what sorts of beliefs we may attribute to it is guided by our assessment of the sort of information the animal utilizes during learning to articulate, develop and refine its discriminatory and classificatory repertoire. If we are talking about an instrument, something that doesn't learn, then its representational powers, what it represents things as being, is a function of the information to which the instrument is sensitive. Since the altimeters are not sensitive to information about the gross national product, no matter what I happen to write on the face of the instrument, an altimeter cannot represent or misrepresent the gross national product. But since the instrument is sensitive to information about pressure and, some would say, in some situations at least, to information about altitude, it is capable of both representing and misrepresenting these magnitudes.

This principle (the principle, namely, that the representational powers of a system are limited by its informational pick–up and processing capabilities) underlies many of our judgements about the conditions in which someone can and cannot learn. Why can't you teach a normally endowed child her colors in the dark? Because information about the *color* of the objects is not therein make available for shaping the child's discriminatory and identificatory responses. Even if the child succeeds in picking out all the blue objects (in virtue of the fact, say, that all and only the blue ones are furry), she will not, by this procedure, learn the concept *blue*. She will not *believe* of the next furry blue object she finds that it is blue. The most she will believe is that it is furry. Even if we taught her to say "blue" every time she encountered a blue object in the dark, we would not, thereby, have given the child a *color* concept. We would merely have given her an eccentric way of expressing her concept of furryness.

The moral of the story is this: to learn what an *X* is, to acquire the capacity to represent something *as an X* (believe it to be an *X*), it is not enough to be shown *X*'s and non–*X*'s and to successfully distinguish between them. Unless the information that the *X*'s *are X* is made available to the learner (or instrument), and it is *this* information that is *used* to discriminate and classify, the system will not be representing anything as an *X*. Even if some concept is acquired, and even if this concept *happens* to be coextensive with that of *X* (thus allowing the subject to successfully distinguish the *X*'s from the non–*X*'s), the concept acquired will not be that of an *X*. The subject will not be able to believe of *X*'s that they are *X*. For the concept acquired during learning is determined by the kind of information to which the learner becomes sensitive, and if no information about the *X–ness* of objects is made available during learning (despite the availability of *X*'s), no such concept can develop.

I have begun to talk more and more about information, so let me pause a moment to explain what I mean by this way of talking. I mean nothing very technical or abstract. In fact, I mean pretty much what (I think) we all mean in talking of some event, signal or structure carrying (or embodying) information about another state of affairs. A message (i.e., some event, stimulus or signal) carries information about X to the extent to which one could learn (come to know) something about X from the message. And, in particular, the message carries the information that X is a dingbat, say, if and only if one could learn (come to know) that X *was* a dingbat from the message. This does not mean that one *must* learn the X is a dingbat from a message that carries this information. One may not, after all, know the code. The message may be in Chinese. When I say that one *could* learn that X was a dingbat from the message I mean, simply, that the message has whatever reliable connection with dingbats is required to enable a suitably equipped but otherwise ignorant receiver, to learn from it that X is a dingbat.[2]

I think it is this sense of the term "information" that is operative in a wide variety of ordinary contexts, and it is for this reason that I feel safe in saying that I am using the term as it is commonly used. We say that a pamphlet contains information about how to probate a will because we believe that someone could learn something about how to probate a will by consulting the pamphlet. Information booths are called information booths because the clerks working there either know, or can quickly find out, about matters of interest to the average patron. One can *come to know* by making inquiries at such places. Similarly, when scientists tell us that the pupil of the eye is a source of information about another person's feelings and attitudes, that a thunder signature contains information about the lightning channel that produced it, that the dance of a honey bee contains information as to the whereabouts of the nectar, or that the light from a star contains information about the chemical composition of that body, the scientists are clearly referring to information as something capable of yielding knowledge. And *what* information a signal carries is identified with what one could learn from it. This, I submit, is the very same sense of "information" in which we speak of books, newspapers and authorities as containing, or having, information about a particular topic.

This is not intended to be a philosophically illuminating analysis of information. At least no epistemologist would find it of any special interest. Rather than telling us anything important about knowledge, it uses the concept of knowledge to tell us something about information. But this merely indicates that information is a member of that constellation of epistemic terms that can be interdefined in fairly trivial ways.[3] This though, is unimportant for my present purposes. What is important is the epistemic character of the concept of information and its connection with knowledge. For if this connection is as I have expressed it, then the upshot of my argument so far can be expressed as follows: what *concept* a person acquires during learning, and hence what beliefs he is henceforth capable of holding, is restricted to the kind of information he is capable of picking up and processing. But, in virtue of the connection between information and knowledge, we now see that this is equivalent to saying that the beliefs a person is capable of holding as a result of learning are restricted to the sorts of things that that person (given his information processing resources) is capable of knowing.

The argument is rather simple so let me recapitulate. To learn what a dingbat is, and hence to acquire the conceptual resources necessary for believing that something is a dingbat, one must not only be exposed to dingbats, but to the *information* that they are dingbats. Not only must this information be made available, it must be *picked up* and *used* by the learner to guide his discriminatory and identificatory responses if he is to be credited with the relevant concept. Since this is so, the learner cannot come to believe something is a dingbat unless he has the cognitive (i.e., information processing) resources for knowing something is a dingbat.[4] Only someone who *can* know (or could know—the learner may have lost his capacity for picking up the required information) that this is a dingbat can believe it to be a dingbat.

It should be emphasized that this is a thesis about the relationship between what is believed and what is, or can be, known, not a thesis about what, if anything, can be known or believed. The thesis is, in other words, quite independent of one's views about what or anything, dolphins, frogs, or people can know (or believe) to be the case. I have not said that frogs can (in their natural habitat) know when a bug flies by. Nor have I denied this (e.g., by saying that they could only know that there was a small dark spot moving by). And for purposes of this paper, I don't particularly care what a dolphin can know, or believe, about a cylinder immersed in its pool fifty feet away. I have my own ideas about these matters, but they are not relevant to the thesis I am presently defending. What I am arguing is that whatever view you take about what a creature can believe, you thereby commit yourself to a certain level of sophistication in the creature's capacity for picking up and processing information; if it can't pick up information about bugs, then it cannot hold beliefs about bugs (just as the altimeter that can't pick up information about the gross national product cannot represent the quantity). So if the frog does believe that there is a bug in front of it, then, it is the sort of creature capable of picking up, processing, and responding to information that there are bugs in front of it. It is this conditional thesis for which I have been arguing. When we combine this conditional with what has been said about information, we reach the conclusion that anything the frog believes is the sort of thing it is (was[5]) capable of knowing.

III. LANGUAGE AND BELIEF

With appropriate modifications, the same can be said about our own conceptual situation: the conditions that must obtain for the acquisition of simple concepts are the same conditions that make possible the *knowledge* that these concepts apply. In our own case, though, the possibilities for confusion about this matter are much greater. For we not only believe things, but we say things, and we sometimes say things we don't believe. That is, unlike the altimeter, frog and dolphin, we have *dual* representational systems and they are not always synchronized. It is therefore, easy enough to attribute to the one representational resources of the other — thus blurring the intimate relationship between belief and (the capacity for) knowledge.

Let me illustrate the problem in a simple-minded way. We will turn to a more interesting case in a moment. If I teach a child her colors and have her say "circular" whenever a blue object is presented, what will this show (assuming the child learns her lesson) about what the child believes or about what kinds of mistakes she is capable of making? Clearly, when the child looks at a blue cube and says "circular " she will be misrepresenting, linguistically misrepresenting, the properties of what she is talking about.[6] This, though isn't very interesting. It certainly isn't a symptom of any *cognitive* or *conceptual* misrepresentation. The child *says*, "This is circular" but she *believes* it is blue. Through an unfortunate piece of education, she does not use the correct word to express what she believes. What she means by "circular" is *blue*. What we have done with this child is similar to what we earlier suggested doing with the altimeter: printing "gross national product in dollars" on its face. In doing this we can make the instrument "say" that the gross national product is increasing (or, more likely, misrepresenting). We have merely given it a way of "saying" things it does not, indeed *cannot*, believe. And so it is with the child. The child's (linguistic) responses have a meaning that exceeds her (internal) powers of representation.

Something like this happens when children first learn to talk. The toddler who delights his mother by saying "Mommy" whenever she appears disappoints her when he says the *same* thing to his Aunt Mildred. When the child is corrected ("No, Jimmy, *I'm* Mommy, that's Aunt Mildred"), what is this a correction of? A false belief? But does Jimmy really believe that this other woman is his mother? Probably not. It seems more likely that the child simply believes Aunt Mildred is a woman, or a person, precisely what he believed of his mother when he called her "Mommy", and that he is using the word "Mommy" to express this less determinate notion. Correction here is not the weeding–out of false beliefs, but the development of more discriminating set of concepts and the correlative ability to express these more determinate concepts in linguistically appropriate ways.

Since for the most of us, the acquisition of our natural language goes hand–in–hand with the acquisition of the concepts to which this language gives expression, the ability to represent something verbally is developed in close association with the ability to represent something in the internal language of thought. Some philosophers prefer to say that these two abilities are not really distinct. That may or may not be so. I don't wish to take sides on this issue here. What is important for present purposes is the understanding that during learning our linguistic responses to stimuli have a meaning independent of whatever representational capacity the learner himself may have developed. Since this is so, the verbal mistakes that occur in classifying and identifying objects need not reflect a mismatch between the world and the respondent's inner representation of the world. This only mismatch may be between the world and the respondent's external (verbal) representation of the world.

This point is, I think, easy enough to accept when we are dealing with obvious examples like those described above. There are, however, profound implications for epistemology. Perhaps the best way to exhibit these implications is by another, less obvious, example.

Hilary Putnam has described a place, Twin Earth, in which there are two substances H_2O and XYZ, chemically different but both having the superficial properties of water.[7] By "superficial" I mean the properties we (Earthlings) rely on (outside the laboratory) to identify something as water: taste, smell, feel, capacity for quenching thirst, etc. Some of the lakes and rivers on Twin Earth are filled with H_2O, others are filled with XYZ (here I depart from Putnam's example). It rains H_2O in some parts of the country, XYZ in other parts. Twin Earthlings called both substances "water" since the liquids are (apart from elaborate chemical analysis, an analysis which they haven't yet perfected) indistinguishable.

Consider, now, a Twin Earthling (call him Tommy) being taught what water (or what the Twin Earthlings call "water") is on a part of Twin Earth in which there is both H_2O and XYZ. As it turns out, quite by accident, Tommy learns what water is by being exposed only to H_2O (it only happened to rain H_2O on the days he was outside, no XYZ ever happened to come out of his faucets at home, etc.). After learning what water is to the complete satisfaction of his parents, friends, and teachers, Tommy is miraculously transported to Earth where there is to be found *only* H_2O (XYZ cannot exist in the earth's atmosphere). Since there are no other difference between Twin Earth and Earth, Tommy blends in without trouble. Everything Tommy says about water (using the word "water") will correspond to what his Earthling friends say and believe about water (also using the word "water").

As you may have expected, the question, once again, is not what Tommy says, but what Tommy believes. Tommy, I submit, does not have the same concept as his earthling associates. Therefore, what Tommy *believes* when he says "This is water" is not what his Earthling friends believe when they say "This is water". What Tommy means by "water" is *either* H_2O *or* XYZ. This, of course, is how we (knowing all the facts of the case) would describe it, not Tommy. If asked, Tommy will say that he means *water* by "water" and he surely does mean this. But the point is that more things qualify as water for Tommy than for the Earthlings. If we should reverse the scenario and imagine an Earthling miraculously transported back to Twin Earth with Tommy, Tommy's belief of a puddle of XYZ that it was water (i.e. an instance of the concept he expresses with the word "water") would be true while his Earthling friend's belief would be false. Since this is so, they must be expressing different beliefs with the words "This is water".

Putnam takes this result as showing that meanings are not in the head. Tommy and his Earthling friends can be identical in all relevant respects; yet, they have different concepts, different beliefs, different meanings. My intuitions (about this example) agree with Putnam's, but the moral I want to draw from this story goes beyond, and in some ways contrary to[8], the moral Putnam draws from it. I think this example neatly illus-trates a principle expressed earlier, the principle, namely, that a system's representational capabilities are determined by its information handling resources. Or, to give a more restricted (not to mention cruder) expression of the principle, an individual can believe (and, in this sense represent) only what it has the information handling resources of knowing.

The difference between Tommy and his Earthling friends is to be found in the difference in the kind of information to which they were made responsive during the learning period when they acquired their respective concepts. Given the situation on Twin Earth, Tommy, though repeatedly exposed to H_2O (and never XYZ) never ex-posed to the *information* that the liquid he saw was H_2O. All he ever received, pro-cessed, and responded to was a piece of disjunctive information, the information, namely, that the liquid was *either* H_2O or XYZ. This is all the information Tommy got because, on Twin Earth, this is all that one could learn about the character of the liquid from ordinary sensory transactions with it. Since it was this piece of information that was used to shape Tommy's discriminatory and identificatory responses, *this* is the concept he acquired and *this* is the kind of belief he subsequently has about the liquids he describes as water.

Since XYZ cannot be found on earth (and this is no mere accident by a law of nature), Earthlings acquire a different concept because their discriminatory responses are shaped by a different piece of information: the information that the liquid is H_2O.[9] Since the lawful regularities prevailing in these two worlds are different, the kind of information to be found in physically indistinguishable signals is also different. Hence, the concepts developed in response to these physically indistinguishable signals are also different. This is why Tommy and his Earthling friends, although they *say* the same thing, although they were exposed to exactly *the same* liquids during learning (viz., H_2O), and although they developed their ideas in exactly the same way, have quite different beliefs about the liquid they see and describe.

The important point to notice about this example is how the concepts one develops, and hence, the sorts of beliefs one is thereby capable of holding, neatly reflect one's epistemological strengths and limitations. There is, as it were, an epistemological pre–established harmony. We (Earthlings) have a more determinate concept than Tommy, a concept that if he possessed it on Twin Earth, he would be incapable of knowing (by ordinary sensory means) whether it ever, in fact, applied to the liquid running out of his faucet. Given the widespread prevalence of XYZ, Tommy would make frequent mistakes. He would, in other words, have a real epistemological problem *if he had our concept of water*.[10] But he doesn't have our concept of water and, given that he learns in roughly the way we learn what water is, there is no way for him to get it. The concept he does acquire (a concept the extension of which I am expressing as "either H_2O or XYZ") is a concept that he is cognitively prepared to apply to his surroundings. He *can know* that the liquid coming out of his faucet is what *he* means by "water".

To put the point in its most general form: if someone lives in a place where it is impossible to distinguish A–type things from B–type things, hence impossible to know that this particular thing is an A (or a B), then it is likewise impossible, under ordinary learning conditions, to develop a way of representing something as an A (or as a B). The most that will be developed is a way of representing something as A–or–B. And in this case we needn't worry about *mis*taking an A for a B (or *vice* versa) since we can never *take* anything as an A or as a B.

IV. CONCLUSIONS AND QUALIFICATIONS

I have been arguing for a perfectly general thesis and I am afraid that it cannot be defended in its most general form. There are exceptions that I have suppressed for expository purposes. So, before trying to state the upshot of this argument, let me briefly describe the qualification that is essential.

My thesis is meant to apply to simple or primitive concepts (representational structures), concepts that are not themselves composed of simpler conceptual elements (representational structures). In arguing that the possession of the concept X requires the possessor to have the resources for picking up, processing and responding to the information that something is X, the argument works only for simple, ostensively learned concepts. I do not wish to argue that we cannot *manufacture* out of a corpus of simple concepts, and the appropriate syntactical machinery, complex concepts for the application of which we lack the requisite information processing capabilities. That is, there are obviously beliefs involving complex concepts. (e.g., the belief that X is a miracle, that Y is a random sequence, or that there are no unicorns) that we lack the cognitive resources for knowing to be true. And it certainly seems that with linguistically sophisticated creatures such as ourselves, these complex concepts will be commonplace. But there can be no complex concepts without simple concepts, and it is to these latter primitive representational structures that the thesis of this paper is meant to apply.

The upshot, then, of this paper is that no matter how we choose to describe the conceptual sophistication of an agent, whether it be a frog, a dolphin, a computer or a human being, we are committed to that agent's having the cognitive resources for *knowing* how things stand with respect to the situation being represented — at least with regard to the agent's primitive concepts. This, I think, completely turns the tables on the skeptic. The traditional arguments that we cannot know what we purport to know because we lack the appropriate cognitive endowments, because the information on which we rely is always equivocal or ambiguous in some fundamental respect, is an argument which, if successful in relation to simple concepts, shows, not that we cannot know what we believe, but that we do not believe what we think we believe.[11] If the information we receive about X's is always too impoverished to specify an X as an X, then, admittedly, we have an epistemological problem about how we can ever know that there are X's. But we also have a problem about how we can ever believe that there are X's.

University of Wisconsin–Madison

NOTES

[1] Some philosophers, I know would deny this. I make the assumption, nonetheless, because (1) I believe it, and (2) it makes my argument that much more difficult and, therefore, that much more significant if correct.

[2] I assume here some kind of reliability account of knowledge or justification.

[3] Although they can be interdefined in fairly trivial ways, they needn't be. In *Knowledge and the Flow of Information* (Bradford/MIT, 1981), I give an independent (of knowledge) analysis of information thus making the concept available for the analysis of knowledge.

[4] Obviously one can believe something is a dingbat when it is not a dingbat—hence, believe things that cannot be known (because not the case). I hope it is clear from the wording in the text that I am not denying this obvious fact. The thesis is, rather, that if one has the concept of a dingbat (hence, capable of holding beliefs to the effect that something is a dingbat) then that something is a dingbat is the *sort* of thing one can know.

[5] The temporal qualifier should always be understood. A creature may have acquired a concept *at a time* when he possessed a fully functional sensory system, one capable of picking up and processing information of a certain kind. Once the concept is acquired, though, the creature may have *lost* the information processing capacity (for example, have gone blind), hence, losing the capacity to know what he can still believe.

[6] I earlier (*circa* second draft) thought that what the child *said* when it said "This is circular" was false. I thought this because it seemed to me that what the child was saying (with these words) was that the object was circular. Jon Barwise convinced me that this was not so. What the child is saying when it uses these words is that the object is blue. Hence, what the child is saying is true.

7 "The Meaning of 'Meaning'" in *Language, Mind and Knowledge*, Minnesota Studies in the Philosophy of Science, 7, Minneapolis: University of Minnesota Press (1975); reprinted in *Mind, Language and Reality* — *Philosophical Papers*, Vol. 2, Cambridge, England (1975).

8 "Contrary to" because the conclusion I draw from this example (as embellished) is that the extension of a concept (like "water") is *not* determined by causal factors. The same things (for example, H_2O) *caused* Tommy to use the word 'water' during learning as caused his Earthling associates to use this word during learning. What determines the extension (and, hence, the concept) are not facts about causal relations, but facts about the kind of information available during learning. Information and causation are related but only indirectly.

9 I here assume that it is a law on Earth (but not, of course, on Twin Earth) that anything exhibiting the normal sensible properties of water *is* H_2O. If this is too strong, then I assume that on Earth (but not, of course, on Twin Earth) one can come to know that something is H_2O by looking, tasting, smelling, etc. It is this fact that supports my claim (in the text) that on Earth (but not on Twin Earth) the ordinary sensory stimulation associated with our perception of water carries the information that it *is* water (that is, H_2O).

10 As I understand the Causal Theory (of natural kind terms) Tommy would (according to this theory) have our concept of water since, by hypothesis, H_2O figured *causally* (just as it did for Earthlings) in his acquisition of this concept. This, I think, shows what is wrong with a causal theory.

11 If the reader thinks it *could not* show this (*viz.*, that we do not believe what we think we believe), so much the worse for the view that we could entertain (simple) beliefs that we could not know to be true.

THOMAS TYMOCZKO

BRAINS DON'T LIE: THEY DON'T EVEN MAKE MANY MISTAKES*

The major task of epistemology, according to many, is to show how knowledge is possible at all, or, in other words, to solve the riddle of skepticism. Several years ago, in his book *Reason, Truth and History*, Hilary Putnam purported to solve that problem by proving that we are not brains in a vat. I am now inclined to believe that Putnam's argument is, in all essential respects, correct.[1]

Nevertheless, Putnam's own presentation is difficult to follow, in part because strands of the argument occur in several places throughout the book, often intertwined with other weighty philosophical issues. My aim in this essay is to present a version of the anti—skeptical argument that stands on its own, disentangled, as far as possible, from those other issues. Since the purpose is not Putnam exegesis, I'll not attempt to correlate my remarks with Putnam's text but instead make the argument in my own terms (although a careful reader will find almost everything I say here also in Putnam rearranged and with a different emphasis).

From my perspective, the key insight is that brains in a vat don't make many false statements — not any more than we do. Such brains are not making false statements about our environment, they're making true statements about theirs. If this point be granted, the skeptic's problem by and large disappears. This essay begins by explaining why this is so, and why it's plausible to assume that the brains speak and think about their environment. Next we'll consider the objection that this way of looking at things just shifts the skeptic's problem about the external world to a skeptical problem about language (no small shift, if the truth be known). I'll argue that the attempt to retreat to linguistic skepticism can not be carried through, in part by showing that the analogous move in a case of mathematical skepticism is transparently incoherent. Finally, I'll try to assuage psychological doubts about this anti—skeptical maneuver. Can we really distinguish our world from the phenomenally indistinguishable world of brains in a vat? Yes, if we use a logical argument and not an empirical discovery. Can we rely on an argument for which a brain in a vat could give a formally equivalent analogue? Yes, this is an essential feature of any transcendental anti—skeptical argument.

I. WHY IT MATTERS WHAT BRAINS TALK ABOUT

Suppose we traveled to a far–off planet and came across a colony of vat brains of the usual sort.[2] These brains are all connected to a giant computer that stimulates and monitors their nerve firings is such a way that the brains' inner experiences just happen to match our own. A minor addendum is that the apparatus just happens to be hooked up to loud speakers so we can hear the brains 'talking' to one another and miraculously, it sounds just like English. Well, perhaps not so miraculously because the neural events in their brains are exactly like the neural events in human brains.

"Hi, Fred. How's it going?"

"Not too bad, Stan. Say, that's a nice lilac bush you have there".

M. D. Roth and G. Ross (eds.), Doubting, 195–213.
© 1990 *Kluwer Academic Publishers. Printed in the Netherlands.*

Has Fred said something false? Should we assume, better *can* we assume that 'lilac bush', as he uses it, refers to certain plants on earth and that Fred says, falsely, that Stan has one of those plants? This rather incredible assumption has two parts: that Fred refers to earth objects which he has no inkling of, let alone contact with, and second, that Fred avoids referring to features of his immediate environment.

For consider the reasonable alternative, that the vat brains refer to aspects of their environment by their language, that 'lilac bush', for example, refers to a subprogram of the computer. After all, the vat brains *interact* with these various subprograms: the computer feeds the brains experiences partly in response to signals it receives from the brains. Not only are individual parts of the program responsible for individual brain experiences, but the brains cause the program to run as it does. There is presumably something like a generic 'lilac bush' program (at least a pattern common to many subprograms) with variant subprograms scattered throughout the computer's store and one of these variants causes Fred to experience 'lilac bush' appearances as he experiences 'approaching Stan's house. But Fred activates this subprogram by generating the experiences of approaching Stan's house (he could have chosen to 'go to Susan's house' instead). For the computer must react to Fred's intentions and his cerebral activity. Similarly, Stan causes the 'lilac bush' program to run a certain way, to produce more 'blossom' experiences among the brains, by 'pruning it' every year. If he did not initiate certain events by desiring, as he puts it, 'to prune the bush', by 'reaching for the pruning shears', by 'going to the bush', then the lilac program would have to 'keep the dead blossoms on the bush' and, since the story supposes fidelity to our experience, Stan would not experience as many new blossoms on his bush. And so on.

Traditionally, the skeptic makes the first assumption that the brains' thought and talk is about the real world of lilac bushes et al., and not about their own environment. Consequently, the skeptic regards the brains as making lots of false statements and having lots of false beliefs (eg., 'it rained yesterday'). And if we were in the position that the brains are in, then we would be making lots of false statements and having lots of false beliefs. On the other hand, if we assume the brains' thought and talk is about their environment, then the traditional skeptic is in deep trouble. The brains in the vat are not deceived, they don't go around making lots of false statements, so they don't present the kind of general, all purpose epistemic contrast to the ordinary case that the skeptic presupposes. When a brain in a vat says 'Here is a lilac bush' with the same kind of evidence we have for the analogous utterance, the brain says something true, just as we do.

The skeptic usually argues as follows: "Your evidence for the lilac bush is not sufficient to show that you know there's a lilac bush there. For a brain in the vat could have exactly the same evidence for its assertion 'here is a lilac bush'. Yet the brain is wrong, its utterance is false. Consequently no experience can establish that there really is a lilac bush."

But it's the skeptic who's wrong if the brains do talk about their environment. For then the brain in his story does not utter a falsehood and, consequently, the skeptic has not presented the contrast he intended.[3] We don't have a case of two subjects with the same experiences making the same statement, in one case the statement being true and in the other, the statement being false. We have two subjects making two different statements both of which are true. There remains nothing in the brains in a vat scenario which threatens anyone's knowledge.

To appreciate the significance of this point, recall Moore's argument against skepticism: "Here's one hand. Here's another. Therefore, there are at least two external objects." The received opinion is that Moore begs the question against the skeptic. How does Moore know there is a hand there? A brain in a vat, in analogous circumstances, would be deceived and so would not know — or so the received story goes. But Moore begs a question only if we assume that the brains don't refer to their environment. If, when a brain says 'here's a hand', it refers to a certain kind of subprogram by 'hand', then it doesn't make the same statement Moore made in a circumstance where that statement is false. It makes a different statement which is true.

The skeptic reads the brains in a vat scenario as establishing a certain contrast: same evidence, different environments, same statement, different truth values for statement. That contrast fuels the skeptic's arguments; without it, he doesn't even have a reply to Moore. I'm arguing that the required contrast presupposes that the brains don't talk about their environment. For if they do, the situation becomes: same evidence, different environments, *different statements,same truth value for statements.* The brains in a vat no longer function as an example of deception.

Indeed, we can go further for the same kind of story can be told about the brains' assertion 'We're not brains in a vat'. It's true! When they say 'brains' they refer to a generic subprogram connected to their experiences in a certain way, and similarly for 'vat'. And they're absolutely right; those organic, pulsing brains are not subprograms of any sort.[4] Here we have the nub of Putnam's anti–skeptical argument that the assertion 'we are brains in a vat' is self–refuting. If it's not made by brains in a vat it's obviously false. But if it's made by brains in a vat, it's also false since 'brains' would no longer refer to brains. In other words, if we can raise the question 'are we brains in a vat?' we're not and we know we're not because we know the brains can't raise that question.[5]

More generally, we know we're not brains in a vat because we refer to many things the brains don't refer to. We refer to lilac bushes, rabbits, etc.[6] We know 'lilac bush' refers to lilac bushes and we know — always assuming that vat–language refers to vat environment — that when the brains use the word 'lilac bush', they refer to a species of subprograms. Since they don't refer to what we do by the same words, we are not they. To those who can hear, our use of language endlessly repeats the message: we're not brains in a vat.

We'll return to this part of the argument again (I know it seems suspicious). The first half of the argument — if the brains talk about their environment, then an essential contrast that the skeptic presupposed vanishes — is more straightforward; the second part — if the brains talk about their environment, then we can know that we're not brains in a vat— is less so. For now I will be content if you agree to the relevance of the claim that the brains in a vat talk about their vat environment. If that claim is true, then we have to look at skepticism in a new light.

In order for skepticism about the external world to succeed, the skeptic must explain how vat language or vat thought does connect to the non–vat world (thereby justifying the claim that the brains are deceived). Failing that, a skeptic might try to adopt a fall back position. He could concede that empirical knowledge and knowledge of language are bound tightly together, but try to recast the skeptical problem on the metalevel as a problem about language. How do we know which language we speak?

In the next section of the paper I'll argue that the first alternative requires an utterly implausible, magical theory of reference. Indeed, the 'theory' amounts to no more than the claim that the vat language just is connected to the non–vat world, that 'lilac bush' is intrinsically connected to lilac bushes in whatever context the word occurs. Elsewhere ("In Defense of Putnam's Brains") I offered the much weaker argument that if a direct theory of reference, or a causal theory, were true, then the vat language could not connect to the non–vat world. Here I will argue that no reasonable theory of language can make the connection. After that, we'll consider whether the skeptic can reformulate his problem on the metalevel.

II. WHAT *DO* BRAINS TALK ABOUT?

If Quine has taught us anything about language, it is that translating or interpreting another's language is no trivial task. There is a plethora of *possibilities* (even if, contra Quine, there are correct and incorrect choices). Now among the wealth of interpretations of the language of brains in a vat, there is a consistent, coherent interpretation which takes their words to be about those features of the computer that determine their experiences. There is also, of course, the homophonic translation which the skeptic assumes is correct (their word 'lilac bush' means the same and refers to the same as our word 'lilac bush). My basic point is that once the former interpretation of vat language as about the vat environment is broached as a candidate, it is hard to see how it can be avoided. What theoretical mechanism could achieve out–of–vat reference for the brains? Any plausible mechanism is more naturally explained as achieving in–vat reference. Take images for example.

Could the skeptic argue that Fred refers to terrestrial lilac bushes because Fred has an image in his mind that's an image of terrestrial lilac bushes? But what makes it an *image of* those bushes — because it's more similar to terrestrial lilac bushes than to anything else? No, I don't think anyone would accept that nowadays. Berkeley's point that a mental image is more similar to other mental images than it is to anything non–mental is still valid. In the absence of a natural match between image and object, any connection between them must involve a projection scheme of some sort. But the mental lilac–image is just as reasonably construed as an image of a computer subprogram as it is an image of an organic plant — it's simply a matter of which projection scheme is used. The decisive point is how speakers of a language use those images in their linguistic practices. For example, suppose that the image Fred associates with the word 'Stan' is exactly like the image we associate with 'Hilary Putnam'. Then when Fred says 'Hi, Stan', is he referring to Putnam and not to Stan with whom he communicates? Surely he is not. It does no good to point to the interaction as a relevant factor for the issue was whether reference could be achieved by the content of the internal image alone

Observe that I did not deny that the meanings of words were images (although they are not), nor that images play a role in fixing reference (although they don't). My claims are just that images don't fix reference themselves (because there's no intrinsic similarity relation) and any story we tell about how images play a role in fixing reference will apply in the case of the brains to connect their images to features of the vat world. Analogous claims hold with respect to any more plausible theory of meaning.

Not too many people are tempted by the thought that images in the mind secure reference. Maybe concepts (or properties or universals) secure reference. Associated with the word 'lilac bush', for example, is a concept, or a conjunction of simple concepts, or perhaps some more complex construction built from simple concepts. I can agree to this much. But the skeptic must go on to argue that we and the brains associate the same concepts with our words and in the case of 'lilac bush' this concept is true of terrestrial lilac bushes but not of anything in the vat world.

Let's look at a simple example. Fred says 'Susan is the only philosopher I actually *talk to* (although I communicate by Bitnet with several others)'. I claim that the concept the brain associates with the words 'talk to' is that concept which is true of any of a class of brain–brain interactions mediated by the computer in a certain way ('sound experiences' are involved as opposed to 'reading/writing experiences'). So what Fred says is true, if he's not lying. The skeptic, on the other hand, claims that the brain associates with 'talk to' a concept that is true of human interactions involving mouths and ears so what Fred says is false since the brains have no mouths or ears. My argument is that the skeptic can never give a coherent account of why this should be so.

Obviously this is true if concept acquisition requires interaction with an environment, either the short term interaction of individuals with their environment or the long term evolution of a species in an environment. If rational beings acquire those concepts appropriate to their environments, then we and the brains acquire different concepts. Yet if the skeptic retreats from interaction with the environment and insists that concepts are acquired on the basis of pure mental experience, then he has to explain how the resulting concepts can be applicable to any non–mental realm, let alone explaining how they apply to one realm and not another. It does no good for the skeptic to insist that there are certain basic concepts — distance, space, mass, liquid — because each of these has a perfectly good vat analogue. For instance, the computer programs determining spatial object experiences will realize an abstract metric space satisfying all the metric relations spatial objects do, or else the brains' experience of 'going from place to place' won't be the same as ours. The question for the skeptic is why one set of basic concepts (involving real spatial distance, for example) is acquired by the brains and not the other, more appropriate set (involving vat metric).[7]

Nor would it help the skeptic to raise the old distinction between natural properties and artificial ones — for the distinction between natural and artificial is relative to one's point of view. Of course the concept of water is more natural than the concept 'water in my immediate environment, acid elsewhere', but *that* distinction among concepts carries over to the vat concepts. Vat concepts may be artificial from our point of view but not from the perspective of brains in a vat.[8]

Finally, if it were possible to draw the referential connections that the skeptic needs, the result would be an embarrassment of skeptical riches. There would be a new skeptical problem: the inverted brains–in–a–vat. Imagine that there really are lilac bushes which we really see, smell and prune. Unfortunately, whenever we say or think things like 'Nice lilac bush', we say or think falsehoods. Why? Because we've accidentally acquired vat concepts true only of subprograms, not of real lilac bushes. It's just the mirror image of the situation the skeptic presupposes — we and the brains do have the same concepts, but we have theirs! So we really don't know anything, not because the stuff isn't out there but because we think the wrong thoughts. (How ironic: so near and yet so far.) Now how do we know we don't have vat concepts?[9]

Of course this story is a fantasy. There are lilac bushes although our concept of lilac bush doesn't pick them out? Who's supposed to be saying this? Yet it is just such a fantasy that the skeptic must invoke to make his reading of the brains in a vat story come out the way he wants it to.

I have been arguing that even if our words have senses, even if there were concepts associated with them by which reference was secured, then it is only reasonable to regard those senses as determined in part by our environment. Whatever mechanism would lead us to associate a concept with 'lilac bush' would lead the brains to associate a different concept with those words. Appealing to definite descriptions as giving the senses of words does no work for the skeptic. It just pushes the issue of connection one step further back.

Nowadays, many philosophers are dubious about the alleged role of concepts in determining reference. Proponents of causal theories or of direct theories of reference argue that words like 'lilac bush' refer to lilac bushes directly, without the mediation of concepts. Of course, if 'lilac bush' is not a disguised description but is, instead, a rigid designator that just directly refers to an object, then the situation is even worse for the skeptic. This remains true whatever variant of the causal theory of reference we choose. It does not matter whether we hold that reference is a primitive, undefinable notion fixed by a chain of borrowings from some initial naming, or whether we try to define reference in terms of a causal chain of suitable type between speakers and objects. Nor does it matter whether we treat referential terms as contributing only their referents to the semantics of thoughts and sentences, or we treat the actual causal chains as the senses of the terms. On any of these alternatives we end up with us and the brains referring to different things by "lilac bush". The appropriate type of causal chains lead from the brains' utterance of "lilac bush" to a species of subprograms in the computer, not to lilac bushes.

There is one remaining loophole to be closed. If the anti–skeptical argument turns so critically on the role of the environment in interpreting language, then we could escape it by abandoning environments. Maybe we can eschew all talk of environment. Perhaps all we can talk about is experience and all our concepts apply to mental experiences only. If that were so and phenomenalism were correct, then our words can only refer to sense data and we and the brains would be speaking the same language in all respects. But this alternative gives no solace to the skeptic for it obliterates the very distinction he wanted to make between us and brains in a vat. If phenomenalism is true and all we can talk about is experience, then all there is experience (Can there be something beyond experience? No, 'something' now means some experience). Once the skeptic specifies that we and the brains share the same experience, then our situations become not only epistemically but ontologically identical. To think that we can draw a contrast by positing material objects behind experience in one case and computer programs in another is, as Berkeley would have pointed out, just so much nonsense from a phenomenalist point of view.

This point is critical for it puts the skeptic between a rock and a hard place. It might have seemed that the anti–skeptical argument presupposes that there is something non–mental out there for our words to refer to. What the discussion of phenomenalism reveals is that if there were nothing non–mental out there, then we could continue to speak and to reason only if our thought and language could be unpacked in experiential or phenomenalistic terms (unlikely as such an unpacking seems). In contrast, the skeptic must argue that even though there might be nothing non–mental out there, our thought and talk is essentially thought and talk of external things — for he has to get it to come out false in the absence of external things! There is nothing in the brains in a vat story that supports this claim. Indeed, the only way I can make sense of the claim is to imagine that once we *were* in the world but have somehow or other *lost contact* with it. It would take us to far afield to pursue this variety of skepticism here, but the theme of loss figures prominently in Cavell's work on skepticism.

However, if we reject phenomenalism, we are left with the environment and its contribution to our language. I don't know of anyone before Putnam who so forcefully raised the possibility that the brains in a vat would be making generally true statements about their environment.[10] But once this possibility is raised it seems very hard to argue against. And once we admit it, we have the basis of the powerful anti–skeptical arguments we saw in the previous section. Moreover, we can defend this position without invoking any substantial theory of language. Instead, it's the skeptic who needs a substantial theory of language to get his reading of the brains in a vat scenario to come out right. Not substantial in the sense of content, for what can the skeptic say in the end but that 'lilac bush' in the vat language just somehow hooks on to lilac bushes outside the vat (and could he even say this much unless he were outside the vat, unless there were lilac bushes?). The crucial step in the anti–skeptical argument is to interpret the brains' language as about their environment and we don't need a causal theory of reference for that. The skeptic needs a magical theory of reference to avoid it.

III. WHAT DO *WE* TALK ABOUT?

In the previous sections I argued that the brains in a vat have, by and large, true beliefs about their environment and because of this, skepticism about the external world ceases to be a serious problem. Now let's turn to the skeptic's fall back position. Can he coherently maintain that the above argument just pushes the problem of skepticism about the external world back one level to a problem about language? I don't deny that there is a strong psychological urge to an affirmative answer. It might seem that the preceding arguments, at best, only tie knowledge of the world to knowledge of the language we speak. So a committed skeptic could simply replace the challenge 'how do we know we're not brains in a vat?' with the challenge 'how do we know which language we speak, English or vat English?'.

Before going on, let's pause to note that the need for a fall–back position would be, in itself, an interesting epistemological result. It used to be thought that knowledge of language was one thing, a rather uncontentious one at that, and that knowledge of the external world was something completely different. But if the price of being skeptical about the external world is to be skeptical about the meanings of our words, then the cost of skepticism goes up considerably. Indeed, if linguistic skepticism is pushed too far — how do we know we *have* a language? how do we know we reason at all? — then the result is, as Putnam notes, intellectual suicide. The skeptic can remain a philosopher, a reasonable being who can articulate arguments and positions, only by acknowledging that he does have considerable linguistic prowess. And that admission opens the door to the argument that the linguistic prowess he has enables him to know what language he speaks.

A common way of formulating the metalinguistic response to Putnam's argument is this: how do we know what question we ask by the words ' are we brains in a vat?'. Beings outside the vat ask one question with these words, brains in a vat ask another. Doesn't the anti–skeptical argument turn on knowing which question we ask? Of course, if it did matter which question we ask, then this issue ought to concern the skeptic even more than Putnam. Before he could raise a challenge with the words 'are we brains in a vat?' or even 'how do we know which language we're speaking?', the skeptic would have to specify which question he's asking! But it doesn't matter. The basic point, and it is a trivial one, is that there is only one question we can ask by those words. The question 'are we brains in a vat?' is not ambiguous like 'where's the nearest bank?' or 'does the shooting of the hunters bother you?' To know which question we ask is not a difficult accomplishment; it comes free with knowing how to speak our language. And the skeptic has to concede that both we and he do know how to speak our language if he is to avoid intellectual suicide. A secondary point is that the argument does not presuppose that we ask one question as opposed to another. The argument can be put in the form — the question we ask when we ask 'are we brains in a vat?' is such that no brain in a vat asks it when it asks 'are we brains in a vat?'; so we're not brains in a vat. The irrelevance of the question of which question we start with is shown by the fact that the brains in a vat, starting from their question, could give an argument of exactly the same form establishing that they aren't, in their words, 'brains in a vat'.

Let's try another way of making the skeptic's point. There are two syntactically equivalent languages, English and vat English. The would–be metalinguistic skeptic asks how we know which of these we speak. Well, what is the difference between them? Among other things, in English, 'lilac bush' refers to lilac bushes but in vat English, 'lilac bush' refers to a certain kind of computer program. In that case, our language is English and we know our language is English. Our language is the one in which 'lilac bush' refers to lilac bushes and, moreover, we know that 'lilac bush' refers to lilac bushes. We know this in virtue of our mastery of our language, in virtue of our ability to use words like 'lilac bush' and 'refers'. There isn't any more to knowing we speak English.

The skeptic, when he is forced to the metalevel, imagines that there is some further task that remains to be done to establish that we're not brains in a vat. We have to say something, find some form of words that will *fix* the interpretation of our language. I am arguing that there is no such task. The interpretation is fixed, if you want to put it like that, by our speaking as we do. Nothing that can be said in our language can serve to further fix the interpretation in any non–trivial sense because it is talk within our language, within the interpretation. Of course we can trivially specify the interpretation — it's this one, the one we're using now. Or if we want to be more prolix, we can say that it's the one in which 'lilac bush' refers to lilac bush, 'apple' refers to apples, etc. What can be done non–trivially is to specify alternative interpretations. So we can imagine a different language, like ours except that 'lilac bush' refers to apples and 'apple' refers to lilac bush — speakers of that language say 'Never eat apples'. But it's no more than a joke to turn around and ask how we know whether we're speaking our language or the different one in which 'lilac bush' refers to apples. The skeptic makes a similar joke, albeit unwittingly, when he asks how we know we speak English as opposed to vat English.[11]

This argument can be very frustrating, I admit. It is easy to feel that there must be much more to knowing we speak English. Or rather, we feel driven to the conclusion that there must be more to knowing we speak English in light of the powerful anti—skeptical consequences that seem to turn on this claim. Prior to Putnam's arguments, even the most ardent skeptic would have willingly conceded that we know our language is English. In the next sections of the paper, I will try to explain why there isn't any more by presenting a model—theoretic analogy to Putnam's argument. It's easy to see that there isn't any more in the analogue and that what there is quite sufficient to refute skepticism.

The analogy is useful in another respect. What fuels the fire of metalinguistic skepticism is the recognition that brains in the vat can give arguments, of the very same form that we gave above, to prove that their language is what they call 'English', not 'vat English'. It is tempting to believe that if the brains can do this, then we must do something further to distinguish ourselves from them. This belief is incorrect as the analogue will show. The brains' ability to give arguments of the same form we give does not undercut our claims to know we are not brains in a vat and to know that we speak English and not vat English. Indeed, in the conclusion of this essay I will argue that the brains' ability to make an anti–skeptical argument of the same form as ours is a criterion of a good anti–skeptical argument, not an objection to one.

IV. A BRIEF DIGRESSION: THE DIAGONAL ARGUMENT AND SKOLEM'S THEOREM

The mathematical analogy to the anti–skeptical argument involves a digression into model theory, but the situation is so similar to the preceding that the results will be well worth it. In fact, if the situations are viewed as strictly equivalent, then the analogy is a powerful defense of Putnam: one can only object to the Putnamian argument by succumbing to an implausible form of mathematical skepticism. Even if the situations are only analogous, the analogy is close enough to show why the knowledge of our language that we have is sufficient to block the skeptic's retreat to the metalevel. Readers familiar with Skolem's Paradox can skip the next section, but for the rest, I'll provide a quick overview.[12]

A set is countable if it is finite or can be put into 1–1 correspondence with the natural numbers, otherwise it is uncountable. There are plenty of uncountable sets, the reals, the set of all subsets of natural numbers, the set of all countable sequences of 0's and 1's. Call the latter set S; it is the set of functions from the natural numbers to 0, 1. Cantor showed how to prove S is uncountable. Suppose, for reductio, that S were countable. Then we could list its members by the natural numbers, eg.,

1.   011011011011...
2.   110111001111...
3.   100001110010...
4.   010010101000...

and so on.

Construct a new sequence by looking at the digits on the diagonal (in bold face) and replacing each 0 by 1 and vice–versa.

NEW   **1**0**1**1...

Obviously, NEW is not on the list since it differs from the Nth sequence at the Nth place. But NEW is a member of S, so not all members of S have been listed (indeed, the vast majority have not). Hence S is not countable.

Later Skolem showed that any consistent theory, including the set theory that Cantor needed for the above proof, had countable models. A version of one of his proofs uses the axiom of choice and the assumption of a standard model and gives a particularly elegant model which is an elementary submodel of the original. All its elements are sets and the membership relation of the model is the real membership relation. Intuitively, the proof works like this.[13]

You tell me specific sets that are in the universe, eg., $\emptyset$, S, and so on and I put them in the universe of the model. Then you point out that sets like $\{\emptyset, S\}$ and the power set of S must exist, and so I add these. Then you point out that this necessitates further sets like $\{\emptyset, \{\emptyset, S\}\}$ and the power set of the power set, and I put these in. Since the original language is countable (because each of its formulas is finite), you can only specify a countable number of sets, so my model M' will have only a countable number of sets. Yet it will be a model of set theory since for every true formula $\exists xFx$ there will be something in M' satisfying F. (For ease of exposition, I equivocate a bit by sometimes treating M' as the domain or universe of a model and sometimes as the model itself, i.e., an ordered pair consisting of the domain and the membership relation.)

One final twist: although M' has only countably many sets, some of the sets in it, like S, will be uncountable. However, since most of the members of S aren't in M', their presence is irrelevant to the model structure, and so I can replace S and other uncountable sets by their countable intersections with M' (that is, the domain). If we label the resulting model M, then M is a countable model of countable sets.

More formally, the proof goes like this.

1. If the language has any constant symbols, 'a', 'b', 'c', etc., collect the objects a, b, c, etc. into a set, M_1. M_1 is the first approximation to a countable model. Since the language is countable by definition, M_1 is countable.

2. For every existential formula like $\exists xFxyz$, apply it to a pair, say (a, b) from M_1, and if $\exists xFxab$ is true, choose a set that makes it true, say d such that $Fdab$, and add the d's to M_1 to make M_2. Since the number of formulas is countable and the number of pairs in M_1 is countable, M_2 will be countable.

3. Repeat Step 2 to get M_3, M_4, and so on; and then let M' be the union of all the M_i's.

4. It is fairly easy to show that M' is the domain of a model of set theory and that M' is countable. M' is countable because it is the countable union of countable sets. We prove M' is a model by induction on the logical complexity of formulas. Quantifier–free formulas assert the same facts inside and outside M'. True formulas of the form $\forall xFx$ will be true in M' when $\forall$ is restricted to elements in M', and true formulas of the form $\exists xFx$ will be true in M' by construction.

5. Finally, we can use a tamping down lemma to get rid of extraneous elements. That is, b might have members which aren't in M'. There is a systematic way of replacing each set b by its intersection with M' to remove extraneous elements while still preserving model–hood. M, as opposed to M', is a transitive model: members of members of M are members of M.

What the Skolem proof shows is that if set theory has a standard model (and it has a model if it is consistent), then it has a standard countable model, M. The nice feature of M is that it contains real sets and the membership relation is the real membership relation restricted to M. So M is not some weird reinterpretation of set theory using natural numbers for sets and some bizarre arithmetical relation for membership.

V. THE COUNTABLE MATHEMATICIAN AND HER SIMILARITY TO A BRAIN IN A VAT

Now let's imagine how the mathematical world looks from the perspective of a mathematician in M. The fancy of a mathematician in M, call her a 'countable mathematician', is heuristic, like the inhabitants of Abbott's *Flatland*. It allows us to convey a lot of information simply. Equally important, it permits a neat analogy to a brain in a vat — only the countable mathematician is like a brain in a countable vat! I claim that our ordinary mathematical situation vis–a–vis the countable mathematician is relevantly like our situation vis–a–vis a brain in a vat.

Consider what happens when the countable mathematician starts doing set theory. She can define 'the set S' of 'all countable sequences of 0's and 1's' as we did and *prove* 'S is uncountable'! How can she do this? Because M is a model of set theory, all the axioms of set theory are true when interpreted over M. Every general principle we used to prove the uncountability of S is true in her model! But since everything in her model is countable, the set that she proves to be uncountable must be really countable. But then how could she have proved S uncountable? This is called Skolem's Paradox.

It's not hard to dissolve the paradox. The countable mathematician might be in the same internal states as we are, and she might give the same implicit meanings to her concepts as we do (she adopts the same axioms we do). But she refers to different things than we do by certain key terms. Her S is not our S. Our S is actually the set of all countable 0—1 sequences. Her definition of 'S' picks out S_M, the set of all 0—1 sequences in her model that are countable in terms of her model. This set really is countable since it's a subset of the countable M. But it looks uncountable to her because the function that 'counts' S_M doesn't exist in her model.

In fact, she doesn't even make the same statement we make by the words 'the set of all countable 0–1 sequences is countable'. She can't even refer to S, which is outside her model. Instead she refers to S_M and says of that set that it is M–uncountable, i.e., there is no 1–1 correspondence in M between S_M and the natural numbers. So S_M really is countable — from our perspective — but the countable mathematician has not made any error by asserting — in her language — 'S is uncountable'. Sound familiar? It's just like Fred's talk of vat–lilac bushes.

Of course we know that our situation is different from that of the countable mathematician. We can, after all, prove that S is uncountable. But can't she do that to?

Not quite: she can't even refer to S or to real uncountability as we just noted. What she can do is give a proof of the same form that 'S is uncountable' or, as we say, that S_M is M–uncountable. Furthermore, she can even construct a countable model M_M relative to her countable model and prove that she is not in that model! That is she can 'duplicate' our proof that she is not in a countable model — just as the brains in a vat can prove, in Putnam's account, that 'we're not brains in a vat' expresses a truth in their language.

Let us review the situation. The countable mathematician speaks a mathematical language syntactically identical to ours. She may even have the same meanings if by 'meanings' we mean ideas or implicit definitions. Nevertheless for a large class of terms, including 'S' and 'countable', the terms of her language pick out different objects than our terms. Her reference is restricted to her model, the things in M, so she can't even make some of the statements we make, like S is uncountable. When she utters the same words, she refers to a different object and attributes a different property to it. Both her statement and ours are true. In precisely the same fashion, Putnam suggests, the brains in a vat speak a different language. When they say 'there is a lilac bush before us' in the usual context, they make a true statement, only 'lilac bush' and 'before us' have shifted reference in the vat world, exactly like 'S' and 'countable' shift reference in the model M. The brains in a vat can't even make many of the statements we make such as the one we make when we say 'there is a lilac bush before us' for exactly the same reason that the countable mathematician can't make the statements we make. The skeptic tried to construct a situation that radically changed our environment while holding the meanings *and* truth conditions of our utterances constant. Putnam's argument is that this can't be done, the radical change of environment *forces a new model on our language* — a new interpretation that changes the truth conditions of utterances. The brains in a vat can no more referentially reach back to our world and make *false* statements about it than the countable mathematician can referentially reach out of her world and make false statements about ours.

The only difference between the cases is this. In the case of *Skolem's paradox*, the alternate model (i.e., the countable model) of language is explicitly given as part of the set up. In the brains in the vat case, we have to *argue*, following *Putnam*, that the skeptic's scenario implicitly forces an alternate model of language.

Nevertheless, for all the similarity between the universe of set theory and the countable model (the same formulas are true in both), we can tell we're not in the countable model. We can prove that S is uncountable, therefore we can't be in a countable model. And of course the countable mathematician can do something very similar, she can give a formally identical proof that she is not, as she says, 'in a countable model' (as the brains in a vat can prove, in their words, 'we're not brains in a vat'). There is nothing untoward about this although many people are bothered by this feature of Putnam's argument. But if you think about it, it seems plausible that a good anti—skeptical argument ought to work for brains in a vat. It can't point to some facet of experience that differentiates the situations, so it must be a logical or conceptual argument, and how can such an argument fail to apply to brains in a vat? It certainly can't fail if we grant Putnam that the model of the language spoken is partially determined by the environment of the speakers. To think that this situation is untoward is rather like my thinking that a precondition of my proving 'I'm not over there' is that you not be able to prove the claim you express by the words 'I'm not over there' (and my attitude is not excused by the fact that I can see that you're over there).

VI. MATHEMATICAL SKEPTICISM AND ITS RELATION TO EMPIRICAL SKEPTICISM

But perhaps I'm being too hasty. Is it so obvious that we're not in a countable world?[14] Perhaps the analogy between countable mathematicians and brains in a vat should be read as revealing a new form of skepticism, as showing that we don't know that our world is uncountable. No; this way lies madness, or at least incoherence. In the first place the mathematical skepticism that results is far worse than skepticism about the external world. A skeptic of the latter kind wonders how we can know we aren't brains in a vat given that our experiences would remain the same if we were. The mathematical skeptic wonders how we can know our world isn't countable given not only that our mathematical experience would remain the same if it were, but even given that we now have a mathematical proof of uncountability! If a mathematical proof isn't sufficient, what does the mathematical skeptic expect of a philosophical argument? What does he mean by the claim that we lack knowledge of what we can prove?

More important, the mathematical skeptic's position is deeply incoherent. If the words in the question 'is our world countable?' have their usual meaning, then the answer is an easy 'no', as the diagonal argument reveals. To make that question non–trivial, the skeptic has to invest 'countable' with some new meaning; he can't take the word that we use. He must suppose that he can detach himself from our world and our language and, from some hypothetical vantage point, look back on us and ask something like "Is *S really* countable?" For as we just saw, the required meaning of '*really* countable' can't be got to from our language, any more than the ordinary meaning can be got to from the language of the countable mathematician. In the skeptic's question, as he wishes to ask it, '*really* countable' has no more force than '*XXX YYY*' — both are meaningless strings of symbols. So the skeptic faces a dilemma. The only questions he can ask are in our language and those admit a trivial answer: the diagonal argument shows our world to be uncountable. The skeptic would like to ask a particular non–trivial question but the words in our language are not sufficient for his task.

It is at this point that the mathematical skeptic, if he is persistent, must attempt to retreat to metalinguistic skepticism. How do we know which language we speak, he can ask, real set theoretic or countable model set theoretic? We can answer him as we answered the empirical skeptic earlier. What's the difference between the two languages? Well, in real set theoretic, 'uncountable' refers to uncountable sets but in countable model set theoretic, 'uncountable' refers to those countable sets in M that aren't countable by a function in that model. In that case, we know we speak real set theoretic because in our language 'uncountable' means uncountable.

I'm sorry that I keep giving trivial answers but it's the skeptic who keeps asking trivial questions. Of course, you and I both know that he does not want to ask trivial questions. He wants to ask deep questions about how we know which language we're speaking, which referential scheme is operative. But since he's forced to frame any question in terms of our common language, the one we share with him, we can always answer back — we speak *this* language.

I don't mean to malign the skeptic. To be sure, I argue that the metalinguistic skeptic, be he mathematical or empirical, is forced to ask trivial questions. But the point of contention between us is far from trivial. The metalinguistic skeptic sees the situation as follows. We have a language, English or set theoretic, and we seem to see that it can be hooked up to the world in radically different ways as exhibited in this diagram.

$$L \rightarrow V \quad \text{(the universe of sets, or the real world)}$$
$$L \rightarrow M \quad \text{(the countable model, or the vat world)}$$

Indeed, to the skeptic it seems that it is Putnam and I who are promoting this very diagram. Isn't it what lies behind the anti—skeptical argument? Then, the skeptic continues, how do we know which line of the diagram portrays our true circumstance?

Putnam's reply, and I agree, is to reject the diagram as a picture of the situation for *from whose point of view is the diagram supposed to be drawn?* Certainly not from the viewpoint of the countable mathematician or of the brains in a vat. They are locked into the second line of the diagram; their conceptual systems only permit them to draw down from there (and so to consider countable models within the countable model or to consider brains–in–a–vat in the vat). But equally important, and this is the essence of *internal* realism as far as I can see, the diagram can't even be drawn from our viewpoint — it aspires to a God's Eye point of view.

Putnam is surely right as far as set theory and model theory go: the diagram is fundamentally flawed. It cannot be expressed in set theory for the simple reason that the set theoretical universe is not one model among many. The universe of set theory, V, is not a set. It provides the framework for all set theoretic talk including any talk of models at all, and any model talked about, even a standard one, is not the universe of set theory. Similarly in speaking of any model, we set up a referential connection ($\rightarrow$) between L and the model. But real reference is not one of *these* connections, any more than the universe is one of the models talked about in it; so we don't have to worry about how we can choose the right referential function from these alternatives.

Moreover, the situation would not be substantially changed even if we adopted a radically different set theory, like Aczel's elegant version of non–well founded sets, in which V is a member of itself and reference is a relation that includes itself as a relata There would still not be a problem of which language we speak, which universe we inhabit, which relation 'reference' refers to. Once we've acknowledged V as the universe and 'reference' as referring to reference — which we're bound to do to accord with our usage — we're not free to disown this knowledge. Which language do we speak? This one, the one in which 'V' refers to V, 'all' means all, 'reference' refers to reference. Any alternatives we can consider are just that, alternatives to the linguistic arrangements we now have. We know that none of them obtain because we know we have the linguistic arrangements that we do.

And so the mathematical skeptic cannot retreat to metalinguistic skepticism. He can't restate his skeptical problem as a problem about language because the only questions he can pose about language yield trivial answers. I believe that the case of the external world skeptic is similar in all relevant respects. There is nothing special about the mathematical case that grounds our knowledge of which mathematical language we speak. There is only the recurring recognition that we speak that language that we're now using to carry on this discussion. In the end, we know we speak English because we know that's the language in which 'lilac bush' refers to lilac bushes and we know that's true of our language. It might not seem like much to know that, in general, '*t*' refers to *t*, but that's all we know about reference and all we need to know to defeat metalinguistic skepticism.

VII. REMOVING PSYCHOLOGICAL MISGIVINGS WITH TOM'S TWIN TIM

The general considerations from model theory provide a powerful support for our anti–skeptical argument. Yet many readers can still harbor serious doubts. Can an *a priori* argument really establish that we're not in a vat? Can an argument avoid begging the question if the brains in a vat could give an analogous and equally good argument? I have been arguing that the answer to both questions is yes because the claim that we're not brains in a vat is a lot less empirical than it's sometimes taken to be. But abstract arguments can just seem suspicious in the face of strong psychological doubts. In conclusion, I present a brief exercise designed to help allay those doubts . Let's look at an anti–skeptical argument we all agree with. Consider Descartes' Cogito argument, 'I think, therefore I am', or as Putnam might put it, if I can raise the question 'do I exist?', then I exist. I assume that the Cogito argument works; it's sound and valid and leads me to the knowledge that I exist, if that knowledge was ever in doubt.

The argument is essentially indexical. One way of putting this is that the *assertion*, 'I don't exist', is self–refuting. Whoever utters it makes a false statement. To be sure, the proposition expressed by my utterance 'I exist', that is, 'Thomas Tymoczko exists' is hardly necessary. We can easily imagine worlds of which it is false. Yet I take it that we will all grant that I *know* that ours is not a world in which I don't exist. I exist and I know it. In so far as I can conceive of a world in which I don't exist, I must conceive of it as other than this world. Putnam's argument purports to be indexical in this sense; it is the assertion 'we are brains in a vat' that is self–refuting', not the proposition that there are no brains in a vat.

Now the cogito is not an empirical argument: I don't discover I exist by careful observation. Permit me to dramatize this obvious point in a somewhat extreme fashion. Suppose that I was conceived as one of a pair of identical twins but suppose further that very early on (as early as you'll permit and still accept his existence) my unfortunate twin brother was spontaneously aborted without anyone being the wiser. Next suppose the following twist of fate. There is a possible world (call it *B* as opposed to this world, which is *A*), in which I and not my now fortunate twin was aborted. My twin, call him Tim, goes on to live my life. I mean that he literally retraces my footsteps; at any moment of time when I was at *P*, he was at *P* (in world *B*). He saw every sight I saw (and with the same weak eyes), he heard everything I heard (as I heard it). He talked to the same people, said the same words, and felt the same feelings. In fact at this very moment in world *B*, Tim is typing "these very words". World *B* and world *A* are virtually indistinguishable. Each contains the same totality of 'inner experiences'; each contains the same atoms in virtually the same arrangements (except for a few details about Tom's and Tim's biology). Yet for all that, I *know* that this is world *A* and not world *B* and I know this not by looking around and saying 'this — these experiences

— could never be duplicated' (they can), but by a simple logical argument: I can raise the question 'do I exist?', hence I exist and so this is world A.

Now should we regard this as an impressive accomplishment, that I can distinguish between worlds A and B, which are, after all, more alike than our world and a brains–in–vat world? I think not, I think we should regard this as a simple logical consequence of how language works, roughly on a par with the contention that 'I'm not here' is self–refuting. Moreover, I suggest that a full–fledged anti–skeptical argument which shows that we are not brain in a vat need not be regarded as any more remarkable than the Cogito argument. It's not as if the anti–skeptic must find some subtle way of distinguishing between the virtually indistinguishable, some hitherto unknown scientific fact about the non–vat universe. For anti–skeptical arguments to work there need only be some simple logical point about the way language works that gets us to the desired conclusion.

But perhaps one should doubt the efficacy of the Cogito argument. Suppose I worried as follows: "I seemed to have proved the assertion 'I exist'. But just suppose it were false, that I didn't exist, and that this is world B. Then my twin Tim could give exactly the same formal argument concluding that he exists, or, as he puts it, 'I exist'. So the mere ability to give a sound argument to the effect that I exist is insufficient. How do I know that it's me and not really Tim that is giving the argument?"

My worry seems rather like a comedy routine, like the lost explorers who, consulting a map, conclude 'we're on that mountain peak right over there'! The facts of language that render the worry inapplicable are patently clear. But recall that an analogous worry, that our proof that a set is uncountable was undercut by the fact that the countable mathematician could give a formally similar proof, felt more serious. It took some work to explain the facts of language that made that worry inapplicable.

Finally the analogous worry with Putnam's brains in a vat argument seems convincing to many. This conviction, I claim, is totally unwarranted. Not that any doubt about the argument is unwarranted, only that this particular criticism is. The mere fact that brains in a vat could give a formally similar argument to establish their assertion that 'we are not brains in a vat' cannot be used to undercut Putnam's argument. No more than Tim's proof of 'I exist' or the countable mathematician's proof that 'S is uncountable' can undercut the analogous arguments we give for our assertions. Indeed given that Putnam's argument is conceptual or *a priori*, and given the claim that concepts are partially determined by speakers' environment, it is an inevitable consequence that brains in a vat can give a form of anti–skeptical argument (it's not the same argument because the statements involved are different). This fact generates a psychological worry, not a philosophical one.

To fully convince oneself of this, one need only consider the alternative. Suppose one demanded an argument that only worked for beings outside the vat. It's to be sound if used outside the vat, but not sound if used inside, eg., Moore's argument. Would such an argument be more convincing? Not at all, for the skeptic would object that it begs the question. Before we could believe it, he would say, we'd have to prove that we're not brains in a vat! The only non–question–begging anti–skeptical argument must be able to be given by brains in a vat. That's a mark of success, not of failure.

Putnam's anti–skeptical argument is a very powerful one. It turns on the novel idea that the brains in a vat aren't consistently deceived. From this point, a clear anti–

skeptical position follows. And the insight seems to be supported by any reasonable theory of language. If the skeptic tries to restate his problem as one about language, he fails because the only questions that he can ask that are both relevant and coherent have trivial answers. But perhaps its misleading to suggest that Putnam has refuted the skeptic. It might be more accurate to say he's deprived the skeptic of certain conditions that the skeptic had presupposed. It that case, Putnam's position might be similar to Wittgenstein's: "Skepticism is *not* irrefutable, but obviously nonsensical, when it tries to raise doubts where no questions can be asked." A minor difference is that I've allowed that the skeptic can raise some questions, but, as I've tried to show, those questions he can raise cannot satisfy him.

The riddle of skepticism does not exist.

Smith College

NOTES

* This essay grows out of my previous work on the subject, "In Defense of Putnam's Brains". When that paper was read at the University of Rochester Conference on Skepticism, 1989, I was prodded to rethink the matter by suggestions from Dorit Bar-On, Earl Conee, Ernest Sosa, and especially by John Bennett who provided an insightful commentary. For the form of the present paper, however, I am deeply indebted to Jonathan Vogel. It is not too far off to say that I presented him with a block of philosophical marble and that he chipped away at everything that wasn't the following argument. I'd also like to thank Murray Kiteley for reading a draft of this paper and providing many helpful suggestions.

1 Perhaps I exaggerate slightly. There are many forms of skepticism and a complete refutation would have to catalogue them all and follow each to its bitter end. In my opinion, the major contrast is between philosophical or 'evidence—transcendent' skepticism which questions the very possibility of knowledge and the milder forms of skepticism which question whether we actually have knowledge in particular situations or just reasonable beliefs. Putnam's argument essentially refutes philosophical skepticism. In "In Defense of Putnam's Brains", I argue that the only variants of the brains in a vat scenario which avoid Putnam's argument are those of mild skepticism, i.e., those for which empirical evidence is relevant.

2 For stylistic reasons only, I assume we're outside the vat and hence that the skeptical questions are whether, and how, we know that we are. The assumption isn't necessary; we could contrast two abstract cases, one of beings in a vat and one of beings outside the vat, but this way of speaking is too cumbersome. Similarly, I tend to focus on language and what statements the brains make, but we could consider, just as easily, thought and what the brains believe.

3 Throughout this essay I refer to the skeptic by the masculine pronoun, not because I am unsympathetic to feminist concerns about language, but because I believe that skepticism, in some sense, represents the masculine component of ourselves. Further, since skepticism might turn out to be a kind of infirmity, an inability to know, I see no reason to be gender inclusive and insist on saying 'he or she' all the time.

4 Hence their utterance "We are not brains" comes out true on this interpretation. But since the interpretation also makes true any sentence of science or philosophy that's true in our world, this amounts to a relative consistency proof of non—materialism. We've found a model in the materialist universe that makes all our theories true but the sentence 'we are brains' false.

5 The closest they could come to the question is 'are we in a vat?' thereby referring to brains by 'we' but 'vat' would still not refer to real vats. In any case, it's important not to get hung up on modalities here, that is, on the issue of what the brains can do. The brains don't refer to lilac bushes by 'lilac bush'; we do; therefore, we're not brains in a vat.

[6] For a specific term, such as 'rabbit' or 'unicorn', there is always a legitimate worry as to whether it refers. That worry is answered by empirical investigation. But as long as we refer to something outside mental experience, we'll be able to defeat the skeptic by a long disjunction: either 'rabbit' refers to rabbits or 'unicorn' refers to unicorn, etc. As Peter Klein emphasizes, we can know that the preponderance of a set of beliefs is true without having to know of any one that it's true (eg., lottery cases). This leaves open the possibility that none of our terms refer. I try to deal with it in the discussion of phenomenalism in the next section.

[7] Am I presupposing too much about the inner workings of the master computer? Maybe the skeptic could say that it's a very different kind of computer from the ones we have now. Yes, but he could also say that it's a very different kind of vat from those at Gallo's Winery, maybe it's actually a gravitational field. And maybe the 'nutrient fluid' that the brains are bathed in is very much like air and the brains are actually attached to complete nervous systems which have to be covered by a fleshy layer to protect them. In that case "brains in a vat" is just a funny way of talking about human beings in the world. To avoid this conclusion the skeptic has to avoid metaphorical stretchings of terms, by 'vat' he means vat, by 'brains', just brains and by 'computer' he means something very much like modern computers only bigger in scale, and so my suppositions are justified.

[8] I'd like to remind readers of note 2. Nothing crucial turns on the assumption that we're actually outside the vat. It's the skeptic who must insist that brains in a vat (or we, if we're in their 'shoes') have concepts that are appropriate to other circumstances.

[9] This puzzle looks rather like the new form of skepticism that Kripke finds in Wittgenstein. If it is, then it is a serious challenge to the claim that our words express concepts. However, in this essay I have tried to avoid criticizing theories of meaning so I make a more restricted use of the puzzle. My version is meant only to show how unreasonable it is to insist that we and the brains have the same concepts.

[10] With the possible exception of O. K. Bouwsma who took a position similar to Putnam's in "Descartes' Evil Genius". Bouwsma argued that minds wouldn't be deceived by a Cartesian demon because they would still have true beliefs in this setting. Although his essay seems not to have been very influential in epistemology, it does point to the deep Wittgensteinian sources of this argument.

[11] At this point we might interject Nagel's complaint that Putnam's argument, at most, merely deprives the skeptic of saying what we all feel to be the case. "What follows? Only that I can't express my skepticism by saying, "Perhaps I'm a brain in a vat." Instead I must say, "Perhaps I can't even *think* the truth about what I am, because I lack the necessary concepts, and my circumstances make it impossible for me to acquire them?" If this doesn't qualify as skepticism, I don't know what does." (p. 74) My reply is that Nagel's worry is not skepticism, not a problem about the possibility of knowledge, but a form of free—floating anxiety. That the skeptic feels anxious, feels deprived of something, be it the world or the words that he needs to connect himself to the world, is a serious issue. As noted earlier, it is a theme explored by Cavell.

[12] The analogy between Putnam's argument and the standard resolution of Skolem's Paradox was a focal point of "In Defense of Putnam's Brains". There I emphasized the overall similarity between the cases. Here I use the analogy more particularly to block the empirical skeptic's retreat to linguistic skepticism. This emphasis was suggested by Jonathan Vogel.

[13] See Cohen for a proof.

[14] In my essay "Mathematical Skepticism: Are We Brains in a Countable Vat?" I tried to find other arguments that showed why we knew the world of mathematical objects was uncountable. After reviewing ideas of Benacerraf and Wright about informal practice and forms of life, I concluded that the best explanation was just the analogue of Putnam's argument given here.

BIBLIOGRAPHY

Abbott, Edwin: 1986, *Flatland* (Penguin Books, Suffolk).
Aczel, Peter: 1988, *Non—Well—Founded Sets* (Center for the Study of Language and Information Lecture Notes, Stanford).

Bouwsma, O. K.: 1949, "Descartes' Evil Genius" (*Philosophical Review*, LVIII).

Cavell, Stanley: 1979, *The Claim of Reason* (Oxford University Press, Oxford).

Cohen, Paul: 1966, *Set Theory and the Continuum Hypothesis* (W. A. Benjamin, Inc., New York).

Kripke, Saul: 1982, *Wittgenstein on Rules and Private Language* (Harvard University Press, Cambridge).

Moore, G. E. 1959, *Philosophical Papers* (George Allen & Unwin Ltd, London).

Nagel, Thomas: 1986, *The View From Nowhere* (Oxford University Press, Oxford).

Putnam, Hilary: 1981, *Reason Truth and History* (Cambridge University Press, Cambridge).

1983, Realism and Reason (Cambridge University Press, Cambridge).

Quine, W. V.: 1960, *Word and Object* (MIT Press, Cambridge).

1969: *Ontological Relativity and Other Essays* (Columbia University Press, New York).

Tymoczko, Thomas: "In Defense of Putnam's Brains", *Philosophical Studies*, forthcoming.

1989 "Mathematical Skepticism: Are We Brains in a Countable Vat?", Philosophica 43.

Wittgenstein, Ludwig: 1961, *Tractatus Logico—Philosophicus* (Routledge & Kegan Paul, London).

INDEX OF NAMES

INDEX OF SUBJECTS

PHILOSOPHICAL STUDIES SERIES
IN PHILOSOPHY

Editors:

WILFRID SELLARS, Univ. of Pittsburgh and KEITH LEHRER, Univ. of Arizona

Board of Consulting Editors:

Jonathan Bennett, Allan Gibbard, Robert Stalnaker, and Robert G. Turnbull

1. JAY F. ROSENBERG, *Linguistic Representation,* 1974.
2. WILFRID SELLARS, *Essays in Philosophy and Its History,* 1974.
3. DICKINSON S. MILLER, *Philosophical Analysis and Human Welfare.* Selected Essays and Chapters from Six Decades. Edited with an Introduction by Lloyd D. Easton, 1975.
4. KEITH LEHRER (ed.), *Analysis and Metaphysics.* Essays in Honor of R. M. Chisholm. 1975.
5. CARL GINET, *Knowledge, Perception, and Memory,* 1975.
6. PETER H. HARE and EDWARD H. MADDEN, *Causing, Perceiving and Believing.* An Examination of the Philosophy of C. J. Ducasse, 1975.
7. HECTOR-NERI CASTAÑEDA, *Thinking and Doing.* The Philosophical Foundations of Institutions, 1975.
8. JOHN L. POLLOCK, *Subjunctive Reasoning,* 1976.
9. BRUCE AUNE, *Reason and Action,* 1977.
10. GEORGE SCHLESINGER, *Religion and Scientific Method,* 1977.
11. YIRMIAHU YOVEL (ed.), *Philosophy of History and Action.* Papers presented at the first Jerusalem Philosophical Encounter, December 1974, 1978.
12. JOSEPH C. PITT, *The Philosophy of Wilfrid Sellars: Queries and Extensions,* 1978.
13. ALVIN I. GOLDMAN and JAEGWON KIM, *Values and Morals.* Essays in Honor of William Frankena, Charles Stevenson, and Richard Brandt, 1978.
14. MICHAEL J. LOUX, *Substance and Attribute.* A Study in Ontology, 1978.
15. ERNEST SOSA (ed.), *The Philosophy of Nicholas Rescher: Discussion and Replies,* 1979.
16. JEFFRIE G. MURPHY, *Retribution, Justice, and Therapy.* Essays in the Philosophy of Law, 1979.
17. GEORGE S. PAPPAS, *Justification and Knowledge: New Studies in Epistemology,* 1979.
18. JAMES W. CORNMAN, *Skepticism, Justification, and Explanation,* 1980.
19. PETER VAN INWAGEN, *Time and Cause.* Essays presented to Richard Taylor, 1980.
20. DONALD NUTE, *Topics in Conditional Logic,* 1980.
21. RISTO HILPINEN (ed.), *Rationality in Science,* 1980.
22. GEORGES DICKER, *Perceptual Knowledge,* 1980.

23. JAY F. ROSENBERG, *One World and Our Knowledge of It*, 1980.
24. KEITH LEHRER and CARL WAGNER, *Rational Consensus in Science and Society*, 1981.
25. DAVID O'CONNOR, *The Metaphysics of G. E. Moore*, 1982.
26. JOHN D. HODSON, *The Ethics of Legal Coercion*, 1983.
27. ROBERT J. RICHMAN, *God, Free Will, and Morality*, 1983.
28. TERENCE PENELHUM, *God and Skepticism*, 1983.
29. JAMES BOGEN and JAMES E. McGUIRE (eds.), *How Things Are, Studies in Predication and the History of Philosophy of Science*, 1985.
30. CLEMENT DORE, *Theism*, 1984.
31. THOMAS L. CARSON, *The Status of Morality*, 1984.
32. MICHAEL J. WHITE, *Agency and Integrality*, 1985.
33. DONALD F. GUSTAFSON, *Intention and Agency*, 1986.
34. PAUL K. MOSER, *Empirical Justification*. 1985.
35. FRED FELDMAN, *Doing the Best We Can*, 1986.
36. G. W. FITCH, *Naming and Believing*, 1987.
37. TERRY PENNER, *The Ascent from Nominalism*. Some Existence Arguments in Plato's Middle Dialogues, 1987.
38. ROBERT G. MEYERS, *The Likelihood of Knowledge*, 1988.
39. DAVID F. AUSTIN, *Philosophical Analysis*. A Defense by Example, 1988.
40. STUART SILVERS, *Rerepresentation*. Essays in the Philosophy of Mental Rerepresentation, 1988.
41. MICHAEL P. LEVINE, *Hume and the Problem of Miracles. A Solution*, 1979.
42. MELVIN DALGARNO and ERIC MATTHEWS, *The Philosophy of Thomas Reid*, 1989.
43. KENNETH R. WESTPHAL, *Hegel's Epistemological Realism. A Study of the Aim and Method of Hegel's Phenomenology of Spirit*, 1989.
44. JOHN W. BENDER, *The Current State of the Coherence Theory*. Critical Essays on the Epistemic Theories of Keith Lehrer and Laurence Bonjour, with Replies, 1989.
45. ROGER D. GALLIE, *Thomas Reid and 'The Way of Ideas'*, 1989.
46. J-C. SMITH (ed.), *Historical Foundations of Cognitive Science*, 1990.
47. JOHN HEIL (ed.), *Cause, Mind, and Reality*. Essays Honoring C. B. Martin, 1989.
48. MICHAEL D. ROTH and GLENN ROSS (eds.), *Doubting*. Contemporary Perspectives on Skepticism, 1990.